A Second Dose of Sandy's Daily Diaries

A Second Dose of Sandy's Daily Diaries

ANOTHER 101 DAYS OF SOCIAL DISTANCING

Sandy Thomson

This book is dedicated to M, with thanks
for keeping me sane, keeping me fit and,
most importantly, keeping me fed.

Introduction

In March 2020, as the United Kingdom was beginning to feel the full effects of the Covid-19 pandemic, I began to write a daily diary on social media, just for the amusement of family and friends. During social distancing, followed by a full lockdown, I recorded my everyday events and activities and tried to see the funny side of daily life.

Thanks to the encouragement of all those followers, plus my family and close friends, I published the first 101 days of my diary in a book - "Sandy's Daily Diaries" - which proved to be popular both at home and in other countries around the globe.

Here, then, is the follow-up. I began this volume on the first day of 2021 and kept it going for the next 101 days. And as before, this is a book for everyone. Nothing controversial, nothing offensive and nothing political, just gentle humour all the way through. You can share it with your five year old child or your ninety five year old granny.

These diaries are simply a record of how a pensioner in the north of Scotland spent his days living with covid restrictions, and my aim was to try to find a little humour in every activity and event. My first diaries made a large number of people smile during a very difficult time, and I hope that these new ones will make you smile today.

Stay well, my friends.

Sandy Thomson
August 2021

1

Day 1 – a day of looking back. And forwards. And sideways.

Today is the first day of January, and also the first day of a whole new year. Hoorah! Is there anyone who's sorry to see the end of 2020? Oh yes, of course, the makers of facemasks and hand gels for whom business has been booming since Covid-19 and its variants arrived on the scene.

Also, newspaper headline writers. Today alone, we've had photos of empty streets entitled "Gappy New Year", a farewell to 2020 described as "Happy Phew Year" and with the suggestion that closed pubs should be used as vaccination centres, "Jabby Hour".

January, as every schoolboy knows (or did in my day) is named after Janus, the Roman god who is often depicted with two faces, one looking back and the other looking forwards. A bit like me when I'm halfway to the shops and realise I've left my mask in the car.

I was always slightly envious of Janus, because I imagined

how smart he must have felt in school, looking attentively at the teacher with one face and chatting up the girl in the seat behind with the other one. However the invention of the rear view mirror (by Elmer Berger in 1921 – thanks Google!) probably stole Janus's thunder because now we could all see what was behind us. Although some of us don't bother using it once we've passed the driving test.

Contrary to the stereotypical image of Scots at this time of year, I no longer mark the new year by sitting up until midnight, drinking vast quantities of whisky, partying until the wee small hours then emerging next morning with a king-sized hangover. I was in bed by 11pm, and falling asleep when rudely awakened at midnight by multiple, and very loud, fireworks being set off in the village. This is a relatively new phenomenon here in the north, and one which I suspect has come from America. They probably consider it revenge for us sending them Donald Trump's mother in 1930.

When I was young, the only sounds were the firing of a shotgun, usually by the local gamekeeper, one shot just before midnight to see the old year out and another a few seconds later to welcome the new year in. Only in Scotland could firing a gun signify a welcome. No wonder the Romans turned back when they reached the border.

Today, then, started quietly for M and me. We're still under Tier 4 restrictions, so largely confined to home and not allowed to visit Baby A on her first New Year's Day. We hope that Nicola (Sturgeon, First Minister of Scotland) will ease these restrictions in a week or two, but today's newspapers are full of doom and gloom so I'm not too optimistic. The Daily Mail alleges that the virus is "running out of control", but then they also describe Boris's Brexit deal as "amazing for Britain" so let's not place too much faith in their opinion.

It was a nice morning so after breakfast we headed out for a long walk which took around an hour, then sent a WhatsApp message to M Junior wishing her, Farmer J, Baby A and Dog F the traditional "Happy New Year". Later we were treated to a video call in which we were able to see Baby A smiling and reaching out for the phone.

After fifteen minutes the video call had to be terminated to allow for nappy changing and feeding. Well, you wouldn't want me to be wet and hungry, would you?

2

∽

Day 2 – a birthday. And a half birthday.

And here we are on the second day of 2021. I think it's Saturday, but it may well be Sunday because every day feels the same during this so-called "festive" period. In my mind the word "festive" suggests feasting and indeed I seem to have spent the last week or so stuffing my face with all sorts of bad things, mainly composed of sugar, salt, fat and of course alcohol. And there's no point in kidding myself that the diet starts tomorrow because we all know my willpower is every bit as strong as the skin of a rice pudding. Mmmm rice pudding...

Anyway, I've promised myself that all this will change when M goes back to work on Tuesday. I will start weighing myself every morning, walking more and eating less, in the hope that I can repeat last summer's feat of losing a stone in a month. I just hope M will know which day is Tuesday because I won't have a clue.

Yesterday, which may have been Friday, or maybe not, the weekly "jumbo" crossword appeared in The Times and by

4

lunchtime today I had finished it. Completion in less than twenty-four hours is a great achievement for me, and even then I had to resort to my friend Mr Google for help with strange words, like "aphelia" and "chiasm".

Aphelia Chiasm, eh? Wasn't she a character in a "Carry On" film? Oo-er missus!

And following the successful completion of the crossword, M and I walked to Dingwall to pop it into the mail. And yes, I know there's a post box five hundred yards from our house and Dingwall is more than a mile away but the walk is good for me. It allows me to feel smug and self-righteous, and I feel able to justify scoffing a chocolate biscuit when I get home. If only I could stop at one.

There's a prize for the first correct crossword solution out of the hat and I always hope that one day it'll be me. But with a daily circulation of almost half a million readers, many of whom do the crossword, I realise it's a bit of a long shot. But if you're not in it you can't win it, as Napoleon might have said as he faced Wellington at Waterloo. And look how that turned out for him.

And so to the birthday - Dog F is two years old today so Happy Birthday to her. M Junior posted a photo on Facebook of Dog F posing in front of some mini sausages arranged into the figure 2. And, showing considerable restraint, Dog F is refraining from attacking the sausages until after the photo has been taken. That would never happen here. If M were to place some sausages in front of me they'd be gone before she even had time to get the lens cap off the camera. And anyway there aren't enough sausages in a pack to depict my age.

And Dog F's little sister Baby A is six months old today, so I've invented the term "half-birthday" just for her. Which means that in April she'll have a "three-quarter birthday" and in June a "eleven-twelfths birthday". So I suppose that in a few days I shall be celebrating my "eight hundred and thirty-eight-twelfths birthday."

Oh my goodness that's scary. I wish I hadn't worked it out.

3

⌒∿

Day 3 – a day of weight watching.

A cold and frosty Sunday morning, so where better to spend
it than in bed, listening to M leaving to go and fetch the Sunday
papers at 7.30am. Not for long though, my conscience – assisted
by my bladder - soon got the better of me and I arose (I'd like to
say "sprang out of bed" but that would be a lie) at 8 o'clock and
got my thermals on ready for a morning walk. And a very pleasant morning walk it was as M and I walked to the stables and
back. Oh how we enjoyed the wonderful early morning aroma
of fresh frosty air. And horse manure.

Because of the restricted daylight in these northern climes,
I've been tending to delay my daily walks until after breakfast,
sometimes even after lunch, to try and get as much daylight as
possible. But now that the shortest day has passed and there are a
few minutes of extra daylight every day I'm reverting to my previous routine of a two-mile walk before breakfast. And as daylight stretches into spring I shall expand these walks until I'm
back into last year's regime of a five-mile circuit. Already I can

hear my weak ankle crying out: "No, no, stop this nonsense. Get back on the sofa. I prefer being attached to a lazy slob".

What's brought on all these good intentions, I hear you ask? Well, having plucked up the courage to visit the bathroom scales I was shocked at the big numbers I saw there. And trying to fool the scales with my usual tricks of shedding slippers, taking off clothes, even standing on one leg, had no effect at all.

However, our bathroom scales are very old and I'm beginning to doubt their accuracy. They were bought many years ago in a shop containing the word "pound" in its name, which goes a long way to explaining my scepticism about their quality. So I've taken the bold step of ordering a new set of scales, and this set is approved by Weight Watchers, the official UK organization for people like me. By which I mean those who could do with losing a couple of pounds and need a little help to achieve it. So in a couple of days I should have an accurate reading of my weight, which I may, or may not, choose to share with you.

And when I opened the laptop to order the scales I found, mysteriously placed on the keyboard, a page torn out of one of yesterday's newspapers advertising a special offer of begonias. How did that get there? It would appear M has already started thinking about this year's garden display and this was a strong hint for me to get the credit card out and start ordering.

And in the afternoon, just to prove I was serious about my healthy lifestyle for the new year, M and I went for a long walk to give me an appetite for Sunday dinner. And it worked. It also gave me an appetite for some pre-dinner beer, along with a bowl of salted peanuts and a couple of chocolates from the Christmas supplies. Won't be stepping on the scales tonight.

And as the day drew to a close, the news came that the Scottish Parliament is to be recalled tomorrow and there will be a special announcement from Nicola in the afternoon. Another lockdown on the horizon? All will be revealed.

4

∽

Day 4 – a day of telecommunications.

M's last day of freedom before she goes back to work. She's had five days off in a row so I shall miss her tomorrow when I'm left home alone. To compensate for this she's been keeping me busy today, tidying up the spare room – which used to be my music room but is now designated as Baby A's room for when she visits – and relocating the last few remnants of Christmas back into the attic. To describe the attic as "messy" would be totally inadequate, everything that should really be thrown away gets chucked up there, "just in case". Picking your way through all the clutter is like tiptoeing through a minefield, and only slightly less dangerous. The only reason we don't have mice in the attic is that there's no room for them.

We had a couple of phone calls today, which is a little unusual. And the biggest surprise was that only one of them was a nuisance call. While M and I were away on our morning walk we missed a call from what appeared to be a mobile number. After much head scratching and examining of our mobile phone contacts we decided it wasn't from anyone we knew so I googled it. Up came the result – a cold call from India, pretending to be from a UK mobile phone. They didn't leave a message so I guess I'll never know what they wanted, but it was probably either a) a problem with my computer, or b) compensation for my recent accident.

In a way I'm sorry I missed the call, because sometimes I have lots of fun playing along with them, inventing accidents. Ironically, the one time I did have an accident they didn't want to know. M and I were in a certain Inverness supermarket when a ceiling tile fell on my head. Yes, really. It was as light as a feather so didn't actually do me any damage, but the manager and staff were fussing round me, obviously afraid I might die on the spot, or sue them for every penny they'd got, or cancel my loyalty card and start shopping in Tesco.

So, just on the off chance of a bit of compensation, I called one of these "no win, no fee" companies who are constantly advertising on the telly, told them my tale of woe (massively embellished, of course) and expected them to swing into action and earn me a million pounds. But it wasn't to be. I had to answer truthfully: "Have you suffered any loss of earnings?" and: "Have you incurred any permanent disability?" And because my answers were both in the negative they told me they couldn't do anything for me. And I'm sure that as soon as they hung up on me they recorded my call as: "...just another chancer hoping to make a quick buck".

The second call, which I'm glad to say I didn't miss, was from the optician to say my new specs are ready for collection, so tomorrow I hope to have my 20/20 vision restored, even though it's now 2021. Tomorrow's diary might just have fewer speling misstakes.

As predicted yesterday, 2pm brought Nicola's announcement. And as we expected, it wasn't good news. Scotland is basically back in lockdown with travel restrictions, no meeting indoors, limits on meeting outdoors and, of course, schools closed until February at the earliest. The result of that last announcement, of course, is that our carefully planned exam timetables and invigilator rotas are now in total confusion, for the third time.

My lovely SQA Co-ordinator is still on holiday until Wednesday so I've decided not to bother her until she returns to work, but I can just imagine some of the adjectives which will be thundering down the phone line when she does.

5

∾

Day 5 – a day of sight and sound.

I got my new spectacles today. Hoorah! I can see with both eyes, for the first time in months.

I've been struggling to read with my old specs for months now, all through the last lockdown. Somehow one eye is ok and the other one is blurry, and sometimes, bizarrely, the reverse is true, and I often catch myself reading the paper or watching the telly with only one eye. Maybe that's why M says I don't pay any attention to half of what she tells me.

Anyway, when the opticians were allowed to open again after lockdown I was able to get an appointment (although I had to wait until December to get it), got my eyes tested and a prescription for new specs. The eye test was a bit of an unusual experience, the poor optician was entirely wrapped up in protective clothing, plastic apron, visor, gloves. Even wellies for goodness sake. What was she expecting, wet feet? OK the eye test was a little uncomfortable, but not as eye-watering as her prices.

It was reminiscent of undergoing an alien abduction. Without the traditional probing, thankfully.

You will remember from last year's diaries that we've had a great deal of interaction with the local wildlife. Crows, seagulls, hedgehogs, even frogs. We were visited, not to say harassed, by all of them. And that doesn't include a couple of stray cats, El Gato and his scabby orange rival who loitered around in eternal hope of getting fed. And in spite of my determination not to encourage them, they knew M would always surrender in the end and donate that leftover cold bacon sandwich or sausage roll that I had been hoarding for a snack later. Thankfully she spared my Harry Gow's dream rings. Some lines just cannot be crossed.

Well, you would think that when winter came along there would be a marked downturn in the number of hungry beaks/mouths demanding sustenance. After all, the birds aren't feeding their young any longer, the frogs are dozing deep in the bottom of the pond and the hedgehogs are slumbering in hibernation. I hope that one of them is taking advantage of my hedgehog box which I made in the autumn and stuffed full of straw donated by Farmer J, but I don't suppose I'll find out until something (a hedgehog, a mouse, a baby dragon) emerges in the spring.

Anyway it seems like the wildlife, like the poor, will always be with us. Percy the persistent crow is a regular visitor, and he seems to have befriended a group of seagulls with voracious appetites, so now when we feed the garden birds in the morning one of us has to stand, freezing our bits off, on the doorstep until we're satisfied that they've all had breakfast before we allow the scavengers to arrive.

And last night there was an addition to our wildlife. A very noisy addition. We live very close to the edge of our local woodland, the remnants of the old forest of Brahan, and soon after we went to bed last night a group of owls chose that very moment to take up position in the trees and began teaching their young how to hoot.

The American poet Richard Wibur describes the sound of owls hooting as "...who cooks for you... who cooks for you..." which is quite sweet. At least that's what we thought for the first five minutes. Two hours later we were wishing for them to change their tune. Maybe to the more Scottish version: "Hoots! Och aye the noo! ... Hoots! Och aye the noo!"

6

$\backsim$

Day 6 – a day of staying cosy.

Brrr! Awoke to a hard frost this morning. Almost expected
to see last night's wee owls frozen to their branches. That would
have given me a chance to get up close and hoot loudly in their
faces, then we'd see how they liked it.

The thermometer was showing minus five centigrade when I
set off on my morning walk at 7am. All wrapped up in my thermals, and with my reflective jacket to alert sleepy motorists to
my presence, I did my usual walk to the stables and back, a little over two miles. It was so clear and crisp, and the moon was
so bright, it almost felt like daytime. And when I got home the
temperature had dropped another degree, to minus six as daylight came in. And the frost never lifted all day. So while poor M
had to go to work I was able to stay cosy indoors all day, emerging only every couple of hours to scatter food for the birds. And
strangely enough, no seagulls today. They're probably hanging
around beside the canal in Dingwall, where it's a degree or two

higher due to global warming. Or maybe the council's adjacent sewage plant, which is just as warm. With added nutrition.

Another day, another random phone call. Apparently my ipad7 is due to arrive from Amazon within seven days, and I've paid three hundred and ninety-nine US dollars for it. I've had various incarnations of this message over the past month or two, sometimes the currency is UK pounds and on one occasion it was Australian dollars. Strewth, Sheila!

The annoying thing is that it's always a recorded message, so there's no scope for me to indulge in a bit of fun with the caller. I'd love to play the silly old fool and engage them in a prolonged conversation during which I question which eye the pad is for, or assure them that I already have an eye pad, made out of cotton wool.

But no, my only option is to "...press one if you haven't ordered this.." and so far I've resisted that invitation. And the even more annoying thing is that in spite of all these phone messages not a single ipad7, or even an eye pad, has been delivered. Maybe the Australian one is winging its way from Wagga Wagga.

The official "Weight Watchers" bathroom scales have arrived. They're very precise in their measurements, displaying stones, pounds and even fractions of pounds. I weighed myself as soon as they arrived, fully clothed, then again at bedtime without clothes, and there was a difference of three pounds. Who knew clothes were so heavy? No wonder I'm exhausted by the end of the day.

My ideal weight is 10 stones 12 lbs but I have to confess I'm a little above that right now. Well, when I say a little I mean, erm, quite a lot. I'm hoping, now I've restarted my exercise regime following a lazy Christmas break, that I'll achieve that goal within a few weeks. Every Friday morning will be "weigh-in" time and I'll keep a chart to record my losses. At least I hope they'll be losses. But the maximum range is 24 stones so even if I gain some at least I won't break the scales.

And tomorrow is bin day, so the old ones have been consigned to landfill. I expect the council workers down at the recycling centre will have a lot of fun trying to get them to work. Good luck with that, lads, because I've taken the battery out.

7

∽

Day 7 – a day of slipping and sliding.

Oh boy, was it icy this morning? Last night we had frost, followed by rain, followed by more frost. The end result was that all the roads and pavements (or, if you're reading this in the USA, pavements and sidewalks) were fiendishly slippery. Poor M had to walk on the village playing field instead of the normal path on her way to the shop, otherwise she was in danger of falling over and breaking her wrist. Or worse, my eggs.

So no morning walk for me, instead I tiptoed out very gingerly spreading salt on all the paths around the house, which wasn't easy. Luckily it was still dark at 7am so the neighbours were spared the sight of me inching along with one hand clinging on to the wall for stability. I can imagine them shaking their heads and tutting to each other: 'That's Sandy just getting home from a wild night at the Mòd'.

Later, when I thought the temperature had risen a little, I did venture out with the intention of walking to the stables. But the roads and paths were still very icy so I curtailed those plans and made do with a short walk through the woods instead. I met a number of people, some with kids and some with dogs, and one or two with bruises having slipped and fallen on their, erm, dignity. And all of them were younger and more sure-footed than I am, so it's a miracle that I made it all the way round without incident. Although to be fair I was averaging a speed of around half a mile an hour.

Yesterday I had a Zoom meeting with M Junior, which is the only kind of meeting we can have right now. And in the middle of it she had to dash out of the room to take a phone call, so I was able to have a nice conversation with Farmer J and Baby A. Baby A's conversation was nice and loud but a little hard to decipher, so we were completely compatible with each other.

M Junior and I had been trialling a whiteboard program online, as an experiment for her remote teaching to see how she and her pupil (me!) could communicate visually. So while she was out of the room I used the whiteboard to draw things for Baby A's amusement. It's very difficult to do accurate drawings using a mouse pad, but I was quite pleased with my efforts. Especially my drawing of a noble Aberdeen-Angus bull, which was belittled somewhat by Farmer J saying: "Look Baby A, Grandad drew a goat". Some farmer he turned out to be.

Following on from that, we made up a parcel of gifts and sent it off addressed to Baby A. A couple of books and a pram toy for her, some sweeties for M Junior and Farmer J, and of course a toy and some treats for Dog F. I defrosted the car and popped into Dingwall to post the parcel, along with instructions from M to get a loaf of bread. Not for myself of course, but for the birds. "Don't get one of those cheap wholemeal ones, they prefer a nice fresh seeded one".

And so, of course, I got them their highly expensive seeded loaf, and at various points during the day I threw scraps of it out to them, along with grated cheese, chopped up ham and last night's left over salmon skins. And how do they repay me? Yes, you've guessed it – by depositing vast quantities of evil smelling sticky goo on my nice clean windows/car/head.

8

~

Day 8 – a day of official interaction.

I had a phone discussion with my favourite SQA Co-ordinator yesterday. Well, it wasn't so much a discussion as a mutual moaning session, she's as frustrated as I am with our ever-changing exam arrangements. Our Prelim exams which usually happen in December, then were delayed until 18th January, then delayed again until 25th January, are now cancelled altogether. Schools are closed until February at the earliest so I've had to write to my entire invigilation team telling them their services aren't required.

Hopefully we'll get back to a normal exam situation next year, by which time the virus will be under control and we'll all have been vaccinated. I don't know exactly when my turn will come for vaccination but I can't wait. I've been sitting here with my sleeve rolled up since the first of December.

A brush with officialdom this week. I've been in touch with the Driver and Vehicle Licensing Agency, who had the cheek to write to me in December telling me that my driving licence was about to expire in a couple of months when I reach "a certain age" (which, please note, can never be mentioned out loud). Advancing years? How impudent! I know what my birth certificate says, but in my head I'm still in my late thirties.

Anyway, they seemed to be serious so I thought I'd better play along with their demands so I filled in their application form. Most questions were pretty straightforward, ie:

"Do you suffer from any major illnesses?" - answer, thankfully: "No".

"Have you ever been convicted of any crime?" - answer, truthfully: "No"

"Can you read a car number plate from a distance of 20.5 metres?" - answer: "haven't a clue what 20.5 metres looks like but I can read the logo on my neighbour's sweatshirt from all the way across the street. It appears to say "SUPERDRY", although I may be mistaken because it's pouring rain.

And somehow they must have been pleased with my answers because my new licence has arrived. I see it's only valid for three years so it looks as if I'm going to have to answer the same questions in 2024. I've heard horror stories about drivers renewing their licences and finding that their motorcycle entitlement has been accidentally removed so I thought I'd better check that mine was still valid. After all, you never know when the midlife crisis will strike and I head off into the sunset on Route 66 astride a throbbing Harley. Or, more likely, along Dingwall High Street on a rattly moped.

Looking at the licence, it seems to show my photo, date of birth, address etc but doesn't show the vehicle classes, so I thought I had better get on to the website and do some research. Of course it wouldn't tell me until I had proved my identity – driver number, national insurance number, mother's maiden name, neighbour's sweatshirt logo, you know the usual thing.

And when I complained about this tortuous process to M she snorted, grabbed my licence and showed me the reverse side, on which all my entitlements are clearly listed. When will I learn?

Happily, my motorbike licence is still intact. The only thing that's missing is my minibus licence, which expires at "the age we daren't mention" and can only be renewed upon successful completion of a medical examination. Which I would have to pay for. Not only that, but after much reflection I've asked myself: "do I really want to be responsible for a bus load of other people's kids at my age?" And anyway, I've had a good long run of ferrying sweaty adolescents around the hills and glens of Northern Scotland after several days hiking, camping and not washing, so I think my sense of smell deserves a break.

9

∽

Day 9 – a day of caffeine intake.

The frost has gone and it was a nice morning. And it's Saturday, which is bed-changing day, so M sprang into action, stripped the bedding and popped it into the washing machine. An hour later it was ready for hanging out, just as the rain started. Luckily, we have an alternative means of drying the washing – in M's greenhouse we have an electric airer which has the dual benefit of drying the clothes and keeping the greenhouse frost-free.

Yesterday I told you I had written to my invigilation team to tell them about the exams being cancelled, therefore they wouldn't be getting their pocket money this year. And all we get really is pocket money, no-one gets rich invigilating on the minimum hourly wage. But it's handy all the same, my SQA pay usually comes in at the start of the summer break, so that's what I use as beer money for my holidays. This year, of course, it looks like there won't be any holidays. And to add insult to injury I shall have to buy my beer with my own money. Unless I can get access to M's private drawer, wherein resides the royal purse.

Anyway, having written all these letters I had to get to the Post Office to buy stamps and get them posted. And in line with my new fitness regime I walked to Dingwall instead of simply jumping into the car, which is always my first reaction. The Post Office, sadly, is at the far end of the High Street so it's a round trip of more than four miles and at my comfortable speed it takes me just under two hours. Except when M is with me, in which case we manage it in less than an hour and a half.

And that's what happened today. M needed to get the electric meter token thingy topped up, which is one of the services provided by the Post Office, so in spite of my protestations: 'I did it yesterday', I was obliged (forced) to walk exactly the same distance again today. At a much higher speed. Phew, I was glad to get home for a warming drink from our new coffee maker.

Yes, in a post-Christmas fervour helped along by M Junior, who also has one, we've become a 21st century family and bought a coffee making machine. Quite a change from a lifetime of drinking instant coffee, sometimes made by world class brands but more usually purchased from a cut-price bargain shop with a fake lookalike label and comprised mainly of sawdust, ground-up rice and a smattering of actual coffee just to make it smell vaguely authentic.

And in keeping with my own long-held traditions, as soon as any new device comes home the first thing I do is cast the instructions aside unopened. 'Won't be needing these!', I cry as I plug the thing in and start pushing buttons, 'This is gonna be the best coffee you ever tasted!'.

My first attempt yielded half a cup of hot water, and the second produced a quarter of a cup of evil-smelling black tarry liquid. Good for filling in potholes but sadly not drinkable. So - at M's insistence – the instructions had to be consulted after all. And as a result I discovered that: a) you have to put a pod in the machine before you start, and b) you have to insert it the right way up. Now that these skills have been mastered we are enjoying regular supplies of freshly brewed coffee, better than anything a Starbucks barista can produce. And to make it an authentic experience we write our names on the cups. Spelt wrongly, naturally.

10

∽

Day 10 – a day of bike madness.

And once again, it's Sunday. A day of rest? No, not with M encouraging me to get up, get out and get exercising. And so we set off on our usual morning walk, only to find that there had been some frost early in the night followed by some rain, so the roads and pavements were very slippery indeed. To keep ourselves safe we each carried a stick and adopted the well-known method of staying upright on ice – walking like a penguin. Yes, waddling along slowly with feet splayed and hands held out by our sides like stabilisers. Not very dignified, but it keeps us safe and gives the neighbours a laugh.

Although I did think the lady across the road who threw us a fish was being a little disrespectful. And her cat thought so too. After all, it was his fish.

There were quite a few people out, some walking (gingerly) or driving slowly, and we were quite surprised when a man appeared from one of the side streets on a bicycle. Pedalling along confidently, we commented on his bravery. Then, wouldn't you just know it? As soon as he was past us we heard a thud followed by a groaning sound which soon developed into string of expletives that would make a sailor blush. Turning round, we saw that he had attempted a right turn, obviously touched his brakes, and his bike had dumped him unceremoniously in the middle of the road. And the road is a very hard surface on which to be dumped, especially when it's frozen solid under a layer of water.

Rushing to his aid, penguin-style, took a little time. But because he was lying in the middle of a junction, entangled in the frame of his bicycle, I was worried a car would come and cause him even greater injury. When I reached him he was still lying down, swearing ferociously. I managed to at least extricate him from the bike, and was just trying to remember my first aid training course of more than twenty years ago, when with a final deep groan he managed to haul himself upright. Safely off the road, we established that he wasn't seriously injured, apart from a bruised hip and a badly dented dignity. His bike wasn't quite so lucky, the left handlebar appeared to have developed a desire to go the opposite direction from its right-sided colleague.

As we set him off homewards, pushing his bike, I remarked to M: "I think I'll get my own bike out today". "That's fine", she responded, "I'll have the ambulance service on speed dial".

The rest of the day was less eventful. After a two or three hour session with the Sunday papers (and the crossword), and a nice coffee from the new machine (made by M), the weather had improved so we had a longer walk in the afternoon. Up through the village of Conon Bridge and home via the A835, there was a surprising amount of traffic around. So the fresh air we had hoped for was tempered by a less healthy dose of carbon monoxide.

And that was followed by a video call from M Junior and we were able to see Baby A doing her usual baby things. Trying to crawl, throwing her toys around, looking to be fed. She gets more like her grandad every day.

11

∽

Day 11 – a day of feeling fed up, cheered up, and fed up again.

Oh dear what a start to the week. Monday morning, and we awoke to torrential rain. It was so bad that M had to take an umbrella to the shop when she went for the papers. And instead of leaping out of bed in time to see her off to work, to my great shame I dozed on until after she'd gone. And when I did eventually get up the weather was no better, so no walkies today. It poured all morning until lunchtime, at which point it snowed. My motivation was at rock bottom, I couldn't be bothered doing anything. Luckily I still had enough energy to eat, drink and lounge in front of the telly.

In desperation, and in an effort to combat my state of boredom, I turned to last year's diary to see if anything would inspire me. And I saw that a year ago last night, I was at the first Burns Supper of 2020. I know it was a little early because Burns wasn't born until 25th January, but the organisers wanted to get in early so they could grab the cream of guest speakers. And in most cases they succeeded, but when it came to finding someone to propose a toast to the Immortal Memory they'd run out of options and so they chose me.

"The Toast To The Immortal Memory Of Robert Burns", to give it its full title, is the keynote speech of the evening and although I've sung at many Burns Suppers over the years this was to be my first experience of serious speech-making. And knowing that a number of people in the room would be much more familiar than I with the life and work of Burns, I decided that I'd better knuckle down and do some serious preparation. Unlike when I was in school sitting my exams, all my study leave was spent fishing and dreaming about motorbikes.

And so I took myself off to the public library. Remember the days when we could actually go to the library? I settled down in the reference room with some books on Burns and my A4 memo pad, and as I looked around I felt very outdated because all my fellow library users were students with ipads, laptops and tablet computers. And there was me with my paper and pencil, scribbling notes and quotes while they were simply pointing their devices at the material and photographing it. I realized then what it must feel like to be a dinosaur who finds himself transplanted into the modern world.

According to all the experts, including Mr Google, my speech should be informative, educational and amusing and last for around 25 minutes. Once I had got home with my notes and written them up I had a trial run, and the speech went on for a full 45 minutes. Horrors! Forty-five minutes of listening to me will send the audience to sleep at best, and kill them with boredom at worst. Some serious editing then took place and eventually I had managed to trim my speech down to the requisite time. I shared this information with my pal, who was due to be in the audience, and his helpful response was: "Well, as soon as you get to 25 minutes I'm going to start clapping, whether you're finished or not".

Well, with pressure like that, I made sure I was finished on time. It all seemed to go very well, and the following day I was visited by the organising lady and given a nice bottle of wine. Which I hoped to squirrel away for later but M insisted on sharing. Oh well, *the best laid schemes o' mice an' men gang aft agley,* as a certain R Burns once said.

In the afternoon, just as I was feeling really fed up, one of my invigilators phoned to say she'd received my letter about the exams. We had a mutual grumbling session about Covid but she's such a cheery soul that she immediately made me feel better, and by the end of the conversation I was much more optimistic. Until I looked out of the window and saw the snow.

12

～

Day 12 – a day of taking part

You will be impressed to hear that I have been "chosen" by the grandly named Office for National Statistics (ONS) to take part in a UK-wide online study. Not a survey or an opinion poll such as ordinary people might be invited to take part in, but a UK-wide national study. There, I knew if I said it often enough you'd be impressed.

This all started a week or so ago when an official-looking brown envelope arrived, addressed to "The Resident". After some debate about who should open it, M decided that I should be "The Resident", just in case it was a parking fine or a demand from the tax office. And if it turned out to be a lottery win or a legacy from a long-forgotten relative then of course the title of "Resident" would revert to her.

It turned out to be from the Director General of the ONS, one Iain Bell, bearing the good news about my selection and asking me to go on to their website and complete the study. Two questions immediately sprang to mind – firstly, is it compulsory, and secondly what's in it for me? And the answers to those questions appeared to be – firstly, no and secondly, nothing. So straight into the recycling bin went Mr Bell's letter, along with his brown envelope.

After some days had elapsed, another, larger and heavier, official-looking brown envelope arrived. Again addressed to "The Resident", this time it contained a similar letter to the first one, a three-page questionnaire and – joy of joys! – a free gift! A shopping bag, or what you might call a tote bag if you had anything worth toting, emblazoned with the ONS crest. Very important-looking and handy for M to use when bringing home the beer from the weekly shopping trip.

So, in light of Mr Bell's unexpected generosity, I decided to show my gratitude by casting aside my churlishness and taking part in his study. According to his letter it should take between ten and twenty minutes to complete online so I settled down (with a mug of home made café latte, hope you're impressed!) and logged on using the unique household code provided. And up came my address, as if by magic. And it was very easy to take part, there were no probing questions and no deeply personal details asked for. Just names and dates of birth of residents in the household, how many students, how many working full time, how many in receipt of benefits, that sort of thing. Unusually, they didn't even want to know my mother's maiden name, unlike every other government agency I've ever dealt with.

What is this obsession government departments have with my mother's maiden name? Next time I'm asked I shall say

"Trump", or "Putin". That should set a few alarm bells ringing in the murkier reaches of Whitehall.

Anyway, having completed the survey – sorry, I mean UK-wide online study – I was gratified to be told that, along with Mr Bell's undying gratitude, I was also to be rewarded with a £15 gift voucher which would be emailed to me without delay.

And, three days later, no gift voucher has yet arrived. And, to rub salt into an already well salted wound, another letter arrived today in which Director General Bell tells me I have only until 19 January to take part in his UK-wide online study. And, he goes on, if I don't take part online, "one of our interviewers may call you".

Ooh I hope they do. I can have a lot of fun with interviewers on the phone.

13

~

Day 13 – a day of deep freezing.

For the second day in a row, the temperature failed to register above zero. Bad news for sun worshippers but good news for penguins, polar bears and well wrapped up pensioners. The best part of it is that the ground is nice and hard, even in the muddiest areas, and so walking is easy, clean and pleasant. As long as you manage to stay upright.

Mornings are still too dark for venturing out as we're still less than a month on from the shortest day, so I've been delaying my walks until after breakfast. Yesterday and today I've been avoiding the tarred road to the stables and reacquainting myself with the local woodland walk. It's a really interesting walk which gives the opportunity to spot wildlife including roe deer, woodpeckers and today, a rare sight – a teenager up and about before 9am.

Schools are closed and lessons are being conducted via the internet, so I imagine most pupils will register online and then retreat to the sanctuary and comfort of their cosy bed. And as long as they remember to switch their webcam off, teacher will never know.

We've been notified by our local medical practice that covid-19 vaccinations are on the way, and will commence shortly. We are not to contact them, they will call us forward when they're ready for us, and we'll be done in order of priority, ie the over 90s, then the over 80s, and so on. The Health Secretary estimates that all over 70s will be vaccinated by Valentine's Day. So all you old romantics will be able to pop out and buy a bunch of flowers and a slushy card for your wife/lover/cat. So that'll be three cards for some of you, then.

Not me, though. Even if everything goes to plan, I'm not due to get my covid jab until the beginning of March so M will have to remain in a Valentine card free zone this year. Again.

But I shall be very relieved to get my vaccination, because I've been sitting here with my sleeve rolled up since early December and my left arm is beginning to feel the cold.

Another day, yet another telephone recorded message about this phantom ipad which I have allegedly ordered from Amazon. Not Australian this time, but British. The biggest shock is that the price seems to have rocketed, from £399 to a massive £1049. I understand about inflation, but that seems excessive. Maybe they think that a higher price will make me more likely to press the button to speak to their adviser but sorry chums, I'm still not gonna bite.

This afternoon Nicola Sturgeon announced some even stricter measures to try to stop the spread of Covid-19 in Scotland. She's restricted the "click and collect" scheme, which I wasn't familiar with and which turns out to be a shopping service. I thought for a moment she was referring to my increasingly noisy arthritic knee joints, which are more likely to "click and collapse".

And the other major change is that we're no longer allowed to drink alcohol outdoors, in these days of the so-called "takeaway pint". Yes, I know that's a difficult concept to understand in the middle of a Scottish winter, but believe it or not some customers have been doing just that since the pubs were forced to stop serving drinks indoors. It must be difficult though, you'd have to gulp your beer down quickly because it freezes at minus two degrees Celsius, and your wine will turn into a rich red pinot noir ice lolly at minus five.

Best bet for an al fresco winter tipple is good old Scotch Whisky, which will remain liquid in the glass until it reaches minus twenty-seven. And by that time all your fingers will have fallen off and you won't be able to grip the glass anyway.

14

～

Day 14 – a day of online inspections and refunds.

A horrible day of rain and snow, gardens waterlogged, roads slippery and footpaths too muddy to walk upon. So no walkies today, apart from a wee stroll to the mailbox to post a couple of letters left for me by M. And I had to use one of MY OWN stamps on one of them, imagine! Therefore today's calorie intake was, I fear, much higher than calories burned, although I did clean the whole house so I suppose that would account for the equivalent of half a chocolate bar. Although in my experience it's impossible to eat only half of a chocolate bar.

Education news – announced in today's papers is the Scottish Government's plan for school inspectors to continue to carry out their inspections, even in these times of remote learning. Teachers are finding online learning to be very taxing, with problems getting pupils to log in, and to pay attention once they have logged in, but at least the threat of a school inspection was no longer hanging over them. Well it is now.

Having worked in and around schools for many years, I'm

well aware of the feeling teachers have of impending dread when inspections are on the horizon. In Scotland there's usually be a period of a couple of weeks' notice before the arrival of the inspection team, and these couple of weeks are spent by teachers in feverish activity, getting records and lesson plans up to date, making classroom displays look professional, and persuading the less, erm, "compliant" pupils to take a couple of days off. Not that that last one ever happened in any of my schools, of course.

So how are these inspections going to take place? In normal times the inspector sits at the back of the class and takes notes while the teacher takes the lesson. It's a very anxious time for the teacher, who's trying to concentrate on the lesson whilst praying silently all the while that none of the little darlings shout out the wrong answers (usually girls) / start throwing things at each other (usually boys) / break wind loudly and deliberately (also usually boys).

With remote learning, I suppose the inspector will simply be able to log on to any lesson and appear by magic as an extra face on the teacher's screen. How unnerving will that be? Suddenly a screen crammed with ten-year-old fresh faced cherubs is joined by an extra pupil with grey hair, specs and a severe expression. And he's the only one, including the teacher, not wearing pyjamas.

Those of you with exceptional memories, or who are anal about record keeping (tip – don't google "anal record keeping") will remember that way back on the 17th of July last year Boris addressed the nation, in his usual Churchillian style. He wanted to share his vision of how the Covid-19 pandemic would pan out, and was widely quoted as stating it would be: "...all over, in time for Christmas".

Well, on the strength of that optimism I went ahead and booked a return flight to London in February this year in order to make my annual visit to one of my favourite motorcycle shows. And as time went on and Boris's predictions were obviously wildly inaccurate I realised that it simply wasn't going to happen. Should I cancel my flights and lose the money, or would easyJet be forced to cancel them, in which case I could get a refund? As the year turned, and as January progressed, it was a question of who would blink first, me or Stelios. And today I got the email I was hoping for: "dear customer, with regret your flight EZYxxx will not be operating. Please select an alternative, or apply for a voucher".

Being an old hand at navigating the easyJet website, I neither selected an alternative nor applied for a voucher but went straight to the "refund" option, which they don't publicise and which appears in the small print. The very small print. And back came an email stating my refund is "in progress". It probably won't appear for several weeks, but in the meantime the score is: Sandy 1, easyJet 0.

15

⌒⌒

Day 15 – a day of money saving.

Following yesterday's easyJet refund application, I had another couple of financial successes today. But before I tell you about them, I need to report that I've had an email from easyJet which begins: "Dear customer, as you will shortly be flying with us here are the rules on mask wearing aboard our aircraft..." Well Mr easyJet, I won't shortly be flying with you, because yesterday you cancelled my flights and told me that my refund is in progress. Evidently there's been a breakdown in communications between easyJet's refund department and their mask enforcement department. Or maybe they're so fully masked up that they can't understand a word they say to each other.

Anyway, back to today's achievements. Firstly, remember I told you a few days ago about taking part in the Office for National Statistics' survey? And they said I would be rewarded for my input? Well I'm happy to say that an email has arrived telling me how to claim my reward, a £15 voucher for the retailer of my choice. All I have to do is select the retailer from the list supplied, many of which I've never heard of and aren't suitable for me anyway. Whittard of Chelsea? Too far away. Lookfantastic skincare? Too late for my leathery complexion. Miss Selfridge? Now I know you're having a laugh.

So I've done the sensible thing and opted for a Tesco voucher, and very generously given it to M to help with her weekly shopping. Although it would be wrong of me to consider advising her what to buy with it, I just thought I should mention that you can get a pretty respectable bottle of beer

The other financial gain also relates to M, whose car insurance is due to be renewed in three weeks or so. I had a bit of a disagreement with our current insurer last year, when they declined my suggestion that they might give me a wee rebate in consideration of the fact my car didn't move for three months while I was in isolation. I declared that I would never deal with them again and rather annoyingly they didn't seem too perturbed at the thought of losing my valued custom. I imagine they have files on all their customers, and mine is labelled: "Cantankerous old cheapskate. Handle with care".

And so, in December when my own car insurance was due for renewal I did a lot of research and I was pleased to discover that I was eligible to apply for a policy with the grandly named "Civil Service Insurance Society". Yes, it may surprise you to learn that I was once civil enough to be classed as a civil servant. And all these years spent counting paper clips have finally paid off because I'm saving a massive £120 a year on car insurance. Of course there are terms and conditions, as you might imagine.

You have to prove you're a genuine civil servant so I'm glad I hung on to my briefcase and bowler hat.

And the CSIS were happy to insure M's car, just as they had insured mine, and saved her £120 a year too. Surely, I enquired, I deserved some sort of reward. "Certainly, my dear" said M, handing me a £15 Tesco voucher.

16

~

Day 16 – a day of reliving trauma.

Instead of telling you about my day today, I must tell you about the drama I had last night. Luckily I had finished writing my diary before it happened, but I'm still traumatised and think I might need counselling. Or beer.

It was a typical Friday night, 8pm, M was watching football and I was just settling down to enjoy a music show on "Facebook Live" when, bang! Off went the lights! And with them, off went the telly, the wifi and the central heating. My first reaction was to check the electric meter to see if it had run out of credit but, naturally, without power it was completely dead, so couldn't display any figures. Of course I should have expected that. "That's just what I expected", I informed M upon my return from the meter cupboard.

Next – look out of the window and see whether the neighbours have lights on. And what a shock! The whole street was in complete darkness, no house lights, no street lights, so obviously it wasn't just we who were affected. Funny how a power cuts is like a cold shower - it never seems so bad when there's someone else in there with you. Unless you're in jail of course.

Luckily we have a supply of candles for just such an emergency, and they were quickly retrieved from storage and lit, so even though we couldn't watch telly at least we could see each other. Which meant that M was obliged to look at me rather than at Cristiano Ronaldo. He may be younger and fitter, but I do more dribbling.

Armed with a torch, I ventured out in the pitch black night to check on our elderly neighbour. And after making sure she was ok I walked along to the end of the street, from where I could see that the entire village was in darkness. Obviously there had been a major failure in the supply, so nobody for miles around was able to watch telly. Husbands everywhere were having to speak to their wives, some of them for the first time in years.

Whenever there's any kind of domestic drama M and I have a solution, which is - make a cup of tea. Tea is our cure for everything from a blocked drain to the common cold, but without a kettle I would need to find, set up and remember how to use my camping gas stove, which I hadn't used for a couple of years. We agreed that to give the engineers time to get the power back on we'd wait half an hour before making tea. We lasted all of five minutes.

So there I was, juggling a torch, a gas cooker, a bottle of gas and a set of instructions while M stood by with a pan of water, waiting for to me to coax the device into life. It's funny how Stone Age man was able to make fire using only sticks and flints, but 21st Century man needs matches, gas, and a degree in engineering to do the same thing. Anyway, once I'd got the gas to light and waved bye-bye to my eyebrows M was able to make us a calming cup of tea.

Eventually, after around an hour of darkness, the power came back on just after nine so normal life was able to resume. And luckily the football was still on so M was able to watch the end of the second half while I blew out the candles and dismantled the camping gas cooker. Than later, when she went off to bed, I settled down to watch episode 1 of the latest Simpsons series, which I had set the Sky box to record at 8pm. And of course, one minute into the show, up came the message: "Recording failed due to power interruption". No wonder I'm traumatised.

17

〜

Day 17 – a day of weight loss.

Sunday again, and after Friday night's events I can report
that the rest of the weekend went without any dramas. Saturday
morning was wet so we abandoned our plans for a morning
walk. Which gave me all morning to read the papers and complete The Times prize crossword, which was a minor miracle –
it usually takes me at least twenty-four hours and involves exten-
sive googling.

After lunch the rain appeared to have stopped, so M and I
walked into Dingwall to post the crossword. It was quite a pleasant walk on the outward journey, with a nice breeze behind us
to help us along. But on the way back the heavens opened again
and by the time we got home we were soaked. No harm done
though, and I was soon glowing after a quick change of clothes
and a rub down with an old army blanket. I knew it would come
in handy some day.

Our local medical practice has started doing covid vaccinations for over-80s at weekends. I heard from a couple of friends

that their parents had received theirs today. This is good news because once they've done the over-80s they'll move on to the over-70s and so on, so I'm hoping it won't be too long until I get mine and I can roll my sleeve down again.

And Saturday finished off with a video call from M Junior, to let us see Baby A playing with her toys in the bath, which looks like a lot of fun. I wondered whether I could have some bath toys and M agreed that it would be a good idea. She suggested taking my laptop in with me, or even a hairdryer. First, though, she insisted on me showing her where I keep my life insurance documents.

Then we moved into Sunday, which started with my weekly weight check. Yes, I know I said I'd weigh myself every Friday but I keep forgetting. I tried sticking a reminder on the bathroom mirror, but that led to me missing a bit when shaving. Anyway, I'm pleased to report that after a complete week of no snacks, no beer and exercise (almost) every day, I have actually lost some weight. However I'm not quite so pleased to report the magnitude of this weight loss – a massive four ounces, according to the super-sensitive and accurate weightwatchers bathroom scales. Four ounces? I'm not sure all my sacrifices are worth it but I'll keep going for one more week. And if there's no marked improvement I shall revert to my normal lifestyle, ie sugar, alcohol and full-fat cheese in industrial quantities.

Sunday is always a quiet day in the Thomson household. Except when Baby A and Dog F are visiting, of course. But visits are not permitted right now so it was only M and I who set off for our morning walk. And just like last Sunday, the roads were very slippery, with rain water on top of ice. So, just in case there would be a repeat of last week's bicycle madness, we decided to turn back and wait until later.

And so in the afternoon we had a long walk, up the main road and home via Conon. The path beside the main road is a shared pedestrian/cycle path and so you have to watch out for silent cyclists coming up from behind and whooshing past without warning. Don't they put bells on bikes any more? I was about to write an angry letter to the papers until I checked, and found that actually the compulsory fitting of bells to bikes was scrapped in 2011. I think we should start a campaign to bring back bicycle bells. And while we're at it, let's bring back some other things from the past. Dog licences, cuckoo clocks and bobbies on bicycles. With bells, naturally.

18

～～

Day 18 – a day of feeling blue.

Today is Blue Monday, the most depressing day of the year. There now, that's cheered you up, hasn't it? Apparently it's a real "thing", it's in all the papers today and refers to the day when Christmas jollity has finally faded from memory, the new year resolutions have stalled and the credit card bills have arrived. Although mine didn't, because the postie didn't come at all today. Was it an official post office holiday, or was he having a blue Monday too?

Incredibly, there's even a formula for Blue Monday, are you ready for this? It's [W+(D-d)]xTQ/MxNA where W is weather, D is debt and no-one has been able to stay awake long enough to decipher the rest of it. And you thought algebra was hard in high school? Anyway, I'm happy to say that even if it was a blue day, it was also a nice day and I had a good long walk through the woods once daylight arrived at 9am.

And afterwards I thought I'd cheer myself up by watching a bit of television. I'm a real fan of box sets, and always on the look out for something new to download, so I settled down with the BBC's latest offering, The Serpent. Well, if you're looking for something happy to cheer yourself up on a dull day The Serpent may not be for you. It's a dramatisation of the life of Charles Sobhraj, a real baddy from the 1970s who drugged, murdered and robbed tourists in various Far Eastern cities including Bangkok, Delhi and Hong Kong.

Originally it was planned to do much of the filming in Thailand. There's a well-known city in the southwest of the country, called Trang. Sadly, due to a typing error, a mistranslation or maybe an autocorrect issue, the cast and crew found themselves in Tring, Hertfordshire. The director was heard to declare that autocorrect was his worst enema.

Amongst the most interesting scenes for me were those filmed in Kathmandu. M and I were there in 2012, and I recognised some of the street scenes, which hadn't changed since our visit. Indeed I suspect they haven't changed in a hundred years, except for an increase in rich western visitors. One thing that struck me was the number of cows wandering the streets. Of course the cow is sacred, and any motorist who collides with one, even inadvertently, can expect an automatic jail sentence. Although the roads are so rough it's impossible to exceed 15 miles an hour, so most cows survive these encounters. Much to the relief of Nepalese drivers.

In the market areas, the stallholders have their fruit and veg laid out on tables, for the customers to poke, prod and inspect before buying. Commonly, the cows also take an interest in these displays and it's not unusual to see a cow wander past, help itself to a banana or take a bite from a cabbage or a watermelon. And because of their protected status the stallholder can't stop them or chase them away. If your local Tesco manager complains about shoplifters, just tell him about the four-legged ones in Kathmandu and he'll realise how lucky he is.

And finally, after watching Charles Sobhraj murder his way across the far east, the day ended as blue as it began. The only cheerful time was when M arrived home and cooked dinner. A nice bit of roast beef which served as a revenge upon cows everywhere. Ha! Not so sacred now, are you?

19

∽

Day 19 – a day of traffic disruption.

Another very cold day, M had to defrost her car before she could leave for work. In support, I made sympathetic noises from under the duvet.

After breakfast it was still cold but nice and sunny, so I had a longer walk than usual, through the woods by a different route. And I was cheered by the sight of a wee conifer which had been decorated with red baubles and a wooden ornament inscribed with the words "Happy Christmas". It must have been done before Christmas, and the decorations had been left on it, so it was a lovely bright cheerful sight, which was a great cure for yesterday's blue day.

Walking on some paths which I hadn't been on since last year, I found that in some sheltered areas where the frost hadn't penetrated there was deep mud. Four inches deep in some places, which isn't a problem. Unless you're the little Jack Russell dog I met, whose belly was only three inches off the ground.

The building site in the village has been busy for several

weeks now. A new housing development is being built alongside the road which we use to get access to the main street and thence to Dingwall. And new houses need access to all kinds of utilities, including electricity and gas and, very importantly, water and sewage. Imagine if all these nice new houses didn't have running water and flush toilets? It would be just like my granny's house back in the 1950s, a wee wooden shed out in the back yard with a dry toilet, squares of newspaper hanging on a nail, and more spiders than a whole spiderman movie.

And so, in order for the new residents to benefit from modern water management, the builders have closed the road while they connect the new houses to the existing pipelines. So we're cut off from the world! Actually no, we're not cut off at all, there's a perfectly good alternative road which adds only a few seconds on to our journey time, but after nearly forty years of driving up and down the same street it's hard to change your habits. In spite of large signs, prominently displayed, I still drove down the wrong way today and had to do an embarrassing (twenty-)three point turn with all the builders nudging each other and sniggering.

I just hope none of them filmed the event, I have no wish to become an overnight YouTube sensation. Well, not for my driving anyway.

In fairness, today was my first day driving since Day 5, when I went to fetch my new specs. Travel is banned unless essential, and I've been very good at obeying Nicola's rules. But today I had to go to the Post Office to dispatch a few copies of my (first) book – a couple of freebies for friends and a couple to local newspapers in the hope that they'll review it. Favourably, preferably. And because the Post Office doubles as a grocery shop I was able to buy a pint of milk while I was there, my first time in a shop this year.

Speaking of milk, who remembers when milk was delivered to your doorstep daily? Well first thing this morning I spotted a milk delivery sitting on my neighbour's doorstep so evidently some enterprising dairy has reintroduced the daily delivery service. I wonder whether there's a similarly enterprising brewery who would do the same for me? A daily delivery would be very handy, especially if it arrives early enough for me to pour onto my cornflakes.

20

❦

Day 20 – a day of power executive business naps.

Today is Wednesday, or maybe Thursday, I'm confused. The weather forecast clearly stated that we would have snow on Thursday, and indeed here it is. Yet all of today's newspapers are dated Wednesday. Even one of the more sensational tabloids, which isn't famous for accurate reporting, clearly states that coronavirus is a government conspiracy in alliance with Russia, that the vaccine contains a microchip so Bill Gates can keep us under surveillance, and that today is Wednesday.

Regardless of what day it is, when I got up this morning there was no snow, only a touch of frost. Then, in the space of two hours there was a huge dump of snow which transformed the whole street into a winter wonderland scene worthy of a Christmas card. Complete with a festive robin and a small donkey. No, wait, that's the cat across the road. I'm beginning to regret choosing these new double strength spectacles.

Once it dried up I set off on my morning walk through the woods, hoping to get round as long as it wasn't snowing. And

I was at exactly the furthest away point from home when it started, so no point turning back. And by the time I got home all my nicely cleared paths were white again. Luckily, I had been so lavish earlier with the salt that the snow soon melted and the paths were safe for the postie to walk on. Not that he brings anything exciting, it's almost entirely junk mail. Today's offerings included a funeral plan leaflet, an advert for beds and a holiday brochure from Saga, the travel agency for the over-50s. I didn't know whether to die, lie or fly.

And if you're old enough to travel with Saga there's a good chance you could do all three on the same holiday.

M was at work, of course, so I had to carry out the daily duty of keeping the garden birds fed and watered. I give them a mixture of breadcrumbs, crushed fat balls and mealworms (dead, thankfully) which I dispense three times a day. Keeping them fed isn't as easy as it sounds due to constant attacks by marauding seagulls and crows. Once I throw out the food I have to stay alert for half an hour to watch out for these intruders. Stay alert for half an hour? I can hardly stay awake for half an hour between naps. Or power naps, as I like to think of them.

And I'm in good company, apparently. World leaders, military heroes and geniuses throughout history have all benefited from napping. Churchill napped every day throughout World War 2, even as the bombs were dropping on London. Napoleon could drop off in an instant, even on the battlefield. Even Thomas Edison was a fan of the power nap, although he ruined it for himself somewhat by inventing the light bulb.

And according to some reports, our own Prime Minister

Boris has what he calls "power executive business naps", so that's what I'm going to call mine from now on. Imagine the conversation...

'Were you asleep in the armchair, just then?'

'No dear, I was having a power executive business nap.'

'OK then, any chance you could powerfully execute the business of hanging out the washing?'

21

∽

Day 21 – a day of all-day illumination.

No confusion about what day it is today, I know it's Thursday. How do I know this? Well it's because Thursday is bin lorry day (garbage truck for my American readers), and last night I heard my neighbour putting his bin out. Not only do I rely on him to know the correct day, I also rely on him to know which of our three bins is due to be uplifted. We have brown, blue and green ones, for garden waste, paper/plastic and landfill so we have to be extra careful. Woe betide anyone who puts an oak leaf in their blue bin or whose green bin is found to contain a single sheet of paper. Unless it's your bank statement of course, the bin men love a good laugh.

Speaking of bank statements, We're now four days past Blue Monday and I still haven't received my credit card statement, although M got hers on Tuesday. This is the one with all the pre-Christmas spending on it so it will no doubt be pretty hefty. Maybe it's too heavy for the postie and is coming by special delivery.

Thursday is also housework day. M works full time so it's only fair that I do the domestic duties, dusting, hoovering, washing surfaces and floors, that sort of thing. And because today started out very rainy I tackled the housework immediately after breakfast, instead of going for my walk. After feeding the birds, of course. And twice this week I've had a special bird visitor – a Great Spotted Woodpecker. I've been hearing them tap-tapping in the woods whilst on my walks, and often wish I'd paid more attention to my Morse Code instructor when I was an Army Cadet, so that I could understand what they're saying to each other.

'Rat-a-tat-tat-tat': 'Here comes that old fool with the stick again'.

'Rat-a-tat-tat-tat-a-tat-tat-a-tat': 'He looks quite well nourished. Think I'll follow him home'.

Now he seems to have taken up residence on my neighbour's tree, which overlooks my garden, and when I'm not looking he swoops down and hangs on to my peanut feeder. And no matter how discreet I try to be, if he glimpses me watching him through the window he immediately shoots off back to his tree. Obviously the sight of me puts him off feeding. Maybe that explains why, whenever I visit a posh restaurant, I always get shown to the seat facing the wall.

Watched the final episode of The Serpent this afternoon. Because it is based on a real story, with real people, as the end credits rolled the BBC showed us what these people look like today. The story took place fifty years ago, so they're all in their late 70s/early 80s. What amazes me is that so many of them are still alive, because in every shot of every episode of the entire series, they were rarely seen without a cigarette. I don't know how big the show's budget was, but the tobacco bill must have been immense. And, just as shows featuring insects make you itch, on-screen smoking makes you cough. I felt quite worn out, after coughing my way through eight hours of robbery and murder.

22

~

Day 22 – a day of belated squirrel appreciation.

In an effort to get my weekly weigh-ins into a regular weekly routine I hopped on to the scales first thing this morning. Well, when I say "hopped" I obviously mean stumbled wearily. And how much have I lost? Nothing. And how much have I gained? 5/8 of a pound! In other words, ten ounces, or a massive 283 grammes in less than a week, which is shocking. I shall have to cut something out but I can't decide what. I need my sugar intake to give me energy, I need my fat intake to insulate me from the cold. And I need my beer intake because, er, ah, um, just because I do, ok?

To counteract this dismay, I had an extra long walk today. First, down to the postbox with another of M's letters (there goes another of my stamps!) then up through the village on icy pavements and into the woods. And I met lots of people I knew, mostly with dogs, so I did lots of chatting and I was out for more than two hours. Which meant I wasn't at home for my usual 10am hot chocolate, so there's a few calories saved already.

And we'll just draw a discreet veil around the 11.30am café latte with toast and marmalade.

In all my woodpecker-related excitement yesterday, I forgot to tell you that it was National Squirrel Appreciation Day. Yes that is a real thing, although in the UK it is more correctly described as Red Squirrel Appreciation Day. Supported by such luminaries as HRH Prince Charles, this is a day on which we are encouraged to look out for, feed and protect our native red squirrels. They're under threat of extinction due to the rising numbers of grey squirrels, a non-native American import which is taking over the red squirrel's habitat and spreading disease. Other, more welcome, American imports include Kentucky Fried Chicken, Burger King and McDonalds. That list probably says more about me than about them.

Of course, it was National Squirrel Appreciation Day in America too. And in addition to the nurturing aspect of the day they have a few suggestions as to how you can make it more fun. Examples include: make a squirrel obstacle course, say the word "squirrel" a lot (yes really, I'm not making this up!) and finally - dress your dog up as a squirrel.

How do you do that last one, then? Stick a huge bushy tail on him and make him hop along on his hind legs? Might be OK for Paris Hilton and her lapdog, but try it with your pit bull terrier and see how many fingers you have left afterwards.

The long awaited credit card bill arrived today. And as expected it's a biggie, largely due to the fact that we bought a couple of new sofas late last year which were delivered just before Christmas. Of course paying by credit card gets you an extra month of free credit, as long as you time it right, but the inevitable day of reckoning is always sure to arrive. Sacrifices have to be made, so that's the beer fund depleted for this month. I shall have to rely on M's generosity from now until the pension comes in.

And the pension, just like the pensioner, is small, comes in slowly and is swiftly exhausted.

23

*

Day 23 – a day of American imports.

Overnight snow again, so first job was clearing the paths and applying a liberal dressing of salt. Then, although the temperature was well below zero, M and I had a nice long walk to the stables and back. Walking was easier today than it's been all week, because the freshly fallen snow supplied enough grip to prevent us slipping and sliding. And the sun was shining so it was very pleasant, even though there were clouds of steam rising from the newly-cleaned out horse "bedding". I managed to hold my breath long enough to get clear of the hazardous zone.

Then home for breakfast before M went to Dingwall for the weekly shopping. When she left, I settled down with The Times jumbo crossword. She was gone for an hour and a half, by which time I had solved five clues. It's going to be a long haul this week, unless I enlist the help of Mr Google.

In the afternoon we walked to Dingwall for the usual electric meter top-up. I was very surprised by the number of people walking in the High Street, because most shops are closed. Luckily the street is wide enough for me to avoid getting anywhere near anyone, because now that the new variant of Covid has become widespread I've become even more paranoid than before about keeping my distance.

Following on from yesterday's list of my favourite American imports (KFC, etc), M came home from her shopping trip with the weekly brochure from our local Lidl supermarket. And their upcoming "flavour of the week" theme is – coincidentally – USA! After me mentioning that yesterday, I'm convinced I must have psychic powers. And I'm going to put these psychic powers to good use by picking tonight's lottery numbers.

And when I win the jackpot and become an instant millionaire I shall hire a proper author to write my diaries for me. So, if tomorrow's entry includes talking paintings, flying broomsticks and magic spells you'll know I've hired JK Rowling. If it's full of unsolved murders and dark Edinburgh back streets it will have been written by Ian Rankin. And if it specializes in far-fetched fantasies and tales of horror, it might be by Stephen King. But more likely by me.

Anyway, back to the Lidl brochure and its American theme. Most of the items featured are just what you'd expect, Oreos, chicken wings, Budweiser beer etc. But the one that caught my eye is the exotically named "Smucker's Goober Grape Peanut Butter and Jelly". What exactly are you supposed to do with that stuff? Inject it into your cavity walls? Grout your bathroom tiles? What do you mean, you spread it on your toast? Well, there goes my appetite.

Ordinary peanut butter, though, is a regular feature on M's

shopping list. Not that she or I ever eat the stuff, but she makes peanut butter sandwiches for, yes you've guessed it, the garden birds. Apparently it's high in protein and fat, and good for them on cold winter days. I think I'll stick to crisps, salted peanuts and bacon for my protein, thank you.

And as for fat, I probably have enough in my internal store to see me through this, and a few more, winters.

24

～～

Day 24 – a day of media exposure. But not for me.

Fame comes to the Thomson family! M Junior has made it into the Sunday papers. There's a feature in today's Mail on Sunday about online tutoring, which is a booming business in lockdown, and she was interviewed by the paper. She's been offering online lessons for primary pupils for a few weeks now, and she's finding that demand increases as more and more parents find it difficult to teach their own children at home. When she was setting up and testing her systems, she used me as a guinea pig, to make sure that all the technology was working ok before she went "live" with her lessons. And it was an interesting time, because I had to act the part of a seven-year old child who needs help with his Maths. Actually, there wasn't much acting required.

In an English lesson, for example, she would share her screen with me and show me a passage from a book, then ask me to carry out simple tasks, like: "find the verb in that sentence", or "underline an adjective". I found that easy enough, but when she moved on to "prepositions" and "conjunctions", I began to struggle. Apparently a preposition isn't an offer of marriage, and a conjunction isn't where two major roads meet, it's something you should never end a sentence with. Still don't understand it, but.

Anyway, while one member of the family gains fame in newspapers, another one fails miserably. A few weeks ago I sent copies of my first book "Sandy's Daily Diaries" to a couple of newspapers inviting them to review it. I'd better not mention the newspapers' names, but one of them is a regional daily and the other is a bi-weekly local publication. And so far, neither one has mentioned my book, nor produced any sort of review. Which means that either they're too short of space or that they've read the first few pages and chucked it in the bin. They say there's no such thing as bad publicity but any review, even a mediocre one, might get the book into the public eye and generate a sale or two. Even if the sales are to friends and relations who buy it out of sympathy.

Self published books always start out in debt because of printing and distribution costs, and even when sales commence the author gets a very small proportion of the sale. And because of that I can't afford advertising so my only method of getting publicity is to promote it on my Facebook page. I always try to make my posts funny, usually involving animals doing silly things. My first one was an image of a bear reading a book over a man's shoulder, with the suggestion that the bear liked my diaries so much he would rather read than eat the man. I suspect though, that the second the camera was switched off, the bear thought: "sod this for a lark", the book was swept aside and the poor guy discovered what a bear hug really feels like.

There's no record of this, of course. The photographer was out of there faster than Usain Bolt. Even faster than me when M calls: "Dinner's ready!".

25

Day 25 – a day of ice, salt and haggis.

No walking today due to very icy conditions, but I had to venture out to the Post Office in the car. Every couple of weeks or so we post a parcel to Baby A, with some clothes, a book, a toy, something for M Junior and Farmer J and of course a wee edible gift for Dog F. It's been very hard these past few weeks, not being able to visit, so we feel a little more involved by sending a wee box of goodies now and again. And I know that a couple of neighbours are doing the same thing for their grandchildren. So at least the Post Office are profiting from lockdown, even if the rest of us are miserable.

And when I got to Dingwall with my parcel, the car park was like an ice rink. And I wasn't able to do my usual "penguin" walk (little steps and hands out at an angle) because Baby A's parcel was so big I needed both hands to carry it.

And I was trying to hurry, because I had spotted another customer a few cars along, who was obviously heading for the Post Office too. She'd obviously had a good weekend of sales on ebay because she was juggling a huge number of parcels of all shapes and sizes. I couldn't imagine what she'd been selling , but some of the packages were marked "fragile" so she was treading even more carefully than I was.

We locked eyes, just for a moment, each of us realizing that the other was heading for the parcel queue, then the race was on! And racing on an icy surface is a very dangerous event. It's not speed that wins, it's the ability to stay upright and steer in the right direction. Luckily I managed to overtake her without falling over, and felt quietly smug when I was in the parcel queue and she appeared behind me. I felt sorry for the man behind her because it must have taken half an hour to get all her parcels weighed, priced, stamped and handed over. By that time I was home having a warming cup of hot chocolate.

Today is a special day in Scotland, and indeed for Scots throughout the world. It's the birthday of our national bard Robert Burns, born on this day in 1759. And every year we celebrate by holding Burns Suppers all over the world, eating haggis and drinking whisky in his memory. No Burns Suppers this year of course, so M and I had our own quiet supper of haggis, neeps and tatties.

Overseas readers may need to consult Mr Google to learn the ingredients of this delightful dish.

Make sure you have a strong stomach before you do.

26

∾

Day 26 – a day of mechanical troubles.

M arrived home from work last night, complaining that, just as she reversed onto the drive, her car began showing a warning light, with the message: "check engine". Being the man of the family, it was expected that I would a) know what it meant, b) know what to do, and c) do it. Since my experience of car repairs stretch away back to the days when cars were mechanical, not electronic, I was rather baffled. But of course I couldn't let that show, so with an air of great authority I opened the bonnet, regarded the engine and said "Hmmm" a few times.

M was greatly impressed with this display of mechanical aptitude, so I followed it up by turning off the engine, counting to ten, and turning it on again. Much to my dismay the error message was still showing, so I switched off, closed the door and walked around the car, kicking all the tyres. Then, since M was waiting for my diagnosis, I knew I'd have to make a pronouncement so I declared: "I think we need to leave it until tomorrow".

In the absence of direct action, delay is always a good tactic because it gives you time to consult Mr Google on the quiet.

Mr Google, however, wasn't as helpful as I had hoped. When I described the symptoms and error message to him, his response was: "Do not drive the vehicle. Consult the vehicle's handbook". And when I did consult the vehicle's handbook, its advice was: "Do not drive the vehicle. Contact your Fiat dealership". So then I spent a sleepless night hoping that by some miracle the problem would simply have gone away by morning and I would be treated as a hero, and given extra rations/beer.

Morning dawned, and I waved M off to work in my car, promising I would get to work on hers as soon as I finished breakfast. And as soon as I felt she was far enough away, out I went, turned the key, and aaargh! There was the dreaded "check engine" message, still there, having waited all night just to annoy me. Oh well, nothing else for it but to phone the garage. Our nearest Fiat dealership is in Inverness, a long established and reputable company. That's where M bought the car from, a year and a half ago. So I phoned them and described the situation and they responded exactly as I expected: "Don't drive the car, call your recovery company and get it in to us so we can work out what's gone wrong".

So I called my recovery company, the grandly named Royal Automobile Club, or RAC for short. Every year I pay for a family membership so that M and I are covered for any breakdowns, and I haven't called them out for several years, so I didn't feel guilty about asking them for help. But, because of the pandemic, when you phone them you get a message stating that, unless you're broken down on the motorway or in a dangerous situation you should log your call online, not by telephone. Well, the car was sitting in my own driveway at home, which wasn't a particularly dangerous situation, so I logged my call online. It was really easy, just filled in a couple of boxes and the response was immediate. A text message came saying that a patrol would be with me within 90 minutes. 90 minutes passed, and a further text message arrived telling me that they were very busy and I would receive an update in 30 minutes. 30 minutes later, yes you've guessed it....

Four and a half hours after my initial call, a very nice RAC man arrived. First thing he did was open the bonnet, regard the engine, and say "Hmmm" a few times. See, I know I was doing something right. However, after some computer jiggery-pokery (technical term there), he got the warning light switched off and pronounced the car driveable to the garage. And he came behind in case of any problems, which made me nervous. Do you hate somebody watching your driving, or is it just me?

And so tonight M's wee car is in Fiat Hospital. And there's no visiting allowed. It will be a long night waiting for tomorrow's news.

27

〜

Day 27 – a day of good news. And bad news. And more good news.

Good news! M's car problem is neither fatal nor dangerous, all that's required is a replacement MAP sensor. Of course, I claim to have suspected this all along, even though I have no idea what a MAP sensor is. A google search reveals it to be a small black plastic device, shaped rather like a miniature version of the Starship Enterprise.

Bad news! A replacement will cost a staggering £199. Beam me up, Scotty! And twenty percent of that is so-called Value Added Tax, or VAT.

Good news! Fitting will only take 45 minutes, and the garage will do it while I wait. I expect they're hoping I'll while away the time strolling around the showroom and be tempted by a shiny new car. The salesman will be hovering in the background, ready to pounce as soon as I show any interest in a new model, and if I start kicking tyres he'll be by my side, telling me that this is the best model ever, and his old mum drives one just like it. And this special deal ends today.

Bad news! They don't have a MAP sensor in stock, so will need to order it. And they can't do the job until Tuesday, five days hence. So M will be using my car for work until then, which is all right because I wasn't planning on going anywhere anyway.

Good news! M has decided it's time to trade in this car anyway, and has spotted one on a local dealer's website that she fancies. She's left the financial negotiations to me, so I contacted the dealership and had a good discussion with a very nice salesman. I had to tell him that we couldn't trade in M's car until the MAP sensor is replaced but he wasn't fazed by that and in fact said that he would take the car in in its present state and would get his own mechanic to sort the sensor. And for a much lower price. The downside is that he wants to exchange cars on Saturday, which gives me only three days in which to locate the vehicle documents and the spare keys. Better get searching!

28

~

Day 28 – a day of fuzzy heads. No, not a hangover.

Thursday again, and it's housework day. And bin day. Thank goodness for routine, otherwise I'd have no idea what day it is. I note, though, that we're rapidly heading towards the end of January so maybe, just maybe, lockdown will be eased in a few weeks.

Two stories in today's news, both featuring scruffy creatures with woolly heads who are often stared and pointed at. Firstly, there's a photo in the paper of four alpacas being taken for a walk in Dingwall. Yes, really. The four are brothers who were adopted a couple of years ago and live happily here in the north of Scotland, where the climate is similar to that in the high Andes. But with less risk of being attacked by a bear, or photographed by an American tourist.

A year or so ago, before covid restricted my walks to my own area, I was fond of walking the path alongside the canal in Dingwall. It's a perfectly good path but very narrow, so not suitable for social distancing. And one day I saw in the distance what looked like a man leading two camels. But as they grew closer I could see they were more like llamas, and then when we actually met it turned out to be two of the alpacas. And because the path is narrow we stopped to chat, and they were happy to be petted and made a fuss of. So we had a few minutes of getting to know each other and I think they were happy to see me, due to the fact I didn't get spat on. Which is quite remarkable for Dingwall.

So that was the first time I became aware of the alpacas in Dingwall, and when M came home from work I was bursting to tell her about them. And of course she didn't believe me. "Alpacas in Dingwall? Are you mad? Or drunk? Or both?"

However I was soon vindicated, because the following weekend we were both walking by the canal and we met the same two again. M and I have travelled quite extensively in South America, so she was very happy to see the alpacas and tell them she'd met their Peruvian and Patagonian cousins. Of course the Dingwall alpacas have no idea where Patagonia is, or what she was raving about, but they were very happy to be petted. I could see they'd labelled her as "mad, but friendly".

And it was only today that I learned that there are actually four alpacas in the Dingwall family. Perhaps I'll meet the other two sometime, but right now I'm too scared to walk in Dingwall because there are just too many people around. I've developed a morbid fear of being breathed on by a passer by. I'd rather be spat on by an alpaca.

And the other story about scruffy creatures with wooly heads? Well, today Prime Minister Boris visited Scotland. Need I say more?

29

~

Day 29 – a day of (brief) solvency.

A showery day today, and very dull. So dull, in fact, that I had the lights on in the house all day. I had hoped that by mid-January longer days would have arrived, but they seem to have been held up this year. Stuck at the French border, perhaps, Boris?

Hooray! At last it's pension day. Pre-Christmas pensions payments were made early so it's been a long time coming, but because the last day of the month is Sunday, I got my January payment on Friday. It was a good feeling, having money in the bank for a change. But it was only in there for a few hours, until I paid the dreaded credit card bill and was back to square one.

At least that's the new sofas fully paid for now, so I don't feel guilty about reclining for my daily snooze.

And of course I've immediately begun loading the credit card again. I had to put a deposit down on M's potential new car, to reserve it until we test drive it tomorrow. Also, I had to notify her insurance company about the planned change of vehicle so was expecting to pay an extra premium. But I was pleasantly surprised when the agent announced that the difference in price would be sixty-three PENCE, and they don't deal with payments under a pound, so there would be no extra charge. I don't usually have such amicable dealings with insurance companies, perhaps I'm mellowing in my old age. Or, more likely, there's still that note on my file which says: "Cantankerous old fool, be sure to humour him".

In between showers I managed a fairly long walk to the stables and back. The main roads are clear of ice now, but some of the sheltered paths are still pretty slippery so there were one or two brief spells of "penguin walking".

In today's news comes the announcement that Harry Gow, the Inverness-based baker of Dream Ring fame, is commencing home deliveries. This is very dangerous for me, there will be an irresistible temptation to get on the phone and order a dream ring. In fact I've just realized that I haven't had a single dream ring during the whole month of January, which is something of a record because even in deepest darkest lockdown I always managed one at least once a week.

And I don't suppose Harry will send a van all the way to Maryburgh with a single dream ring, so I'd better order a dozen. Or, better still, a baker's dozen.

30

$\sim\!\sim$

Day 30 – a day of wheeling. And dealing.

A cold and very frosty start meant that it was impossible to get into either M's car or mine because the doors were frozen shut. Which was a bit of a nuisance because today was the day for M's car to be traded in, and we couldn't get it out of the drive because mine was in the way. M's solution was to thaw out my car then jump into it and head off for her weekly shopping, leaving me to fight my way into the Fiat, start it and defrost the windows before she came back. I ended up having to enter the car via the passenger door, manoeuvre my way across into the driver's seat (ooh my poor knees) and open the driver's door from the inside. If the circus is looking for a contortionist, here I am.

And once the engine had warmed up the car soon thawed out and windows defrosted, ready for it to leave our drive for the final time. She's had it for two and a half years and was very fond of it, so it's with mixed emotions she's letting it go, but the nice car dealer has made us an offer we can't refuse and we'd be mad not to accept it. So, after M came home with the shopping, we had our morning coffee then headed into Dingwall to conclude the deal. Luckily M had her credit card with her, mine has had enough excitement after paying for the suite.

Buying a car has changed markedly since Covid arrived. Previously, as we all remember, you could wander into the showroom, kick a few tyres, have a chat with the sales staff, wander off again and repeat the process in another dealership until you found the car you wanted, at the right price. Normally there was lots of wrangling, haggling and downright arguing before you both agreed the price, and even then you sometimes couldn't escape the feeling that somehow you'd been ripped off. I remember a certain motorbike dealer from away back in my youth who used to offer a "twenty-twenty guarantee" with every bike sold. Sounded impressive, until you learned that the guarantee ran for twenty miles or twenty minutes, whichever came first.

Now, at least in our local dealership, the whole process begins – where else? – online. You go to their website, browse their stock, see something you fancy and register an interest. You then receive an estimated price for your trade-in, and a promise that someone will contact you by phone the next day. And that's what happened. A very nice salesman phoned me and talked through all the details, took a description of our trade-in and offered a price which tied in almost exactly with the online one. And he explained the Covid set-up in his dealership, which was that no-one was allowed to enter the premises, and he couldn't even meet anyone outside until what he called "transition day" which was the day upon which the car would be handed over. It was necessary for me to pay a deposit to secure the car, and even then, if we decided we didn't want it after all, the deal would be cancelled, the deposit refunded and there would be no hard feelings.

And there was no pressure, he was happy to chat and answer any questions, unlike salesmen of old (and they were all men) who wore shiny suits and brylcreem, and spoke very fast at you until your head was reeling until you would agree to anything just to get him to shut up.

So today was transition day! And it all went smoothly, M took the new car for a test drive, pronounced herself happy, the salesman inspected our trade-in and pronounced himself happy, M's credit card took a hit, and now she's the proud owner of a Vauxhall with less than 5000 miles on the clock. Which is in contrast to her husband, who has in excess of 840 months on his clock.

And now she's got the hang of wheeling and dealing, I wonder when it will be my turn to be traded in?

31

~

Day 31 – a day of ornitol..., erm, oarnothle..., erm, bird-watching.

Very hard frost again, I can't remember what it's like to be warm. Before breakfast M and I walked to Dingwall to pop yesterday's prize crossword into the mail. It's probably a complete waste of time but at least it gives us a reason to get out and exercise. It was a very pleasant walk, and I wore my thermals so I was nice and cosy. And when I got home I ventured on to the dreaded weighing machine – and I've lost more than half a pound! Five-eighths of a pound actually, which is a massive (for me) ten ounces. And when I came to enter this figure on my fridge-mounted chart I realised that I'm back to the same weight I was sixteen days ago. And I'm not telling you how high it got in between times.

Can I keep this up? Well, the signs are looking hopeful because all the Christmas chocolate is almost gone. After scoffing our (my) way through various selections we're down to one box of Celebrations and a chocolate reindeer with a tiny gold medal round his neck. I expect that by this time next week the reindeer will be gone, and his medal will be around my neck.

A quieter day for M and me today, after yesterday's car-buying excitement. A quieter day too, for our redit cards, which will be glad of a rest and the chance to recover from yesterday's excesses. Until later, when I get logged on to Amazon and start ordering loads of stuff I don't really need. Why do I do it? Well, like climbing Mount Everest, "just because it's there".

Today was the day of the RSPB's "Big Garden Birdwatch". M is an RSPB member and takes part in this event every year. It involves counting and listing all the birds in your garden for a certain period of time, then reporting the results back to the RSPB so that they can work out which species are thriving and which are declining. I don't need an official birdwatch to know that crows and seagulls are thriving and everything else is declining. I haven't seen a flamingo, a cockatoo or even a dodo in my garden. Not since my experiment with the home made mushroom soup, anyway.

So there was M, at the appointed time, perched in the kitchen dutifully scanning the garden and taking notes. And in amongst the blackbirds, starlings and occasional robin she was startled by the arrival, right on cue on the right day and at the right time, a fieldfare. Now, I appreciate that the appearance of a fieldfare isn't maybe the most exciting thing that could happen to most of you, but for a keen bird watcher like M it was akin to winning the lottery. I was summoned from my armchair to come and observe this fantastical creature and sure enough, there it was, pecking furiously at an apple and chasing other birds away from it. It reminded me of school dinners, when you had to guard your plate against the ever-ready forks of other diners who were always ready to swoop and carry away one of your sausages. And to be honest, I may have done a little swooping myself.

And he stayed with us for the rest of the day, even though I told him: "You've been counted, you can go now". No, he refused to move on and we had to continue to throw out apple after apple to satisfy his demands. By the end of the day we'd almost run out of apples, so guess what M will be buying along with her newspapers tomorrow morning? And she'll be at work tomorrow so no doubt it will be up to me to keep this monster fed. On the plus side, he seems to chase away the crows and seagulls too, so that saves me a job.

And at last that's us at the end of January. Thirty-one days of lockdown, which felt like a hundred and thirty-one. I hope February will be shorter, with less frost, fewer snowstorms and more chocolate.

32

Day 32 – a day of pinching and punching.

And a new day dawns, and along with it a whole new month because today is the first of February. An historic day, because it was on the first of February 1793 that France declared war on Great Britain. I don't know what we'd done to offend them, but a few days earlier they'd decapitated their King, Louis XVI, so maybe they were annoyed because Wetherspoons had just opened a new pub in England called "The King's Head".

They declared war on the Netherlands at the same time, but they were all so, erm, "relaxed" and casual that no-one noticed at first. It took several days for the news to filter through the impenetrable (but wonderfully fragrant) fog in their smoke-filled "coffee shops". And even then they were too laid back to care.

'What's dat, Hans? Somebody makink der war against us?'

'Ja, ja Willem, but let's not get too excited. Der Brits vill sort it out for us. Pass the matches.'

As usual I lost the inane "pinch, punch, first of the month" ritual. M did the pinching, and the punching (rather harder than necessary, I thought) while I was still asleep and she was bringing me my morning cup of tea. Yes, I know how lucky I am, but for the first thirty-two years of our marriage I was the one fetching the tea in the morning and now that I'm retired I feel I've earned a few privileges. Even if it means putting up with a bruised shoulder on the first day of every month.

No sign today of yesterday's fieldfare. I threw out a succession of apples at regular intervals but he didn't appear. Funny he came yesterday, just as the RSPB bird survey was taking place. How did he know the date? Maybe he has a sore wing today. Perhaps Mrs Fieldfare woke him up with an early morning "pinch, punch..."

It was very frosty again today, but nice and clean underfoot, so I had an extra long walk after breakfast. Took me an hour and a half and probably burned off loads of calories, so I didn't feel too guilty about having a chocolate biscuit with my coffee. I did feel slightly guilty, though, about the three Celebration chocolates I scoffed immediately afterwards. But only slightly.

Then I had to visit the bottle bank to get rid of loads of empty beer bottles which have built up over the past few months. OK, few weeks. Well, if you absolutely insist, few days. We don't have a bottle bank in Maryburgh so that involved a drive to Conon Bridge, our neighbouring village. So when the government starts monitoring beer consumption we Maryburgh residents can smugly point out that we're very light drinkers. But these hooligans in Conon are guzzling so much beer that their bottle bank fills up every couple of days.

33

Day 33 – a day of electrified activity.

Met an old acquaintance on my morning walk today. I haven't seen him for months, but we used to meet every morning during last summer's lockdown and he never once complied with social distancing rules. Yes, it was Angry Dog! Regular readers will remember Angry Dog, he featured in many previous diaries and was, along with El Gato the stray cat, one of my most frequent animal companions. I haven't seen either of them since last summer so it's good to know that at least one of them is still alive and well. And he was pleased to see me too, as I reached into my pocket for the treats.

The most important thing about Angry Dog is that he's not at all angry, but he has these very striking wild-looking eyes that make him appear very scary. He's actually a very friendly chappy, especially when he spots M or me. No matter how far away we are he abandons his owner and comes and sits nicely, gazing hopefully, and hungrily, upwards. Just as I do when M comes home from work.

More drama with that most frequent source of irritation, the electric top-up meter. On the 21st of December our supplier sent us a letter to say that they had incorrectly changed our tariff away back in October and we had been overcharged ever since. They went on to say that their team were "hard at work" and that our meter should be set to the correct date by the end of January. Well, if it takes a "hard at work" team forty-one days to figure out which button to press to adjust my meter price, I'd hate to think how long it would take to do something complicated. Like wire a plug or change a fuse.

But I mustn't be too hard on them. After all, the meter is in Scotland and the button is 4,780 miles away. In Delhi.

Anyway, there's going to be some compensation. They're sending us a £10 top-up credit, which should appear as if by magic when we top up our meter token in our local shop. All we need to do is between three and five top-ups to receive the credit. Well, since December M has topped up the meter six times already, and there's no sign of this credit, so today I decided to risk my blood pressure and phone their helpline to enquire.

The first two calls yielded nothing in the way of human contact, just a constant stream of (not particularly inspiring) music, interrupted every thirty seconds or so by a disembodied voice telling me: 'Thank you for your patience, your call will be answered as soon as possible'. After every tenth 'thank you' I hung up. There's only so much gratitude a man can take.

Perseverance pays off, though, and at the next attempt I was relieved to hear a friendly, and very Scottish, voice offering to help. And she did help. First of all she asked me to read out some figures from the meter, which was quite a challenge. In the dark of the meter cupboard, juggling a torch, a phone and the ironing board and pressing buttons all at the same time isn't easy when you only have two hands.

Satisfied with my readings, she then furnished me with an eight-figure code. She assures me that quoting that code in the shop will result in us getting our tenner next time we top up. We'll find out on Saturday if it works. I have the electricity supplier on speed dial just in case.

34

⌇⌇

Day 34 – a day of repeats

Yesterday was Groundhog Day. I only learned this today, by reading about it in the newspapers. Apparently it's an annual event in America – where else? – which involves a small cuddly creature emerging from a hole in the ground and predicting how long the misery of winter will be with us. Is it purely by coincidence that yesterday was the day that Nicola (Sturgeon, First Minister of Scotland) chose to emerge from her erm, office, and predict that lockdown will be with us until at least the end of February?

So February is looking like a repeat of January, with a continuing travel ban, no visiting and no pubs or restaurants. There's one major difference, though. It is planned that on the 22nd of February schools will reopen to pupils in Primary classes one, two and three, along with pre-school and nursery facilities. And school staff are promised twice-weekly Covid testing, by means of a home-testing kit which will be sent out by post. I guess this scheme will include M, who is a full time employee based in a Primary school. This could be my chance to get tested, even though I'm not eligible. Could she allow me to take every second test and pass it off as her own? Would the authorities ever know? Would the results come back as: "Covid-free but worryingly high in cholesterol. And congratulations on your gender reassignment".

Also returning to school will be some senior pupils who need to carry out practical assessments in order to have their grading carried out by their teachers, because of course for the second year in a row there are to be no formal exams. Which means that the SQA have a huge number of professional and highly experienced invigilators (including me) kicking their heels at home all year instead of overseeing the running of exams. Maybe we could work from home, in line with government guidelines? Could the pupil sit the exam in his own home, supervised by me, on Zoom? Maybe not, I'm not sure I'd like to see inside modern day teenage bedrooms. I remember all too well the state of mine when I was a teenager – unmade bed, dirty dishes, towels and underwear strewn all over the floor. Luckily there was no Zoom or webcams in those days so it was my little secret. Until now.

Remember yesterday's electric meter top-up saga? Well, here's todays. It was a very cold day but nice and dry, so I donned my thermals and walked into Dingwall with the meter top-up device and the magic eight-digit number which the nice lady gave me yesterday. And guess what? It didn't work. The staff in the shop tried it on two different machines and it declared itself to be "not recognised". Why didn't this surprise me?

And in a repeat of yesterday's phone calls to the helpline

(Groundhog Day again!) I spent thirteen minutes on hold before a human voice came on the line. No Scottish accent today, this one was definitely from an exotic location far, far away to the East. She checked my account, declared the code to be "still valid and awaiting to be redeemed". When I told her about the shop's machines rejecting it, she announced that there must a fault with those particular machines and I should try again, in a different shop. I did wonder whether it would be easier for them just to send me a cheque, but she didn't appear to be open to negotiation.

Suitably chastised, I hung up. And tomorrow M will take the gadget to the shop near her school and try it there. And if that doesn't work I don't know what to do. Try every shop in an ever widening radius until we find one that works? I'll let you know how we get on in Perth.

35

~

Day 35 – a day of damp patches and sweet treats

Help! There's a man on my roof! He's not wearing a red coat so I assume it's not Santa Claus making a late delivery. And in any case he'll have trouble getting down the chimney because we don't have one. And it's not the tooth fairy, or if it is she's in for a shock when she finds out how few teeth I have left. No profit to be made here, dear. Try the dog next door.

No need for alarm, last year we had Fence Man, today I have Roof Man. I called him in because I've been suffering from damp patches. Not, as you might expect, in my foundation garments (although there have been some narrow escapes) but in my attic. I suspected a leak amongst the roof tiles, which is something I would have tackled myself just a few years ago, but sadly my days of climbing extended ladders and clambering around on the roof are in the past. Creaky joints and increasing weight gain have put paid to that. Even if I did make it to the top of the ladder there's a very real danger that my vastly increased tonnage might prove to be too much for the roof to bear and I might come crashing down through the ceiling. Which would be ok as long as I could aim to land on the bed, but knowing my navigational skills I'd probably land on the beer fridge and break all the bottles.

After some clomping around on the roof and lifting various tiles to look underneath, Roof Man declared the roof to be sound, and that the attic dampness must be caused by condensation. He recommended the fitting of roof tile vents and something called soffit vents. Soffit vents sound to me like some sort of air intake fitted to Victorian ladies' whalebone undergarments. I'm sure I've seen them on telly, being worn in Upstairs Downstairs. Or being ripped off in Bridgerton.

However it transpires that they're little plastic grills which fit into the woodwork at the eaves of the house and allow air to flow in. And before I knew it Roof Man and his assistant had fitted a series of them at each end of the house. He didn't have time to fit roof tile vents today, but he's left four of them in my shed and hopes to come back soon and fit them. He's also left his roof ladder, I wonder if I could sneak a wee trip up onto the roof, just for old times' sake? Nah, better not, some of the neighbours would be sure to spot me and report to M.

On Day 29, you will remember, I shared the joyous news that Inverness-based baker (and purveyor of the fabled dream ring) Harry Gow had commenced offering home deliveries. And in an idle moment I daydreamed about the possibility of receiving one of his deliveries. Well, dreams do come true! This morning as I was preparing to leave for my walk a white van arrived and the driver approached, bearing a large cardboard box.

"What has she been ordering now?" I wondered, expecting it to be the latest of M's mail-order shopping items. Since the start of lockdown we've had all sorts of articles delivered, ranging from garden plants for M, to toys for Baby A, to an exotic cordless vacuum cleaner. For me. Thanks, dear.

Upon opening this box I was delighted to find it was crammed with goodies from the wonderful Mr Gow, which had been ordered for us by the equally wonderful M Junior, along with a card signed by Baby A and Dog F to say how much they're missing their grandparents. How thoughtful, and what a selection of bakery products was in the box. Biscuits, shortbread, cakes, meringues, and in pride of place - not one, but TWO beautiful dream rings! And the best thing of all is that M isn't a huge fan of dream rings so they're both mine. Hello calories, goodbye waistline.

I don't think I'll bother visiting the bathroom scales this week.

36

～

Day 36 – a day of snow everywhere. But not here.

And we end the week with news of a success. You will remember on Days 33 and 34 I told you about the long-running saga of the missing £10 owed to us by the electric company, and their failure to get our meter topped up properly. And their suggested solution of simply trying a different shop, which I suspected was just a delaying tactic to get rid of me for a few days. Well, I'm delighted to report that M has succeeded where I had failed. She took the electronic top-up device to a shop near her school and the assistant there punched the necessary buttons and declared the process to be successful. Of course M was sceptical until she brought the thing home and insisted that it should be my job to insert it into the meter. On the principle that if it didn't work it would automatically be my fault.

This principle applies in many areas of our life, it has always been "my job" to do anything with the potential to go wrong. Examples include cutting the dog's claws (danger of being bitten and contracting rabies), putting up shelves (danger of collapse), evicting spiders from the bedroom (danger of it crawling into her mouth while she's sleeping). She's read somewhere that in an average lifetime each of us will swallow at least three spiders. I'm sure I've consumed more than that whilst snoozing in my shed on a warm summer day.

Anyway, when I plugged it in the meter display read: "£10 credit successful", so I was much relieved and it spared me from another phone call to my friends in New Delhi. I imagine they're equally relieved.

Coincidentally, when I came home from my walk today there was a message waiting for me on my landline. It was from some customer service survey company asking me for feedback about my recent telephone contact with my "energy company". Interestingly, they didn't name the energy company so I was immediately suspicious. They invited me to contact them on a freephone number and tell them all about my experiences, but I decided not to. I thought it better not to encourage them because sometimes when you make contact with these companies it opens a floodgate and you get bombarded with calls from similar agencies. And I get plenty of nuisance calls every week about my broadband connection, my Amazon account and my recently ordered (and progressively more expensive) ipad7. Or maybe, by now, it's an ipad8.

And the rest of the day was fairly uneventful. It seems that most of Scotland is struggling with severe weather, deep snow, and blocked roads. But we have no snow at all, and the temperature is an (almost tropical) three degrees.

Wouldn't that be a great name for a singing group? Oh, wait...

37

~

Day 37 – a day of piling on the pounds

Saturday morning, a leisurely start because M has no work today. I allow her to have a long lie, so she doesn't have to bring me my tea in bed until 7.30am. See how caring I am?

It was a very cold morning again, so I laid out the ever-reliable thermals in anticipation of (being dragged out for) a walk and headed to the shower. Daily ablutions completed, I emerged from the bathroom, shining clean and smelling beautifully of Kath Kidston Blossom shower gel. Which, according to the label, is rich in glycerine, so that explains the shine. And oops, there goes my macho image.

But before I could commence the daily struggle into my thermals, M called out the fateful words: "Have you remembered to weigh yourself?". Aargh, I had forgotten to tell her about my vow to steer clear of the scales for a few weeks following the Harry Gow bakery delivery! Anyway, dutiful as ever, I hopped on to the scales, and she insisted on peering over my shoulder to confirm the reading. Anyone would think she didn't trust me.

And the dial showed that I'm heavier today than at any time since the new scales arrived, five weeks ago. I've put on almost one and a half pounds since last week, which is shocking. I can't imagine where all this extra weight has come from all of a sudden.

In other news, the aforementioned Harry Gow box is more than half empty. Only the meringue shells, shortbread and biscuits remain. Could this have anything to do with my weight gain? Surely not. If eating cakes made you fat surely someone would have mentioned it before now.

Roof Man is hoping to come and install some roof tile vents over the weekend so I thought I'd better have some cash in the house so that I can pay him. So, following my usual Saturday routine of walk/breakfast/papers M drove me into Dingwall so that I could visit the cash machine. It was only my second time in her new car, that's a week today since she bought it and she's very happy with it. It's much more modern than her previous one, and the terminology has evolved significantly since I last bought a car. What used to be called the heater is now known as the "climate control system", and the radio has become the "infotainment system". I almost expected the steering wheel to be redesignated as the "going round the corners system".

And the handbrake is a button, not a lever. So there's no more of that satisfying *crrrrrk* sound as you pull the handbrake on. On the other hand, hill starts are child's play because the brake releases itself as you accelerate up the hill, which stops the car from rolling backwards into the front of the highly polished and mega-expensive BMW behind you. No need to make up excuses, like: "Oops, my hand slipped", "Oh dear my handbag got caught on the lever" or: "Sorry, the dog released the handbrake before I was ready".

But the bank trip was uneventful. Suitably masked and gloved, I managed to remember my PIN number and the cash machine obediently spat out a fistful of banknotes, so I'm ready for Roof Man to come and do his thing. Then my attic, along with my bank account, will dry up.

38

~

Day 38 – a day of roof repairs

Sunday morning walk to Dingwall with M, to post the Times prize crossword. There goes another wasted stamp but at least it gets me a bit of exercise. M usually has two walks a day but one is enough for me. Not today, however, as we shall see.

In anticipation of Roof Man arriving we moved our cars out of the drive to give him space for his van. And also in case he inadvertently drops a roof tile – M would be furious if her new car got dented so soon. She found a parking space across the street, where dog walkers park their cars before walking round the woods, but there wasn't room there for mine so I had to drive down to the village hall car park and walk home. So that counted as a second walk. Feeling smug already.

True to his word, Roof Man arrived to install the roof tile vents. He estimated he'd only take a couple of hours to do the job, but everything went so well that he was finished inside 45 minutes. He's fitted four vents on one side of the roof, and has ordered another four for the other side. He's had some difficulty in sourcing them, it seems they come from Europe and there's a significant delay in getting building supplies across the channel because of Brexit. So while our lorry loads of Scotch whisky sit in Dover waiting to be allowed to enter France, my roof tile vents are apparently doing the same, in reverse, in Calais. I wonder whether we can do some sort of deal? You keep the roof tiles, Monsieur, and I'll keep the whisky. And I'll just drill a few holes in my roof instead, to let the whisky fumes escape.

Before Roof Man left we asked him to measure and provide a quote for a new shed for M. Regular readers will remember she painted it a lovely blue colour during the first lockdown last year, and during that painting mission she became aware that the whole back wall was crumbling away. Also the roof has been leaking for some time, in spite of the felt being replaced, so she's decided that it's time for a replacement. I hope she doesn't cast her eye over anything (or anyone) else suffering from crumbling components and problems with leaks, otherwise it might be goodbye from me.

Anyway, because we aren't getting a holiday again this year due to Covid, we thought we might as well use our money to enhance our property. So we've asked him to give us a price for a whole new shed, with a concrete slab base so it shouldn't rot from below. She's also opted for a tin roof, which will be completely waterproof, if a little noisy during hailstorms. At least it will scare away any visiting cats.

And then of course after he'd finally gone I had to walk down to the hall and fetch my car home, so that was my third walk of the day. Which meant I didn't feel at all guilty settling down in front of the telly with a couple of beers.

39

Day 39 – a day of election fever

We're due to have Scottish Government elections on the sixth of May, which is only a dozen weeks away. In light of the continuing and seemingly never ending lockdown, we've been fully expecting the elections to be called off or postponed. Everything else I'm interested in is cancelled – music festivals, motorbike events, highland games and agricultural shows – but our glorious leaders in the Scottish Parliament seem determined to get themselves re-elected without delay. I hope we'll be spared the doorstep visits from campaigning candidates. I shall put a notice on my front door – "political canvassers will be sneezed upon".

Like many other villages, our voting takes place in the village hall. They install a couple of rickety wooden booths, each with a wee pencil on a string, and that's where you put your cross on the voting paper. I'm concerned about this arrangement, not only because of the potential of coming into contact with other voters on the way in/out of the hall, but mainly because some of us are in the habit of licking the pencil before scribing with it. I have always done it, my own shed is full of well-licked pencils, and my HB-impregnated tongue is a constant source of amusement to my dentist.

So because of that, M and I have decided that we won't risk exposing ourselves to the risk of infection, and we've applied to become postal voters. This has various advantages, and not only the obvious health-related ones. You get to vote in a nice warm environment, in the comfort of your own home. You don't have to engage in conversation with the polling station staff, who have been on duty in a freezing hall since early morning with very little human contact, and are lonely and desperate for conversation. And of course you get to use your own pencil, or if you're feeling very important, your own pen. And you have time to compose a wee message for the back of your voting slip, to give the counting staff something to smile about. Something like "Save our bus pass", or "Free TV licences for all", or, if you're feeling particularly adventurous, "Active pensioner seeks lady vote-counter with GSOH. And she'll need it".

Anyway, I went online and found the application forms for postal voting, and completed one each for M and me. The forms are very simple, the usual name, address, date of birth etc. They don't ask for any proof of identity, like passport number or mother's maiden name, just a signature and "Bob's your uncle", as we used to say in 1960s Britain. Mind you, we had lots of odd sayings back then. or "I'm off to spend a penny" was a polite way of answering a call of nature. "A tinkle on the blower" was the same thing, but in a telephone box.

And the forms have been posted off to the local council, so I hope M and I get accepted into the ranks of postal voters. And knowing our luck we'll probably be told next week that the whole election has been cancelled for this year.

Heard from various ex-colleagues today, that some of them have had their covid vaccinations already. Which is good news for them, but they're all younger than I am so I'm feeling very left out. Maybe it's because they're all in Inverness and I'm in Dingwall. These Inverness residents have a theory that if you roll up your sleeve in Dingwall somebody will steal your wristwatch. How cheeky of them. Last time I rolled up my sleeve in Inverness they stole my wristwatch, my wedding ring and my "Scotland For Ever" tattoo.

40

❧

Day 40 – a day of automated banking

Today dawned bright and clear, but it was the coldest morning for a long time, minus five degrees Celsius. Brrr. On went the thermals for today's early walk, which kept me nice and cosy but they do restrict my movements due to their very snug fit. Putting on socks always causes a certain amount of grunting, but doing it while wearing tight thermal leggings results in even more grunting than usual. M was concerned enough to rush through to the bedroom, she thought I was watching Serena Williams playing tennis on the telly.

There had been a very slight sprinkling of snow overnight, so I ventured out and cleared the paths around the house. I swept all the snow off them and spread a generous amount of salt. Then I moved over and did the same for my elderly neighbour. She spotted me and we had a nice chat through her window although, with the window being closed, her Italian accent and my ever worsening deafness, it wasn't the easiest of conversations. When she said she didn't like inverno I thought she'd taken a dislike to Inverness. Well, how was I to know that "in-verno" is "winter" in Italian?

Following on from M trading in her car for a newer model, she was happy to receive a refund for the balance of her car tax, which still had ten months or so left to run. And the DVLA sent her a cheque, which was kind of awkward for her because she works full time and can't get to a bank during opening hours. Before covid we always used to go to Inverness on Saturday mornings for shopping, and that was our chance to do any bank business, but we don't feel safe amongst crowds nowadays so M does her shopping in Dingwall on her own. While I stay at home, in isolation. With the coffee machine, the biscuit tin and the Times crossword.

The Dingwall branch isn't open on a Saturday so it was delegated to me to pay this cheque into the bank. And when I got there this morning I dutifully lined up outside the door, in accordance with the instructions. A lady came to the door to ask me what I wanted to do, and when I indicated that I had a cheque to pay in she bade me wait outside until the self-service paying-in machine was free. Gone are the days when you simply went up to the counter and engaged in some social chit-chat while the casher paid in your cheque for you.

Once the previous customer had gone I was permitted access to the paying in machine, but not before the door-guarding lady had liberally doused it in some sort of spray. By the time I reached it I was almost overcome by the fumes of cheap disinfectant. For a moment it felt like I was back in a 1960s pub toilet, which wouldn't be as bad as it sounds as long as the beer was still at 1960s prices.

Anyway, no social chit-chat with this electronic cashier, just a keypad, a screen and a slot for your bank card. Pop it in, press a few buttons, stick the cheque into the intake tray and that's it. And when it spat out my receipt I forgot myself and said "thank you" out loud, much to my embarrassment and the amusement of Disinfectant Lady, who was already moving towards the keypad with her squirty bottle and cloth.

Imagine embarking on a career in finance and ending up doing nothing more than wiping down keypads in between customers. Although I suppose it's marginally better than wiping down customers in between keypads.

41

∽

Day 41 – a day of good news

Last night we had the first significant snowfall of the winter. Significant for us, but nothing approaching the snow in other parts of Scotland. Some areas have two feet of snow, whereas we have a measly two and a half inches. And it was minus seventeen Celsius in a remote part of the Highlands last night, but a positively balmy minus four here. Doesn't stop me complaining though, I've been sitting waiting since early December for the opportunity to have a moan. And I can't wait for summer to come so that I can complain about the heat.

These heavy snowfalls all over the country have disrupted roads and railways, which doesn't affect us anyway because we're still banned from travelling. The one effect it has had on me is that when M went to the shop this morning there were no newspapers. And today is Wednesday, which is one of the two days in the week when I get The Times. And no Times equals no crossword, which equals a long boring day for Sandy. Or, more accurately, two or three long boring days.

And as we all know, the devil makes work for idle hands so something had to be done. So in an effort to keep myself occupied I cleared all the snow in my drive, and my neighbour's drive, and sprinkled salt on all the paths. Then after breakfast I walked (yes, walked) down to the shop and was delighted to find that the papers had arrived. So once again I feel very self righteous by having an extra walk, even though the shop is only ten minutes away.

And after a good hour of coffee, biscuits and papers I set off on my official daily walk, all the way around the woods in the snow. And that was followed by more coffee, biscuits and papers until lunchtime. What's that you say, how's the diet going? Well it's going fine, I had eggs for lunch. And no, they weren't chocolate ones.

Exciting news! I had a phone call from my medical practice to invite me in for my covid vaccination on Saturday, which is only three days away. M is quite miffed because she won't be getting hers until the following week. Serves her right for always boasting about being younger (actually she always says "much younger") than I am. So she's been trying to scare me with talk of side effects, fierce nurses and huge long needles. I have no fear of needles, nor of nurses, none of whom are in any way fierce in our health centre. And as for side effects, if all my remaining hair falls out it will be hardly noticeable, if I grow an extra arm or leg it will come in handy for fetching my beer, and if I turn green I'll be easier to find when I get lost in the snow.

And finally to end on a historical note, it was on this day in 1840 that Queen Victoria and Prince Albert of Saxe-Coburg and Gotha were married. So Happy Anniversary, Vicky and Bert!

Luckily for Victoria, it wasn't necessary for her to change her name to that of her husband. Which was lucky for winners of what would have been called "The Victoria of Saxe-Coburg and Gotha Cross", or "VOSCAGC". Also lucky for Mr Kipling, whose "Victoria of Saxe-Coburg and Gotha sponge" just wouldn't have the same appeal.

42

〜

Day 42 – a day of record temperatures and a broken bear

What's the opposite of heatwave? Coldwave? Deep freeze? Whatever it is, that's what we're having today. It's not usual for us to have extremely low temperatures and we hardly ever dip down into double figures, but today we awoke to a brain-chilling minus 13.1 degrees Celsius!

It was very hard to raise enough enthusiasm to climb out from beneath the duvet, but today is bin day so not only did I have to get up, I had to go outside as well. Luckily I have a very cosy woollen hat and nice warm gloves because while it takes less than two minutes to bring the bin in, it takes more than ten to struggle into my thermals, and even longer to struggle out of them.

So, once the bin was safely home, I did all the hoovering and dusting, and cleaned the bathroom and kitchen surfaces and floors. And I kept my woolly hat on while I did that, much to the amusement of neighbours who passed while I was cleaning the windows.

Some years ago we adopted a bear. See, I knew that would get your attention. Not a real live bear, of course, but a garden ornament in the shape of a teddy bear wearing a pair of dungarees. Incidentally, did you know that "dungri" is the Hindi word for a type of thick cotton, and was brought to this country by British soldiers in the 19th Century? Other words they brought back include bungalow (in which I live), pyjamas (which I wear) and doolally (Stop it. I know exactly what you're thinking).

Anyway, back to the bear. He was a poor soul when he came to us, a neighbour found him abandoned beside the path during her dog walk, probably stolen from someone's garden as a drunken prank and then abandoned when the culprit realised how heavy he was. He was covered in moss and missing an eye and looked like some sort of seaweed-encrusted pirate. Not exactly common in rural Ross and Cromarty.

So we sat him in a prominent position on a nearby wall, in the hope that his original owner would spot him and take him home, but after a few weeks it was obvious that he was indeed abandoned so we took him in and I scrubbed the moss off him, painted him brown with smart blue dungarees, and even sent away to Mr Amazon for replacement eyes so that he could admire his new home. And his new daddy.

And he has sat in our back garden ever since, until a few days ago I noticed he'd been afflicted by a severe dose of frostbite. So severe in fact, that his right ear had fallen off and was lying forlornly beside him. And when I gently scooped him (and his ear) up, I saw that there was a crack right across his face and his nose was about to fall off too. Bad enough being deaf in one ear, but imagine being the butt of the old music hall joke: "I say, I say, I say, my bear's got no nose....".

Anyway, after some Google research into bear's ears and noses, I've discovered that the cure lies in some kind of gluey solution called epoxy resin, which sounds scary enough, but even more scary is that its brand name is Gorilla. I've taken the plunge and ordered some from Mr Amazon, and it's due to be delivered tomorrow.

So if there's no diary tomorrow you'll know I've a) been savaged by a gorilla, or b) glued my own ear to the bear. Either is possible.

43

∾

Day 43 – a day of sticky problems. And solutions.

What a relief! When M got up this morning the temperature was -6C, not nearly as cold as yesterday. And an hour later, when I eventually dragged myself out of bed, it had risen to minus four, so it was with a spring in my step that I set out for my morning walk to the stables, all alone and peaceful except for the rat-a-tat-tat of the ever-present lesser spotted woodpecker. I haven't spotted him (see what I did there?) in our back garden for a couple of weeks now. I suspect he's turning his beak up at our peanuts, which are cheap ones from Poundstretcher, because we can't travel to Inverness for the more expensive variety from the pet shop. And anyway, what does he expect from a poor pensioner?

True to his word, Mr Amazon delivered the epoxy resin I ordered yesterday. Apart from a picture of a particularly fierce gorilla on the packet it seemed to be quite user-friendly. Until I tried to open it. The packaging, as with so many other products, was made of very robust clear plastic. And it was impossible to open without using a knife, which places my fingers in deep danger. Eventually I managed to reduce the packaging to tiny plastic particles and at last gained access to the contents.

If their glue is as strong as their plastic packaging the bear will be strong enough to survive a nuclear attack once I'm finished.

Anyway, once I had gained access to the actual resin, it turned out to be in the form of two syringes joined together, one containing the adhesive and the other containing a hardening agent. And it had a sort of double plunger, so the theory is that when you press both syringes at the same time, the two solutions will come out together. And there was a wee wooden paddle, like a lollipop stick, which was provided as a mixer, so that the two pastes could be thoroughly blended together. What should I mix it in? A study of the instructions revealed that the actual plastic packaging was designed to double as a mixing bowl and should have been kept in one piece. Oops.

Undefeated and ever resourceful, I turned to the place I go whenever life gets difficult. The fridge. But instead of my usual comfort food / beer I opened and consuming a healthy yoghurt, much to the surprise of my taste buds and digestive system. The yoghurt pot then became a handy mixing bowl for the glue. What do you think of that, Mr Gorilla?

And soon the bear had his ear reattached, his nose reinforced and one or two other areas patched up, and is now in the intensive care unit (ie my shed) waiting for his resin to dry. Then once the weather warms up a bit he'll get a vigorous wire brushing and fresh paint, and be put back to sit on his low wall and supervise the garden birds. Not that they show him any respect, you should see what they do on his head.

This afternoon I had a zoom meeting with a group of ex-colleagues. We all worked together in the same school but a few of us have moved on, to other jobs or into retirement. It was really good to talk to someone outwith my own family, I fear lockdown poses a danger of losing the art of conversation. For example, I sometimes get my expressions a little mixed up. But I suppose that's just the way the crow crumbles.

44

∽

Day 44 – a day of two punctures

Puncture number one was brought home by M on Thursday. She arrived home from school with a barrow wheel whose tyre was sadly deflated. Just as deflated as she is herself, on the rare occasions when her favourite football team lose out to their European rivals. Not that there's much of that these days. Thanks to Brexit, by the time the British team negotiates its way through the EU border the final whistle has blown and the host team are already in the nearest nightclub, celebrating their victory with champagne, cigars and wannabee reality TV starlets.

It's not the first time this barrow wheel has been punctured, as I remembered when I levered the tyre off and spotted two previous repairs, both done by me over the past few years. This time, however, there was a split along the seam and it was beyond repair. These modern plastic compounds aren't nearly as robust as the rubber tubes of my youth, I remember the tubes on my vespa tyres had more patches than a Geography Teacher's jacket.

Incidentally, did you know there's a song called "More Patches than Brains", by a Belgian band called Agathocles? No, me neither. Maybe they'll have a revival now that I've mentioned them, and if so I want some royalties. I hear Belgian beer is very good.

Anyway, it was obvious that a new tube was required, so I ordered one from my friend Mr Amazon, and thanks to his Prime service it arrived today, while M was away for her afternoon walk. Fitting it took just a few minutes and minimal swearing, although I did neglect to wear gloves and so my hands have turned a shade of satanic black which seems to be indelible, sadly. Still, it's a good excuse for me not to help fold the white bedsheets.

And when M returned I was able to surprise her with a fully inflated barrow wheel ready to return to school on Monday, and I didn't even charge her for the £9.99 tube. I'm hopeful my reward will be in liquid form, and I don't expect Wild Rose shampoo.

And so to puncture number two, and this time it was personal because my left arm got punctured by a practice nurse wielding a syringe full of Astra Zeneca vaccine. It was a very swift process, from the car park into the door, along the corridor, all the time guided by volunteers, then into the nurse's room. A few routine questions: "Any allergies?" "Any symptoms? "Why are your hands black?" And then bang! It was all over and I found myself back in the car park within two minutes of entering the building.

My second dose is due to follow at the end of April, so I have marked the date on the calendar, in my diary, and set a reminder on my phone. Surely even my unreliable memory will be jogged by one of those systems. And we have fingers crossed that M will get her vaccination soon although as she keeps telling me, she's "much younger" than I am, so she may need to wait a week or two.

Of course when I got home I pretended to M that my arm was so sore I couldn't possibly help with any hoovering/dusting/dishwashing. So far she's sympathetic, but I don't think it will take long for her to see through my excuses. Light duties end tomorrow, I fear.

45

∽

Day 45 – a day of man 'flu (the worst kind!)

Awoke this morning not feeling too well. After a restless night of alternating between roasting and freezing, today finds me with shaky legs, sore joints and a slight temperature. It seems I have had a wee reaction to my covid jab from yesterday, which is very unusual, because normally I don't have any after-effects from vaccinations, not even the flu vac which I get every year. M was despatched to the recycling bin to retrieve the information sheet the nurse gave me yesterday and sure enough, listed amongst the most common reactions are shaky legs, sore joints and a slight temperature. It looks like I'm not about to expire after all, just as M had the phone directory open, looking for a number listed as "undertakers".

Anyway, there's always a silver lining. As I was languishing in my bed of pain, M had to walk to Dingwall on her own to post my Times crossword. And by the time she got home I was up and about, having had a bowl of porridge and two paracetamol, and beginning to feel better already. And after a quiet morning with the Sunday papers and a light lunch (accompanied by two more paracetamol) I felt fully recovered and able to walk to the stables and back. So in fact all I had was about 12 hours of very mild symptoms, which is a small price to pay for being vaccinated against covid. My second dose is due on a Friday, so if I brush up my acting skills maybe I'll be able to squeeze a whole weekend of sympathy and pampering out of it.

Happy Valentine's Day to all you romantics! Yes, today is the Feast of St Valentine, the annual celebration of love and affection. I'm afraid neither M nor I remembered about it until mid-morning, when Baby A sent us a Valentine's Day WhatsApp message. I fear romance may be in decline here at Thomson Towers. I shall have to try and remember it next year, and pop along to the petrol station for a bunch of flowers for M. And she might pop along to Tesco for a crate of beer for me.

And in addition to Valentine's Day, let me say *"xin nian kuai le"* to my Chinese readers. This weekend marks the start of the Chinese new year and for the next twelve months we will be living in the year of the Ox. I'm not sure how to react to this news – are we supposed to start being extra nice to cows? I shall have to seek advice from Farmer J, who's an expert cattle breeder. Will his herd be getting extra pampering for a whole year? Fresh bedding every day, organic turnips from Sainsbury's instead of the usual field neeps, Body Shop "Wild Rose" shampoo to make them more attractive to the bull?

By the way, Wild Rose is the name of the shampoo, not one of the cows.

And coincidentally, Farmer J is featuring in one of the Sunday papers today, in a double page spread promoting his forth-coming TV sitcom "The Farm" which is due to air in a few days' time. It was filmed on location at his own farm and he's play-ing the part of, well, a farmer, so we're looking forward to seeing that. While the BBC were on site Dog F had to be fostered out to M and me for ten days to stop her from barking and disrupting the filming, and more importantly to stop her raiding the all-day running buffet which the BBC lays on for its stars and crew.

All-day running buffet, eh? I wonder if I can wangle my way on to the next show as an extra. An extra what, you ask? An "ex-tra large", suggests M, casting a critical eye at my ever-expanding waistline.

46

❧

Day 46 – a day of metric money

Monday morning, and a couple of bad things have vanished! Firstly, we have a dry day and a warm southerly breeze so the recent snow has almost all disappeared. It was so nice first thing in the morning that I heard M switching on the washing machine, and by the time I got up the washing was all ready in the basket for me to hang out on the line. I waited until daylight before doing that, because I like the neighbours to see what a good housekeeper I am. "Yes", I often boast, "I did a washing first thing this morning", and they usually react with approval. Although I often think that they suspect the truth.

The other bad thing that seems to have vanished is my manflu, after yesterday's post-vac symptoms. Which were very mild, but let's not let the facts get in the way of a good case of attention-seeking.

Anyway, I woke up feeling great this morning, far from my usual lethargic self, and immediately after breakfast I headed into Dingwall to post a parcel to Baby A. Sadly the parcel was too bulky to carry all the way on foot, so I was obliged to take the car. And I got there just as the Post Office was opening so I was first in the queue. Often on a Monday morning there are long lines of customers with multiple parcels, posting all the stuff they've managed to sell on ebay at the weekend. Either that, or returning all the stuff they accidentally bought on Amazon at the weekend, after a few glasses of wine. Well, haven't we all?

Speaking of shopping, today is an important anniversary in the history of our currency. Fifty years ago today (yes FIFTY years!) the UK changed from the old pounds, shillings and pence into the new decimalised system we have today, ie a hundred pennies to the pound. In the old days there were twenty shillings in a pound, and twelve pence in every shilling, and four farthings in every penny, so you can imagine how difficult it was to budget for your weekly shopping. Imagine if you had two half crowns in your pocket, trying to work out how many pints of beer at one and ninepence ha'penny you could afford? Especially if you'd already had a few.

The most sobering thing about this fifty-year anniversary is that I remember it. I was employed as a bank clerk at that time, and it was the only time we ever got paid overtime because we had to work all weekend converting the accounts into the new currency. No computers in those days, we didn't even have calculators, or adding machines as they were called then. And no bank statements either, all the customers had a passbook, in which was recorded their transactions and balances. And so, in advance of D-Day, as it was called, every customer had to hand in their passbook for us to convert. And we had one elderly farmer who steadfastly refused to hand in his book. He insisted he wasn't taking part in "this decimalation", as he called it, but was sticking to the old money.

Poor old chap, I wonder where he is now. Probably sitting in his barn surrounded by a pile of ten bob notes and gazing wistfully at his bank book with its balance, £12/4/6½ for all eternity.

47

⌘

Day 47 – a day of photographic modelling (well, posing)
And it's pancake day! No pancakes for me this morning
though because like Valentine's Day, it passed me by until I read
it in the paper. I really should start looking at the calendar because without a work routine I only ever have the vaguest idea of
what day it is. Luckily M is usually on the ball, and informs me
when important days are coming, like bin day for example. Or
her birthday.

This prompted me to look at last year's diary, and I see that
on this day last year I was on a plane from London to Inverness
on my way home from attending an annual motorcycle show.
At that time Covid was no more than a vague threat, one of
those far away things that we thought we could safely ignore,
like global warming, nuclear war and Brexit. And I'm still ignoring two of those.

So on my London journeys by air, rail and tube I saw a
few people wearing masks, but that wasn't uncommon in cities
around the world anyway so was no cause for concern. And my

own sole concession to the threat of an errant virus was to wear my gloves whenever I was out in public. Which may have reduced my risk slightly, but made a visit to McDonalds rather messy.

Anyway, that's the last time I was on a plane and the last time I was more than 120 miles away from home, because a few weeks later it all became too real and we were plunged into lockdown and every other event in my diary was cancelled for the remainder of the year. Except for M's birthday, of course.

Anyway, for the second time this week I ventured to Dingwall. I drove to the petrol station and topped up the car, before venturing into a deserted Tesco to buy a couple of things. I don't often go into shops, and when I do I'm doubly rigorous about cleaning hands, baskets and trolleys, and I insist on putting on rubber gloves before using the self-service checkout. And even then the staff hover behind and swoop immediately after I've finished, and spray the keyboards with disinfectant. I understand they have their orders, but you'd think they'd at least wait until I've gone more than two steps away.

While I was in there, I spotted their scheme for recycling inkjet cartridges. You can pick up a freepost envelope into which you pop your used cartridge, along with a tear-off slip on which you write your loyalty card number. Then they credit you with a massive 150 points for every cartridge you send them. And apparently 150 points is worth £1.50, and if you convert that into my local currency, three used cartridges equals one bottle of beer.

And finally, today I have taken the first steps towards becoming a media sensation. No, don't get too excited, all that happened is that one of my local newspapers sent a photographer to capture an image of me holding a copy of "Sandy's Daily Diaries". I've had a telephone interview with their reporter and they're going to run a wee feature on me and the book. Must remember to buy an extra paper this week so that I can share this fame with family who live outside the local area.

I was surprised how easy it is getting photographed, all you have to do is stand still, hold up your book (or your fantastic cake, or your pet pig, or whatever you're promoting), smile, and "click-click-click" it's all over. I can't see why Kate Moss and all these supermodels make such a big issue of it. After all, they get to pose in the most exotic of surroundings, while I was stuck in my own back garden. Up to my ankles in bird poo.

48

♒

Day 48 – a day of catering concerns

Almost thirty years ago, when I began working for the local authority, I signed up to be a vote counting assistant for local and national elections. And European ones too, although I guess we won't be having those any longer. It was quite a good ploy in the early days, the polling stations would close at 10pm so we would start counting the votes and, depending on how big the turnout was, we might be there until early morning the following day. It was always a good source of banter and in return we got extra pay plus a day off work. But for me, as you might guess, one of the most important elements was the catering.

The counting usually took place in a sports centre, either Dingwall or Inverness, and both of those had a cafeteria attached, so when it was break time we were able to visit there and avail ourselves of the best snacks and drinks. The café staff were happy because they were getting extra pay, and the sports centre staff were happy because they were getting paid by the local authority, so the food and drink was plentiful, and fresh.

Alas those days of plenty were destined not to last. As public money became scarce and budgets tightened, cuts had to be made. Soon we were cut to one break per session, and issued with vouchers for ONE drink and ONE snack. And eventually that one drink became a cup of cheap coffee dispensed from an urn, and that one snack developed into a pre-packed sandwich of indeterminate origin and content. Still, it was free. And if anyone didn't fancy theirs I was always happy to help them out with it.

And I've remained on the council's list of election staff ever since, even though I'm now fully retired. I haven't been able to help out at the last couple of elections because of my commitment to running exams in schools, but this year there are no exams so I've indicated my availability. As a result I was invited to take part in today's online "Chief Executive's Staff Briefing", which makes me feel very important. And during her briefing, the Chief Executive told us that this year's election count will be carried out during the day, not throughout the night as before. I don't know how this will affect the catering arrangements, but they may use covid as an excuse not to feed us at all. Better have a chocolate bar in my pocket, just in case.

Two very welcome phone calls this afternoon. First, one from a colleague and friend in the Highland Hospice fundraising office to tell me that my Facebook page appeal has raised almost £1500 for the Hospice. And because I'm unable at present to go in and carry out my volunteer role she thought I might appreciate a phone call rather than a simple "thank-you" letter. And she was right, I haven't had a proper conversation with anyone other than family since before Christmas so she really cheered me up. And she promises me that when the day comes when we can be together in the office once more, she'll make sure we can share a Harry Gow's dream ring. That will be lovely, but I'm not too clear on the concept of "sharing".

And the other, even more welcome, phone call was from the doctor's surgery to advise that M's covid vaccination is due on Saturday morning, which is only three days away. She's been envious of me getting mine last week, so this is her chance to get even. I've told her that they use a HUGE needle and that the nurse has the same build (and temperament) as Mike Tyson. That should keep her mind occupied for a few days so she won't notice any of my misdemeanours.

49

～

Day 49 – day of retail therapy (aka impulsive buying)

Housework day today, and I'm sad to report that one of my favourite appliances has given up the ghost. No, I don't mean a personal appliance, or abdominal support, which is the polite name for what used to called a truss. I'm happy to say I don't need one of those. Yet.

No, the appliance in question is my faithful steam mop, or as it's now more accurately called, my faithful mop. Every week I mop the kitchen and bathroom floors with it, and it's really easy. All you need to do do is fill its tank with water, plug it in and wait for the steam to come, well, steaming out. But last week, for the first time in years, it failed to produce any steam and I was obliged to get down on my knees with a cloth and scrub the floors.

But I didn't panic. Last week was a time of hard frost, so I convinced myself that somehow the frost had slowed down the machine's functions (well, it certainly slows down mine) and that once the temperature rose above zero all would be well.

Well today, in a temperature well above zero, the water in the wee tank remained steadfastly cold and not a wisp of steam was forthcoming. Ho hum, into the shed with it and back on the knees for me.

Major shopping expedition this afternoon. Well, five different shops, so that's pretty major for me. I failed in my main objective, which was to buy a replacement floor steamer following this morning's knee-bruising experience. Can't find one in Dingwall, not even in Tesco, so it looks like I shall have to revert to online ordering, which can be dangerous, because they make everything look attractive.

While browsing for steam cleaners, of course I got distracted as usual and began looking at power tools for woodworking. I have the dreaded "birthday that daren't mention its age" coming up and M has been asking for ideas as to what present I'd like. Also, she says Baby A has been asking her granny for hints, and the big day is only three weeks away so I need to come up with some ideas. And that's my excuse for drooling over power tools when I should have been comparing the merits of various brands of steam cleaner.

Anyway, the rest of my shopping went according to plan. First, a picture frame and padded envelope so that I can send a photo of Baby A to her great-granny. And while I was buying those items I bumped into a couple of former Gaelic choir colleagues, neither of whom I had seen this year, so we were able to catch up with each other's news. Main topic, of course, was the covid vac: "Have you had yours yet", "How did you get yours before me?", "Hope your arm falls off", and so on.

Then on to the next shop for a roll of brown wrapping paper for Baby A's next parcel, and some suet pellets for the garden birds. All going swimmingly so far, and all within budget, until the fateful decision to "just have a wee look" in Lidl.

And where do I always end up during my "wee looks" in Lidl? Yes, you've guessed it, in the middle aisle where all sorts of shiny tools, attractive nuts and bolts and other items irresistible to man are to be found. And so, having gone in just for a look, I emerged with a set of three vice grips, a pair of sidecutting pliers and a thirty-six piece pack of screwdriver bits. Luckily I didn't have enough money for a chain saw or a cement mixer.

50

〜

Day 50 – a day of waiting in for a man

The long awaited local paper came out today and I was crushed to discover that I haven't made it into the news, in spite of having been photographed on Day 47. I'm guessing that Tuesday was too late for today's paper, so hopefully I shall appear in full colour next week. Or it might be that when the story and photo were submitted the editor took one look and declared: "Not another story about the Loch Ness Monster! And this is the ugliest photo yet!"

Lovely Italian neighbour has the electricians in today. I'm not sure what she's getting done but it must be something pretty major because they were in all day. Maybe she's getting her fence electrified to stop neighbouring cats from visiting her garden after dark. I had a similar problem last year, especially in my vegetable patch where every cat from miles around used to gather for a game of bears. In the woods.

I've asked Mr Electrician to pop in and see me with a view to fitting a vent fan in my bathroom. You will remember my damp attic problem which Roof Man investigated, and fitted various roof vents to try to combat. Well, he suggests a bathroom vent fan would be helpful for extracting moisture and I'm sure he's right, although I wouldn't like to be standing outside the house when the fan is blowing air out. Especially after one of my microwave curries.

Anyway, Mr Electrician says it won't be a problem for him and he hopes to come and fit one early next week. It will come on every time we turn on the bathroom light, but the actual fan will be in the attic so shouldn't present too much of a noise nuisance during midnight toilet visits. And when men get to a certain age these visits become ever more frequent.

And of course, I didn't know what time Mr Electrician would call on me, so I had to stay in all day and wait for him. So no walks today, apart from regular ones to the fridge.

Some pupils will be returning to school on Monday, and staff will have a covid test twice weekly. This includes M, who has brought home her self-test kit and will start using it next week. They are instructed to carry out their tests on Mondays and Thursdays and the kits contain seven tests, so that's enough to last three and a half weeks. Unless I can surreptitiously purloin a test or two for myself, just for interest. Mind you, I don't have that much interest in sticking swabs up my nose.

For that is what they have to do. One end of the swab down the throat to the tonsils and the same swab inserted up the nose as far as possible. Getting those actions confused doesn't bear thinking about, but you're guaranteed a choke and a sneeze every time, no matter what order you do it in. Then the swab gets placed into a special fluid which needs to be dripped on to a test strip. And in thirty minutes the test strip will give an indication of the result. A single line indicates you're covid negative, a double line indicates you're covid positive.

And although it doesn't mention this in the instruction book, a wee image of a teddy bear indicates that you're pregnant.

51

∾

Day 51 – a day of (recovering from) nocturnal excitement

Picture the scene. It's 1.30 in the morning and M is fast asleep, dreaming of her garden winning the top prize at Chelsea Flower Show, judged by her twinkly-eyed hero Monty Don. And Monty is interviewing her on national television, while she gazes up at him in adoration. And his two dogs, in their turn, gaze up at her in similar adoration, as she plans her new life in the potting shed with the three of them.

And alongside her I lie, equally fast asleep, but in my dream the fragrant Joanna Lumley is about to present me with a cheque for a million pounds from the national lottery and, more importantly, marking the ceremony with a huge comforting hug. And as she pulls me towards her and I pucker up ready for a major snog, suddenly I'm forced awake by an ear-piercing RINGA-RINGA-RINGA, DINGA-DINGA-DINGA!

What's going on? The peace of our quiet suburban street is shattered by a persistent, annoying, siren-type noise. M's first thought was that it might be a police car passing through the village, but it didn't fade away as expected so was obviously something closer to home, and unmoving. Which sounds like a good description of me, but wasn't.

By this time all my visions of Joanna had been shattered, and I was despatched to investigate. I immediately discounted the possibility of a car alarm because neither of our cars has one fitted but when I peeked out of the front door to check on them I was immediately assailed by a wall of sound coming from next door's burglar alarm. I was rather surprised at this, because it hasn't sounded for at least twenty years, and my first thoughts were that perhaps yesterday's electricians had inadvertently done something to cause it to erupt in the middle of the night.

Anyway, I thought I'd better make sure that our lovely Italian neighbour was all right so I quickly got dressed, grabbed a torch and went round to check. Sure enough, there were no signs of burglary so it was obviously an electrical fault. There's a keypad in her garage which controls the alarm but the trouble was that after all these years of not being used, she had no idea of the code number required to silence it. So I carried out the standard practice for these occasions, press 0000, press 1111, and so on until in desperation I was pressing random numbers until my finger was black and blue. And the air was pretty blue too.

I phoned her adult son, who also didn't have a clue about the code number, but he said he'd try to get the electrician out and also he'd tell the police, in case they came rushing round expecting to find a major crime in progress. It would be a nice change for them to have something meaty to get their teeth into, instead of their usual Deas pie at the back door of the bakery in the early hours of the morning.

And the electrician soon arrived and got to work to silence the racket, which must have wakened half of the village by this time. And while he was there two children arrived, a couple of adolescent boys. I questioned them as to what they were doing out at that time of night, and did their parents know, and if they didn't go home I'd call the police.

To which they responded: "Calm down sir, we ARE the police".

And after checking that there had been no crime they left to prepare their report. "Italian lady safe and well, but dodgy character from next door has a serious Joanna Lumley obsession. Potential stalker".

52

~~

Day 52 – a day of pea disappointment

In all of yesterday's excitement, I forgot to tell you that M has had her covid vaccination. To avoid her having to wait for the fifteen minutes before driving after getting the jab, I drove her into Dingwall. In her new car, which was interesting for me because among other modern facilities, it has an electronic handbrake. So there I was, reaching down to apply/release the handbrake but there was no lever there, just a wee button. So having saved fifteen minutes by letting me drive, we wasted ten of them trying to get the car moving so we could exit the car park.

Just like me the previous week, M's injection was completely painless so she came bouncing out of the medical centre in high spirits. "Just you wait, my girl", I warned her. "Just you wait until the side effects kick in. You won't be so merry when you're lying in bed with a temperature and feeling weak, like I was last week". So we did wait. And wait. And wait some more, right through until this morning when it became obvious that M wasn't going to suffer any adverse reaction. She's as full of energy today as she ever was, and succeeded in dragging me out for TWO walks, one to Dingwall then another to the stables. Heaven knows what she'll be like when she gets the second dose.

Today was beautifully sunny and warm, almost like a Spring day. The upside of that is that I got a good dose of vitamin D during my walks. The downside is that I see the grass has already started growing and so soon it will be time to think about this years' garden. And noticing the grass reminded me that when I put the mower away at the end of last season I promised it that I would give it a service "one of these days". Well, as you will have guessed, "one of these days" hasn't come around yet so the poor mower hasn't had its new spark plug, clean air filter and nice fresh oil. And we all benefit from some nice fresh oil, don't we? Although in my case it's cooking oil, with plenty of bacon.

Back in October I sowed some winter peas, as an experiment to see whether we would get an early crop this spring. According to the label they were suitable for outdoor sowing and would survive winter without needing to be covered. I was a little dubious about this claim, so as well as planting a row direct into the ground, as a fallback I also sowed two plastic trays of them in the unheated greenhouse. And they did appear to be surviving, both indoors and out. Our light snowfalls didn't appear to trouble them, and even when the nights were frosty they still seemed to be happy, so I was looking forward to having fresh peas in the Spring without having to open a can. And that was all very well, until ten days ago, when the temperature dropped to -13.1C.

Well, when I eventually thawed my way into the greenhouse I found the poor peas had turned black and were all floppy, and the ones in the garden seemed to have shrivelled away to nothing. I consulted my gardening expert, Mr Google, and he reassured me that they'd survive, rally round and come back to their formal vigour. Today I inspected them and I fear he may have misled me because out of around 100 plants, only three or four are showing any signs of reviving. I suspect that the "surviving in winter" promise on the packet refers to winters in Kent, not the north of Scotland.

M's shopping list this week – milk, bread, and a tin of peas.

53

∾

Day 53 – a day of swabbing and venting

Monday morning, and time for M to do her first covid self-test. As I lay in bed, from the bathroom came the sounds of the test being administered – first the choking, then the gagging, then the sneezing as the swab was inserted into various orifices. Then a long silence, before she burst into the bedroom and said "Can you come and help me with this, please?" "Oh no", I thought, "I'm not trained to cope with swabbing, especially at this time in the morning".

But happily, it turned out that the help she needed was with the recording process, which is done online via the Scottish Government's website. Despite several attempts poor M couldn't get the system to accept her result, hampered by the fact that the reference number printed on the test strip was in such tiny print that it was impossible to read. 'Does that read II, or 11, or I1, or 1I?' 'I don't know, maybe it's a capital "U" with the middle bit missing'.

Anyway, after a few attempts we managed to get the system

to accept her reference number and her test result of "negative" was duly recorded by the Scottish Government. I bet they were pleased to hear it.

As promised, Mr Electrician sent two of his men to come and install my bathroom vent fan. I knew they were coming, so I had the attic ready open with light on and ladder set up. And I had emptied the meter cupboard of its usual clutter (dog towels, blankets, bird's fat balls and the ironing board) so that they could get access to the fuses. They were impressed with my efficiency, but I don't suppose it'll earn me any discount when the bill comes in. They were a cheery pair, though, and quickly set to work while I retreated into the living room and listened out for a flash and bang from the bathroom. Or a foot coming down through the ceiling.

And the job seemed to go smoothly. The fan lives in the attic and blows the bathroom air to the outside world via one of the roof tile vents which Roof Man fitted a couple of weeks ago. That was another bonus for the electricians, because it saved them from having to bore a hole in my nice plastic fascia above the bathroom window. Also it means that any steam will blow upwards, away from the house, so any passers by will be spared a blast of warm air. Along with any other, erm, "bathroom odours". Phew.

The light fitting in the bathroom had to be changed to accommodate the new fan because the fan is supposed to come on at the same time as the light, therefore has to share the same wiring. The current fittings are the original ones installed when the house was built, around 40 years ago. They're the traditional pendant style, which hang down from the ceiling and need a bulb, and they're not compatible with the vent fan. Modern ones are all LEDs, and luckily my sparky chums had one in their van, so were able to fit it without delay.

And in case you're wondering, like I was, LED stands for "light emitting diode" and apparently they last for ever, unlike old fashioned light bulbs which go pop with annoying regularity. Also, they're much brighter so maybe I'll actually be able to see what I'm doing in the bathroom. I'm referring, of course, to shaving, which I have to do without my specs and which is always a bit of a hit or miss affair. You'd think I'd know my way around this face after all these years, wouldn't you? Well if it looks rough from where you're standing, you should see it from the inside.

54

∽

Day 54 – a day of garden plans

Another mild day but with rain forecast, so M put a washing on when she got up, and I hung it out on the line, but not until after breakfast, of course. Breakfast takes priority over everything. It's a long time between bedtime snack and breakfast, at least ten hours, and a man could easily expire from lack of calories.

Then while it was still dry I had my long walk, and half an hour after I got home the heavens opened and I had to run out and take the washing off the line. Thank goodness we have a tumble dryer in the shed. For the rest of the day it was sunshine and showers so I was in and out of the house every half hour, like a wee weatherman. Who remembers these weather houses, built to look like alpine chalets? The man would come out when it was raining and the lady when it was dry. And they never seemed to be both inside the house at the same time, but I suspect they sneaked in together, after dark.

And the mild weather has turned my thoughts even more towards the garden. The grass had begun to grow, which reminds me about my poor mower languishing in the shed unloved because it was due to be serviced "one of these days". Well, I have some good news for it - I've ordered a new spark plug, air filter and fresh oil and as soon as Mr Amazon delivers it I shall give the machine a full service. One of these days.

I've also ordered some plants. M spotted a special offer in one of the Sunday papers for hanging fuchsias and asked me to order them for her baskets, and while I was on the website I was tempted to order nine hardy ones for myself. I'm hoping they'll provide a splash of colour in the border where the much feared berberis lives. And save me from having to do so much weeding, because my fingers are still throbbing after last season's encounters with the berberis spikes. No wonder I can't play the piano.

Still on a gardening theme, following the demise of my so-called winter-hardy peas a couple of days ago I've sown a new couple of rows, direct into the garden. According to the packet, they should germinate in around 21 days so the climate should be a little kinder to them by then. Mind you, the packet also claims they're hardy down to minus 23C, yet our minus 13.1 killed them off a couple of weeks ago. Perhaps the fact that the packet had been lying around in the greenhouse for a few (well, several) years before sowing might have had an effect on their viability. Lying around for long periods certainly makes me lethargic.

Special treat at lunchtime, instead of my usual sandwich I made some spam fritters. Spam, for those of you who don't know, is wonderful stuff. It's spiced pork and ham in a wee tin and has been a staple diet since before the war. Like Marmite, you either love it or hate it, and I love it. I'd never made fritters before, so consulted Mr Google for instructions on how to make batter. Looks quite easy, just plain flour, milk and a little salt all mixed together. What could possibly go wrong?

A search of the kitchen cabinets revealed that we don't have any plain flour, so would self-raising do? Mr Google was silent on the topic so I went for it anyway, and it worked quite well, except my batter turned out to have the consistency (and taste) of pancakes. So that made up for me missing Pancake Day last Tuesday.

And no, there isn't a fritter stuck to the ceiling following the traditional pancake tossing ceremony.

55

∽

Day 55 – a day of make do and mend

Still reeling from Nicola's announcement yesterday afternoon telling us that we're unlikely to be allowed to travel until early April. We'd hoped for a March easing so that we can go and visit Baby A and her family, whom we haven't seen since Christmas. Coincidentally, M Junior phoned this afternoon to remind us that M and I will be needed on the farm when lambing starts in April, and that's classed as essential travel so will be allowed. Not that we'll be doing much lambing, we'll leave that to Farmer J, his mum and M Junior while we step in as child carers for Baby A. It's a very similar environment anyway, constant feeding and dealing with lots of bodily fluids.

Today was so nice I couldn't resist taking the car for a twenty-minute drive to a beauty spot near Inverness for my morning walk. Yes I know, it's not often you see the words "beauty" and "Inverness" in the same sentence, but this one is on a wooded hill overlooking the bridge into the city and has quite spectacular views of the Moray Firth. Too far away to see the legendary dolphins, sadly, but I was blessed with meeting several dogs during my walk so that was almost as exciting. And much less slimy.

It takes a little over an hour to complete the circuit, so that should burn up some calories. And combined with my healthy lunch of sardines on toast should cancel out yesterday's high-fat, high-salt diet of spam fritters. Maybe, just maybe I'll visit the bathroom scales tomorrow morning to see if there's any change for the better.

After my walk I was only ten minutes away from Inverness, so I drove to one of the shopping malls and treated my car to a car wash. I usually do that myself at home with a bucket and hose, but the ground is still very wet after a few weeks of rain and snow, and I don't want to add to the moisture. That's my excuse anyway, for sitting in the car, warm and dry, listening to Popmaster while the machine does the work. Unfortunately some of the washing processes are rather noisy so I couldn't hear half of the questions. And I didn't know the answers to the other half so it was "*nul points*" for me.

My lawn mower oil and spark plugs were delivered today, so all I need now is the new air filter and I'll be able to give it a spring service. I'm not going to start it until I have all the spares, and that's as good an excuse as I can think of for not doing it today.

In any case, I was busy mending a kitchen utensil for M. Quite a few years ago the handle came off one of her pan lids and, rather than throw it away and buy a new one, I improvised a new handle by fitting a wooden drawer knob from B & Q. It looked smart, it was heat resistant and – most importantly -

it was cheap. Sadly, the years inevitably took their toll, and last night the wooden knob disintegrated and the pan was left knobless.

So I was tasked with replacing it, but after a thorough search through the jumble that is my shed I found all sorts of things, but nothing that would suffice as a pan lid handle. Not to be defeated, I found an old broom handle, cut a short piece off it, sandpapered it to make it smooth and screwed it on to the pan lid. OK, it looks a little crude, but it will do the job until I make it to B & Q.

At least the pan is usable, so we'll still be able to boil the potatoes. And the peas, if they grow.

56

~

Day 56 – a day of meetings, real and virtual

As threatened, I stepped on the scales this morning. Three-quarters of a pound down in the past four days! At this rate I'll be down to my proper weight by the middle of 2023.

Met a friend for a socially distanced walk this morning, it was a nice change to have someone to talk to. In a loud voice from six feet away. And she had her dog with her too. Sadly dogs seem to have no concept of social distancing and are always happy to come within patting/feeding distance. Perhaps I was a canine in a previous life.

It was good to catch up with her news, and I learned there's a new baby in our street, born yesterday, so I shall pop round to their house tomorrow with a wee card and a gift. This happy event will help lower the age profile in the street, quite a lot of the residents are over retirement age. In our own wee cul de sac there are eight houses and all but one are owned by retirees. And I'm the fifth oldest. But I'd rather you thought of me as the fourth youngest.

Another day, another online meeting. You will remember that back on Day 48 I was able to take part in the local authority Chief Executive's briefing. Well, by "take part" I mean "sit quietly and listen" because I'm not a permanent member of staff any more, just a casual employee whose sole role is vote counting at elections. But my name is obviously on a list somewhere because I was invited to attend today's meeting, which was held at the next level down from the Chief Exec and chaired by the Executive Chief Officer based in Dingwall. And he attracted more than fifty-five participants, which is close to the maximum number of people awake in Dingwall at any one time.

Today's meeting was held using a computer program called Microsoft Teams, which is a new one to me. In previous online meetings with schools I've used Google Meet, and I've chatted to family and friends on Zoom, so Microsoft Teams was yet another system for me to learn how to use. The main difference I found is that you can't actually see the other participants, just a row of circles along the bottom of the screen showing their initials. And if you want to know who they are you just hover your mouse upon their circle and up comes their name, and in some cases their department. So it was interesting for me to work my way along the list and say to myself "Oh, I remember him from twenty years ago. He still hasn't managed to get himself promoted", or "Oh I remember her from the office Christmas party in 1993. I wonder if she's still banned from using the photocopier".

Anyway, no particularly new information about the elections, apart from an ongoing recruitment drive. I suspect they're struggling to get sufficient polling station staff, which doesn't surprise me because traditionally these volunteers come from the more senior members of the population, and they're the ones most wary of covid. Although they did show us a slide demonstrating all the extra safeguards being introduced this year, which reassures me that the vote counting will take place in a safe environment, so I have no qualms about signing up. The main difference will be that there will be less opportunity for banter and chat with my fellow counters, that's always one of the most enjoyable parts of the job. You'd be surprised how much juicy gossip you can pick up over the Wester Ross ballot boxes.

And you should see what some of these crofters write on the back of their voting slips. Obh obh mo creach!

57

∽

Day 57 – a day of fame. But not fortune.

M came rushing into the bedroom as soon as she returned from the paper shop this morning, brandishing a newspaper and shouting: "You're in the paper!". What could the matter be? What's the worst thing the local paper could be reporting on? Has a smart camera captured an image of my car on a double yellow line in Dingwall? Is there even a double yellow line in Dingwall? You can image how my mind was racing.

But no, it was a case of fame at last! This week's issue of our local weekly newspaper, The Ross-shire Journal, features a wee photo of me on the front page and a bigger one on page three, along with a review of "Sandy's Daily Diaries". A very positive review, I may add in all modesty, and some biographical info about myself. Unfortunately the photos only show my head and shoulders, which is a pity because it was the first time this year that I've been able to wear smart clothes. Including my favourite pink shirt, as featured in the book. Luckily the photo was taken around three weeks ago, before my hair took on its present state of "explosion in a sofa factory".

Leaping out of bed, my first action was to photograph the page and WhatsApp it to M Junior so that Baby A could see how famous her grandad is. My second action was to alert all my Facebook friends and encourage them to buy the paper. And my third action was to have breakfast. It's hungry work being a celebrity, as any cookery show presenter will tell you.

After breakfast I walked down to the shop to buy an extra copy of the paper, so that I could sent it to my elderly aunt, who lives far from the Ross-shire Journal's circulation area. And I wrapped it up along with a copy of a photo of Baby A and walked – yes, walked, hope you're impressed – to Dingwall to post it.

And on the way home as I entered our street I noticed that the fence belonging to the old lady across the road was broken. It's a wooden spar fence which I built twenty-five years ago when we lived in that house, and one of the top spars had become detached at one end and was hanging down. To be honest I'm surprised it's lasted so long, twenty-five summers and winters have come and gone since I made it. I must have used good quality wood, and expensive paint. I wonder where I got the money from?

Anyway, it was an open invitation to vandals to detach the board and walk away with it or, worse, beat someone over the head with it, so "someone" had to do "something". And the poor lady in the house is in her eighties and has failing eyesight so she could hardly be expected to get her boiler suit on and renovate the fence. So off I went to my shed, gathered up a hammer and a handful of nails, and fixed the damaged spar. It felt very odd, memories came flooding back of M and I nailing the spars on in the first place, all those years ago when M Junior was still in primary school. And I was still in control of my hair.

58

～

Day 58 – a day of preparing for spring

Saturday morning, beautifully warm and dry. In bed and out of it.

After yesterday's publicity buzz, it was a bit of a come-down to open the paper and not see me. Instead, today's papers are featuring a younger man, one Alex Salmond, who it seems had something not very complimentary to say about our Nicola yesterday. And next week it's Nicola's turn to say something not very complimentary about Alex. I don't get myself involved in political matters, but I've seen enough playground fights in my time to know it's all going to end in tears. And a summons to the head teacher's office where, in my day, the tawse would be produced and "six of the best" would be administered. Following that, the two delinquents would be forced to shake hands and be friends again. Somehow I can't see that happening this time.

Today I ran out of excuses for not servicing the lawn mower. Couldn't blame the weather because it was perfect, even outdoors without a jacket. Couldn't blame the lack of spares because Mr Amazon had delivered the final item – the air filter - yesterday. And since it is a full two weeks since I got my covid jab I couldn't even pretend I had a flu-type reaction.

So nothing for it but to get stuck in – blade off and sharpened, new spark plug and air filter fitted, oil drained and replenished, fresh fuel installed and ready to go. Would it start? M was sceptical and stood by ready to laugh while I pulled the starter cord once, twice...

Pull number 13, and I was beginning to wonder whether I'd put the plug in the right way up, when the engine burst into life. "Thirteen pulls", I announced to M, "That's about what I was expecting it to take". "Yes, dear", was her reply, as she walked away trying unsuccessfully to hide a snigger.

We have an old tree trunk still standing in our garden, it was one of a group of lime trees which we had cut down a few years ago because they were encroaching on the house, but we left that particular trunk standing so that we could use it to support one end of the washing line. And it has done that duty admirably for all these years until we noticed just these past couple of months, that "something" seems to be attacking it, stripping the bark off and making holes in the trunk. And that has led to it starting to rot, which is bad news for me because if it falls down I will have to erect a proper washing pole. And that involves A LOT of planning, A LOT of digging and probably A LOT of interesting language for the neighbours to shield their grandchildren's ears from.

Today, the culprit was identified. You will remember we have a visiting woodpecker who hangs on our nut feeder. Well today we spotted him flitting from the feeder onto the tree and start pecking his way around the trunk. I suppose he must be doing it during the week when I'm home alone, although I never see him. Maybe he knows my routine – 'Aye, that's him had his lunch, he'll fall asleep in a minute and I can have half an hour on the tree'.

So if the tree falls down I'll be too embarrassed to admit to the neighbours that I was defeated by a woodpecker. I shall have to say it was a lightning strike during a fearful thunderstorm. A very localised one.

59

〜

Day 59 – a day of learning to spell

Sunday again, and our usual walk to Dingwall to post this week's Times prize crossword. Had a little trouble with it this week, the answer to one of the clues was that area of a ship pronounced "gunnels". I was sure it was spelt gunwhales, but of course I couldn't get it to fit in the grid. My normal recourse on these occasions is to consult Mr Google, but I've lost faith in him after his epic failure, telling me my winter peas would survive a temperature of minus 23C when in fact they lay down and died at a mere minus 13.

So to solve my nautical quandary I resorted to the old-fashioned method, and looked it up in Chambers Dictionary. And there it was – gunwales with no "h". All my life I've been under a misapprehension about how to spell it. It's maybe just as well I failed the Royal Navy entrance exam by answering the question: "How would you address an Admiral?" Apparently a wee wave and a cheery "Hello, Sailor!" was the wrong answer.

And this whole spelling thing reminded me of an Army officer I once knew – and this is a true story – who had enjoyed a long and glittering career, had reached the rank of Lieutenant Colonel and had retired to his country estate. And it wasn't until he was in his late 70s that he learned (from me!) that there's an "r" in the middle of "February".

Lucky for him there were no gunwales in the Army. Although I suppose they use funwales to pour fuel into their tanks, and the WW2 prisoners escaped from Stalag Luft III by digging tunwales.

It was a nice warm day again, so very pleasant to be outdoors. I haven't spent so much time out of the house since Christmas, as I have these past two days. Evidently sunshine is a good source of Vitamin D, so I expect to be bursting with health by the end of the weekend. As opposed to bursting my waistband.

Flushed with yesterday's mechanical success, I serviced both of our strimmers. Yes, we're a two-strimmer family, we have "his" and er, "also his". So that got them up and running along with the mower. And while I was doing that, M was clearing the vegetable patch of last year's brussels sprout and broccoli plants, so by the end of the afternoon we were all prepared for spring. Spring's official start date in the UK is the 20th of March, but knowing my luck it probably won't reach here until June. Just in time for the days to start getting shorter.

And while I was in the plastic shed retrieving the strimmers I found a couple of small sheets of plywood which are around the same size as the board I painted and displayed at Christmas, the none with the wee penguin and his santa hat. My plan was to paint over him and create an Easter scene, but now that I've found these extra boards I'll use one of them instead and save the poor wee penguin for next Christmas. If I ever remember where I put him.

So I've cut these two down to a suitable size, sanded them smooth and begun painting them. Today I did two coats on one side of each board, and tomorrow I shall do the same on the other side. And then I shall devise a suitable Easter scene. A chicken, perhaps, or a cute wee bunny. But these are quite challenging for my 1967 O' Grade Art, so maybe I should stick to something I know I can draw.

Easter penguin, anyone?

60

⌇

Day 60 – a day of Welsh traditions

Monday the first of March, and another fine spring-like morning. Surely this good weather can't last much longer, can it? After losing the traditional monthly game of "pinch, punch" I set off for my morning walk and did a five mile circuit before breakfast. It took me almost two hours, which averages out at two and a half miles per hour, which leans much more towards "tortoise" than "hare".

But if you think that's slow, just compare it with a real tortoise. According to the Guinness Book of Records, the world's fastest tortoise can run at 0.63 miles per hour, so he would need almost eight hours to do that journey. And he'd be sure to require a toilet break halfway round so would need an extra half hour to get behind a tree.

St David's Day today, which apparently is a big day in Wales. It's their national day, when they dress up in traditional dress and wear leeks in their lapels. And if they can't get leeks they wear daffodils, which are more colourful but not as high in vitamin K. And they eat a traditional dish called cawl, which is a concoction of lamb and leeks. I suppose the same leeks as you have on your jacket will also do for the cawl, no point in wasting them. As long as you take the safety pin out first.

I wondered whether they make cawl with the daffodils too, but it appears daffodils are toxic and eating them can lead to abdominal pain, stomach disorders and even madness. Which explains a lot when you see what Welsh rugby fans get up to in the pub after a victory over the English. Or the Scots, or the Italians, or the St George's School for Girls under-12s.

Had a busy day today, finished painting yesterday's plywood boards so they'll be ready to have an Easter scene painted on. One of them will, anyway, I'll keep the other one as a spare for the next notable occasion. Mayday perhaps, or Midsummer, or "Official End Of Lockdown" which I expect Nicola will announce on Christmas Eve. Then "Official Restart Of Lockdown", which will be on Boxing Day.

While I was in painting mode, I treated the concrete bird bath with a waterproofing compound, to stop it leaking. Several winters of frost have caused lots of tiny cracks in it and when we fill it up the poor birdies have to be quick to get their bath/ drink before it all seeps away. I was going to buy some resin for that job, but M found an ancient tin of waterproofing treatment buried away at the back of her shed so I'm using that instead. It goes on like a thick white paste, but claims to dry clear. I shall find out tomorrow whether that claim is accurate.

I popped up the street with a card and gift for the new baby I told you about on Day 56. On the way I bumped into one of my neighbours, we had a long chat and compared our reactions to the covid vac. His was worse than mine, he felt very ill for a couple of days with headaches and pains, and was sure it was caused by the Astra Zeneca vaccine.

Or maybe he'd just been eating daffodils.

61

～

Day 61 – a day of pod trouble (coffee, not peas)

I told you a few weeks ago about our new coffee making machine, the purchase of which was a bold step into the unknown for us. Well, for me.

Instead of coffee beans or granules it uses pods, which are little round devices rather like wee flying saucers covered in foil. I keep expecting little green men to emerge, shrink me down to their size

and abduct me into their alien ship to carry out some invasive probing. It hasn't happened yet but there's no harm in hoping.

Anyway, the machine is really easy to use, even for me. You insert the pod, press the button, and the machine punctures the foil and mixes the contents with the hot water and out comes the coffee. Which is fine as long as you've remembered to position a cup under the spout, which I have occasionally forgotten to do. Now it's OK to spill stuff on the floor in Starbucks or Tesco because they will send someone (almost always the Saturday girl, bless her) to clean it up. But when I'm home alone there is no Saturday girl, or indeed any other day girl, so no matter how loudly I yell "clean up in aisle three", no-one is going to come to my aid.

But we've rubbed along quite nicely together, the coffee machine and me, until we hit an unexpected snag at the weekend. M came home from the grocery shopping trip on Saturday, with everything on her list except coffee pods. At least she got the beer, so the trip wasn't a total disaster.

She found that although the shelves were labelled "coffee pods", they appeared to be out of stock. Not to worry, I thought, I bet at this very moment there's half a dozen Tesco lorries heading up the A9. At 50mph, with a trail of frustrated car drivers behind them. And one of them is bound to be carrying a whole load of pods just for us. So I assured M that I would visit Tesco on Monday and buy a supply, and in the meantime we would have to spend the rest of the weekend drinking instant coffee. Just like we did in pre-pod days, two months ago, which we can hardly remember.

On Monday (yesterday) I headed in to Tesco as promised only to find the same empty shelf, but this time with a label attached stating: "out of stock, replacement due 8 March". That's a whole week away, how come it takes so long to get here? The answer, of course, is Brexit. These coffee pods are manufactured in Europe, and so they're probably sitting in a warehouse in Calais waiting for Inspector Clouseau to sign the appropriate forms. In triplicate.

Today, then, I went to Inverness, for the first time this year, in a bid to find the correct coffee pods. And I did find them, in one of the main supermarkets. Just to be safe I bought enough to last us for two weeks, in case Clouseau reads this diary and decides to hold our supplies back for another week to teach me a lesson.

And while I was there I took a walk along the street and through the shopping centre. And what a depressing walk it was. Almost every shop is closed, some of them permanently, and more than half of the main shopping centre is in darkness and closed off behind metal barriers. When I remember the bustling city centre M and used to visit every Saturday, only a year ago, it's hard to equate that with the ghost town I visited today.

On a lighter note, at least the car got a run. And got pooped on by a different class of seagull.

62

~

Day 62 – a day of automated banking

Today started with a visit to the bank. Well when I say started, it was a couple of hours into the morning because breakfast and reading the papers always take priority. And I delayed my morning walk so that I could walk into Dingwall and pay a cheque into my account. Yes, a cheque. Or what my American readers will know as a check. Cheques are pretty rare in these days of electronic banking so this was a bit of a novelty. And paying money INTO my account is even more of a novelty.

And in line with modern methods, you don't just stroll up to the bank counter and hand the cheque over to the cashier to be paid in. Oh no, you have to carry out the transaction yourself, using a machine which looks like a cash dispenser but works in reverse.

So, having queued at the bank door and been admitted by the duty receptionist, I was directed to the machine and, having assured her I was quite capable of using it myself, left to get on with it. Insert card – ok. Insert cheque – also ok. Then, suddenly – not ok! The display read "cheque not recognised, please remove", so I waited for the cheque to be rejected and come gliding out of the slot. But, to my horror, no cheque reappeared, just a rather alarming series of grinding noises followed by an ominous silence.

Luckily the helpful lady who had admitted me was hovering, saw my distress and came swiftly to my aid. And helpfully, she immediately declared: "Yes, it did this yesterday too". I think she intended that to reassure me, but my immediate thought, which I didn't say out loud, was: "If it did this yesterday, how come you haven't had an engineer out to fix it?" And my next thought, which I DID say out loud, was: "Where's my cheque?" Don't worry, said she as she got down on her knees and reached inside the slot with her slim and neatly manicured fingers. I stood well back, waiting for the machine to electrocute her with a huge bang. Either that or pull her inside through the slot, arm first, kicking and screaming and never to be seen again, nothing to be seen of her but her shoes (sensible, flat) lying abandoned in front of the machine.

But my concerns were unfounded, within seconds she had managed to pull the rejected cheque out of the slot, gave it a smooth down on her apron and inserted it again. And this time it was accepted, my receipt came gliding out, and the money was safe and sound in my bank account. But I don't suppose it will be in there for long because as soon as I start visiting Mr Amazon's treasure trove I'm bound to discover something that I really need and can't live without.

Two hours after setting off I was home, in time for my morning coffee break. And the rest of the morning – and much of the afternoon – I'm afraid was spent on the sofa, with my laptop on my, erm, lap, watching the proceedings of the grandly named "Committee on the Scottish Government Handling of Harassment Complaints". I mentioned this on Day 58 when I described Alex Salmond's attendance at the committee, and today was Nicola Sturgeon's turn to be grilled. I shall refrain from making any jokes about grilling people with fish-related names. The Sun headline writers do that much better than I do.

And that was the rest of my day effectively written off. When M came home from work she found me still sitting engrossed in the proceedings. No table set, no dishes washed, and only five clues solved in today's Times crossword.

63

∾

Day 63 – a day of angel numbers. Whatever they are.

Today is the fourth day of March 2021 which, in the way we Brits write our dates, is 4.3.21. And while I was having lunch I glanced at the clock and realised that it was 12.34 on 4.3.21. Furthermore, if you add 1234 and 4321 you get 5555 which is a so-called angel number, the meaning of which is that something big is about to happen to your life. That's what Mr Google says anyway, but we all know what a liar he is.

Anyway, long before my angelic lunch I had a busy morning, and an early start. We don't have any larks here so I was up with the seagull. M had switched on the washing machine and it had finished its cycle by the time she left for work, so I hung the washing on the line in the hope that the early morning dampness would turn into a warm dry day. And it did, so I had the washing dried, aired in the tumble dryer, folded and put away by the time M came home, thereby earning some brownie points to make up for yesterday's slothful afternoon slumped on the sofa pretending I understood any of the questions Nicola was being subjected to. Or indeed any of her answers.

Incidentally, I hope I never get called to answer questions in front of any of those committees. They seem to have a great fondness for asking about things which happened some time ago, such as: 'What did you say to your chief of staff on 17 December 2018?', or 'Who was present at a meeting in your office on the third of April 2019?'. I would have to answer (truthfully, because I would be on oath) 'Haven't a clue, I can hardly remember what I had for lunch yesterday'.

Perhaps I could fall back on my Civil Service training and respond: 'Terribly sorry, I'm bound by the Official Secrets Act and cannot possibly provide that information'.

Back to my busy morning, after hanging out the washing and having breakfast I dusted and vacuumed the whole house. Well, not literally the whole house, you understand. I didn't actually climb up on to the roof with the hoover, or climb into the attic and wield the feather duster, but you know what I mean. And then I washed the bathroom and kitchen surfaces and floors before a well deserved (in my opinion) coffee break and half an hour with yesterday's Times crossword. Half an hour well spent, I might add, because I've increased my clue-solving total from yesterday's five to nineteen. Only eleven left unsolved, which I need to have done by Saturday. I may well need to resort to Mr Google for help, if I can drag him away from today's obsession with angels.

And between coffee and lunch I walked to Conon Bridge, recycled half a dozen bottles (no, NOT all beer bottles, how dare you?) then up through the village and home by the main road. A good two and a half miles, so I felt very self-righteous. And hungry.

Now that we're into March and the days are getting longer, I thought it was time to introduce a little more colour into our environment. So I've bought some polyanthus plants, which are in flower just now, blue flowers with yellow centres and healthy green leaves. And I'm displaying them in a planter shaped like a miniature white cottage without a roof, which I made out of scrap wood a few years ago. After sitting outdoors for a couple of winters it had begin to deteriorate so It's been in the shed since November and had some remedial work done including a new red door and windows and a couple of coats of paint.

It brightens up the area outside the front window, and amuses passers by. It also amuses passing dogs, who are always grateful for a new, erm, convenience.

64

〜

Day 64 – a day of sloth appreciation

Yet another fine morning, but very cold. I did the five mile circuit before breakfast, clockwise for a change. Which doesn't make any difference to the distance but it means the sun is in my left eye on the first leg of the journey, then my right eye once I turn for home. So if I meet you on my morning walk, please don't be alarmed. I'm squinting, not winking at you. And that's what I shall tell the judge.

Postie brought some holiday brochures today. I think he does it just to annoy me. These came from Saga, a UK-based company which specialises in holidays for the over 50s. We've had a couple of holidays with them in the past, one trekking in the Himalayas which I'll tell you about some other time, and one on safari in Africa. We had lots of (very close) encounters with the African wildlife, nearly within touching distance of a male lion who, luckily, had just eaten a large gazelle-flavoured lunch otherwise he might have been tempted by my appetising figure.

One day we spotted a whole flock of vultures up in the trees, looking down at us. Our guide told they weren't a threat because they only eat animals which are already dead. But I'm sure I could read the lips of the leading vulture as he addressed his colleagues: "Don't worry lads, it's a Saga tour. They'll all be dead soon".

My mention of having a slothful day on Wednesday prompts me to share with you the fact that I'm a full member of the Sloth Appreciation Society. Yes, that is a genuine thing, founded and run by a leading zoologist, and Mr Google will take you to its website. But ignore anything he says about garden peas.

Importantly, we're talking here about the furry animals which hang from trees, not the deadly sin of the same name. Although it too has its attractions, but I'm not sure there's an actual appreciation society for deadly sins. Unless you count the rock band from Finland who have called themselves Sinful Society. They won't sell many records in the Vatican City branch of HMV. Mama Mia!

No, the Sloth Appreciation Society (motto – the slow shall inherit the earth) is for those of us who admire the sloth and his perceived lazy lifestyle. The sloth is the master of energy saving, he spends his days hanging upside down and barely moving, except for a toilet visit once a week for which he descends from his tree. Well, there are some things even a sloth can't do in an upside down position.

There are serious sides to the society, of course. Preservation of habitat and conservation are important, but I suspect many members join simply because it's something different, perhaps slightly eccentric, and it's a great conversation starter at parties. The society has a manifesto with six lifestyle rules for members. The first is "slow down", and after obeying that one I'm afraid I haven't yet got around to reading the other five.

Slothville is where all things sloth-related come from. You can order books and calendars, but so far there doesn't seem to be a badge or a tie to help us identify fellow members. And if there's a secret slothy handshake it hasn't been shared with me yet. But I do have a membership certificate, and I suspect it was issued by an actual sloth, because they ran out of energy (or ink) when they got to the end of my name. Anyway, there it is, up on my bedroom wall, evidence that a full member of the Sloth Appreciation Society is one "Sandy Thomso".

65

〜

Day 65 – a day of scrubbing and scraping. But not by me.
You will remember we've recently had a vent fan fitted in our bathroom, by two nice young men who were sent by the electrician. Well the bill for that job came in today, courtesy of the postie. I suppose it was a change for him, from the usual holiday brochures. And just as I was reaching for the chequebook I spotted a note on the invoice that said: 'you can pay online, our bank account details are xxxxxxx'. Which I thought was strange, because my bank account has numbers, not "x"s.

Anyway I did just that, logged on to my online banking app and transferred the payment direct to the electrician's account. How modern am I? Not all that modern, as it turns out – rather than simply trust the system to have made the payment I printed a copy of the receipt, just in case the system gets hacked and the money ends up in some Colombian drug dealer's account.

Somewhat spookily, a few minutes later I received a call on my mobile phone from a suspiciously robotic voice with a mid-Atlantic accent (you know, like the one Lulu puts on when she's not in Scotland) telling me that Her Majesty's Revenue and Customs have issued a warrant against me for non-payment of taxes. Ooh how scared was I? Not scared at all, as it happened, because this is a common and well publicised scam. They invite you to press a button to prevent the enforcement officers arriving, and then they ask for your bank account details and before you've put the phone down your life savings have gone. To that same Colombian drug dealer, probably.

The vent fan was installed, in case you've forgotten, because we were having a wee problem with dampness in one corner of the bathroom. M noticed it some time ago and had stripped away the wallpaper in that corner, exposing what looked like damp patches on the wall. She wasn't sure where the dampness was coming from, and was even casting doubts on my erm, "aim", if you know what I mean. Isn't that a shocking suggestion? I may have dodgy eyesight and creaky joints but there's nothing wrong with my sense of direction.

So today she set to in the bathroom, with a plastic bucket, a scraper and something called "sugar soap" which sounds to me like a very versatile product, sugar and soap combined, and one that I can make good use of. I tried sprinkling it on my cornflakes and then I washed my hair with it. Neither venture was successful. The bright red scalp was bad enough, but the foaming at the mouth didn't half scare next door's grandchildren. Don't try this at home, kids.

Anyway, M scrubbed and scrubbed so ferociously that the wallpaper remnants swiftly surrendered and soon she'd scraped the wall back to the original paint from 30 years ago. I helped of course, by standing over her, nodding my head knowledgeably and making approving noises. Eventually she chased me away to make her a cup of tea and finish the Times crossword. In that order.

And now we wait and see whether the dampness returns, or whether we (she) can repaper that part of the wall. Luckily she has some paper left over from when she first did it so at least I'll be spared being sent to B&Q and tasked with bringing home a matching roll.

Because we all know what can happen. Either I come home with completely the wrong paper, or come home with no paper at all but instead with some new shiny power tool just "because it was on special offer". And M will give up and go and buy the paper herself, which is what I was hoping she'd do in the first place.

66

∽

Day 66 – a day of industry

Sunday morning again, and we had our usual morning walk to Dingwall to post my Times crossword, or "waste another stamp" as M describes it.

And it was a nice day, so after breakfast M headed out to her greenhouse and started sowing seeds for her summer bedding plants. And having sowed them, she's brought them into the house to germinate because there's almost certainly going to be a lot more frost between now and spring. Once they're safely through the compost they'll need extra light, so that's the point at which we'll switch on the greenhouse heater and move them out there to develop into healthy, robust plants. I wonder if a spell in there would work for me?

And all this industry made me feel guilty, so I've embarked on a scheme to further enhance the gravel area at the front of the house. You will remember I have some polyanthus in a wee wooden house out there, and there's also a stone otter which I painted last year plus three wooden toadstools which have been sheltering all winter but can go out soon. And I have a couple of other stone ornaments which I'm going to paint and put on display. One is a baby rabbit and the other is a frog. I plan to sit the frog upon one of the toadstools and leave the other ones free for kids to sit on. There are a couple of local mums who pass by with their little kids and I'm always happy to see them sit on the toadstools and talk to the animals. The kids of course, not the mums. That would be worrying.

So once Mr Amazon delivers some paint I shall get cracking. In the meantime the frog and rabbit are sitting in my shed having been wire brushed. Along with the teddy ornament, who has been sitting there waiting to be painted since Day 42 so I hope they don't expect any swift action.

After my talk yesterday of "shiny power tools" from B&Q, I've taken the opportunity to remind M that I have a (big, but don't tell anyone) birthday coming up. And I've been dropping some pretty heavy hints for a couple of weeks now about how my woodworking skills would be considerably enhanced if only I had a few more. Even if I don't know how to use them, the noises they make will impress the neighbours and raise my hard working, skilled and talented image all along the street. I can hear all the wives already: 'See that Sandy? I don't know what he's making but he's been busy working the whole day in his shed, why can't YOU be more like him?'

On my last, erm, "big" birthday M bought me one of those portable work benches, which is one of the most useful presents ever. I've used it for many projects over the past five years and even though it's now paint-stained and suffering from certain cuts and scrapes following some of my more exuberant sawing endeavours, it's still as robust as ever. I wonder whether it would survive an encounter with a handheld electric planer, which is one of the things I've been hinting for. And if it does survive, will my fingers also escape unharmed? Electric planers are great labour saving devices but very dangerous in the wrong hands. I might even have to read the instructions BEFORE switching it on, for a change.

Anyway, I'm hopeful that my hinting has borne fruit. This afternoon I found M busily engaged on the computer, with her bank card by her side, ordering something which I wasn't allowed to see. And I've been told that if any parcels arrive this week I'm not to open them, so that's also quite a good sign. All will become clear on Friday, when I unwrap my present. Hope I don't find a roll of wallpaper and a pack of sugar soap.

67

～

Day 67 – a day of international women

Long walk before breakfast on a Monday morning, that's the
way to start the week. Or in my case that's the way to startle the
weak. But it stayed dry for a couple of hours, and I only met one
car the whole way round. And one horse, being led from the stables to the field for a day's outdoor grazing. His owner will be
hoping he performs all his, erm, toilet duties whilst he's outside,
to save her having to barrow a huge load of manure in the morning.

A parcel arrived today, addressed to M. In line with her strict
instructions yesterday, I haven't opened it, not even for a wee
peek inside, but it feels quite heavy. I hope it's not a set of exercise weights. And just as I was feeling smug at winning the "who
gets a delivery" game with the neighbours, my immediate next
door neighbour received not one, but TWO separate deliveries.
So today he wins, but never mind. I have paint on order from
Amazon for my garden ornaments, so that should even up the
score.

Today is International Women's Day. I don't know any international women. Unless you count a lady taxi driver in Santiago who, in the midst of the 2019 city centre riots, piloted M and me through the back streets at high speed and got us to the airport without being trampled on or blown up, both of which were real possibilities. South Americans seem to enjoy a good riot, and they usually time it to coincide with our holiday dates. Maybe it's something we said.

And despite all the dangers (snakes, volcanoes, earthquakes, pickpockets) M and I love South America and had planned to visit Ecuador in October last year. Of course that plan was blocked by the pandemic and we didn't have a holiday in 2020. And we're not planning one in 2021 either, but now that vaccines are beginning to have an effect and there's maybe some light at the end of the tunnel (as Nicola is fond of saying) we're begun -with caution - to think about 2022.

I phoned my travel agent, just for a chat and some advice, and he's optimistic that by summer 2022 a trip to Ecuador will be possible. Luckily, our favoured airline plans to reintroduce daily flights to Quito as soon as it's safe to do so, so I've pencilled in July 2022 for our next South American adventure. And if there are riots in the streets I shall phone my favourite Chilean taxi driver to rescue us.

I imagined that International Women's Day wouldn't affect me, but every paper I opened had page after page of stories about inspirational women. Michelle Obama, former First Lady of the United States. Or FLOTUS, which I always thought was a fancy name for plastic waste washed up on the beach. Mother

Teresa of Calcutta, who had an airport in Albania named after her. Her most famous saying was "If you can't feed a hundred people, then feed just one". I think I shall get that engraved on a plaque and hang it up in M's kitchen.

And there are multiple photographs of women doing what was once considered "man's work". In one paper alone, there's a group of lady bus drivers, a lady Police Chief Inspector, even a lady gamekeeper. And why not? In fact M's brother's grand-daughter (whatever relation that is, I can't get my head round it) is a gamekeeper, and a good one. She can skin a deer just like peeling a banana.

Wish I hadn't said that now, there's banana custard for dessert tonight.

And I know it's a little early to predict, but I wonder if Baby A will grow up to be a lady farmer like her dad. Farmer, that is, not lady.

68

∽

Day 68 – a day of slipping, sliding and pecking

A wee change of route for this morning's walk. Along to the stables as I frequently do, but instead of either turning round and coming back, or carrying on and doing the full circuit, I headed down a farm track to the river. Then I turned and walked back home along the path at the bottom of some fields, with the river on my right. It was a nice change but the path was quite muddy, which I didn't mind, and because of the high clay content in the soil here it was very slippery, which I did mind. I had hoped that with the worst of winter behind us my days of slipping and sliding were past, but this mud was worse than ice. And a lot messier when you fall on it.

Then when I reached the outskirts of the village, instead of heading straight home I crossed the railway line and joined the road which comes from Conon Bridge. In fact it's often said that the best thing that ever came out of Conon was the road to Maryburgh but I couldn't possibly comment.

The railway that runs through our village is the main line

from Inverness to the north and west. When it reaches Dingwall it splits, one line goes north to Wick and Thurso and the other goes west to Kyle of Lochalsh. Although in these covid times hardly anyone is going anywhere by train so they often run empty. But even an empty train has the capacity to run me over and kill me, and there are huge signs warning BEWARE OF THE TRAINS so I was very careful about crossing the line. Although to be honest, these are very slow trains, even by Scotrail standards. Instead of being run over I'd be able to jump up and use the windscreen wipers as hand holds. I wonder if I'd be able to hang on all the way to Wick. And would the ticket collector insist on making me pay full fare or would I qualify for a discount for not having a seat?

Our resident woodpecker has been visiting our peanut feeder fairly regularly for a few weeks now. He has also taken a liking to our dead tree, which doubles as our washing pole, and seems determined to bore a hole right through it. And he's even better at boring than I am. It took the combined engineering skills of Britain and France a full five years to construct the channel tunnel. If they'd hired that woodpecker we'd have been saying 'bonjour, Pierre' within a couple of weeks.

And he has become fearless. Usually when we spot him on the nuts or the tree he flies off as soon as he sees us, but not any more. When he notices me watching him he just shrugs his feathery shoulders and carries on pecking. I can almost hear him thinking "It's only the old fellow, he hasn't a chance of scaring me with his waving hands, and she's banned him from throwing things at we birds, so I shall carry on with my woodpeckering".

This afternoon I saw him on the peanut feeder, rushed to get my phone and filmed him for a full minute. Even then he didn't have the good grace to fly off, he just moved on to the tree and began his hole boring routine. I filmed him for another minute, then another, then my phone battery ran out. His battery didn't, however, and he stayed on the tree, tearing huge chunks off it and casting them to the ground, all the while thinking: "Hee hee, when she sees this mess she'll have him out clearing it up and I shall sit and laugh at him from the neighbour's tree".

And finally, this afternoon Nicola announced an easing of covid restrictions. We're to be allowed to meet four friends outdoors from Friday, just in time for my birthday. I wish I had four friends.

69

～

Day 69 – a day of painting and planting

A dry morning with a wet forecast later in the day, so on went the washing machine first thing and out went the washing before my morning walk. Luckily yesterday's woodpecker attack hasn't actually felled the tree yet, so the washing line is still fully supported and my smalls have a chance of staying off the ground. Smalls? Who am I kidding? If these are smalls I'd hate to see mediums. And I don't mean those in touch with the spirits. If there's any spirits to be touched I shall do the touching.

And just to reinforce that point, I weighed myself when I came home from my walk – half a pound GAINED since Friday! How can that be? Surely yesterday's calorie intake wasn't that high, was it? After all, I limited myself to just the one caramel wafer after lunch and a dream ring is just a distant memory.

You will remember my so-called winter peas which turned up their toes (or whatever peas have at the end of their feet) at the first sign of frost. Well today I went through both trays of seedlings and weeded out those which had survived. And they totalled two. Yes, only two wee plants have survived. So I've transplanted those two into a bigger container and given them some twigs for support, and thrown all their deceased comrades in the bin. That's the garden recycling bin, which is due to be uplifted tomorrow for the first time this year. It's due to go out to the kerbside later tonight, but I noticed that my neighbour had his out by lunchtime, so he wins this round of the "who's bin is out first" game.

Some of the paint I ordered for my garden ornaments arrived today. A nice orangey-brown, called sunburst, for my teddy and a nice mid blue for his overalls. So after breakfast I applied a first coat of brown to him, which is doing a good job of covering up my resin repairs. Which, to be honest, are not exactly perfect. If I were a plastic surgeon and he was my patient I fear he'd want his money back.

After lunch I gave him a second coat and tomorrow I shall move on to the blue and give him a nice smart set of overalls. Then all he needs is his nose and mouth neatly marked out in black and he'll be ready to return to his wall in the back garden. Oh, and of course he needs a new set of eyes. I'm hoping to position him so that he can glare balefully at that woodpecker and hopefully scare him away.

Luckily I have a stock of teddy bear eyes left over from the last time I refurbished him. I only needed two but Mr Amazon would only sell them in packs of ten so they've been in a drawer in my shed ever since. And every time I open that drawer to reach for the bottle opener I'm always made to feel guilty by four pairs of eyes staring accusingly back at me. Perhaps I should re-locate the bottle opener to a less judgemental drawer.

And while I was at it I tried some of the sunburst colour on a wee concrete rabbit, it was the nearest thing I had to brown so I thought I'd try it. My plan is to put the rabbit out on display at the front of the house, perhaps sitting on one of my home-made toadstools, to amuse passing kiddies. But now that I see it in all its sunburst glory, I fear that perhaps it's a little bright. Almost fluorescent, which can't be natural for a rabbit.

I also have a stone frog waiting in the wings for a paint job, but I think I'd better wait until the green paint arrives. An orange rabbit is one thing, but an orange frog would definitely scare the kiddies away.

70

❧

Day 70 – a day of garden gripes

The garden recycling bin got emptied for the first time this year, so it's goodbye to all the leaves that have blown in from all corners of the street since November. It seems unfair that we have such a huge amount of leaves in our garden yet we have no trees. Except for the woodpecker's one of course, which doesn't have any leaves and, at the speed he's going, very soon will have no trunk either.

We pay an annual fee to the council to get our garden bin emptied. It started off a few years ago at, I think, £30 but has been increased by a fiver every year since. This year's £5 increase was announced a couple of weeks ago, resulting in much complaining from gardeners. We gardeners are a pretty placid lot, usually nothing gets us annoyed. Except for the weather, slugs, cabbage butterflies, fallen leaves, cats, slow deliveries, the weather, broken tools, lawnmowers that won't start, noisy neighbours, floods, pesky kids, woodpeckers, punctured wheelbarrows, leaky wellies, oh and did I mention the weather?

So as you can see we're slow to take offence but the latest £5 increase was the last straw. Which reminds me, I must ask Farmer J for some straw for my bed. My strawberry bed of course, whatever were you thinking?

Anyway once the local council realised the strength of feeling they wilted (in much the same way as my winter peas) and reduced the increase to £1.35. Result – a saving of £3.65 which, if spent wisely, and in the right shop, can get you two bottles of beer. Cheers!

Yesterday's paint job on the rabbit looks even worse in the cold light of the next morning. A golden teddy is quite acceptable, but a glowing golden rabbit is just too dazzling. He wouldn't look out of place in a James Bond movie, but he just wouldn't blend in here. Coming soon to a cinema near you – Daniel Craig in "The Man With The Golden Rabbit". Cert 18, not suitable for minors. Or OAPs. Or anyone, really.

And when I showed him to M she was equally horrified, so I've ordered some red paint from Mr Amazon to mix with the green I've already ordered, to try to make a more natural looking brown colour for the bunny. But knowing my mixing skills, this experiment could go either way. Maybe I'll get a nice light brown fluffy rabbit, or more likely I'll end up with a drab and dreary looking beast the colour of mud. If that happens he won't be going on display, I shall give him red eyes and station him at the garden gate to keep the cats away.

And the bear, by way of a contrast, is looking good. His two coats of golden paint from yesterday had dried by this morning, so I've now painted his blue overall, also with two coats. Next I shall furnish him with his new eyes, and paint on a black nose and a nice smile, and then he'll be back in the garden, cheering us up as we look out of the kitchen window. And if any bird dares to foul my beautiful bear he will get chased. As long as M isn't watching.

But that won't be happening tomorrow, because tomorrow is my special day. Already a couple of parcels have arrived, and both have an encouraging "glook, glook" sound when I shake them. What kind of liquid can be in them? We'll find out tomorrow but I'm hoping it's not paint.

71

~~~

Day 71 – a day of surprises

This morning I woke up and was immediately a year older. How did that happen? Well, at last the birthday has arrived, and I move into another decade. Yes, this is one of those that ends in a zero and it's been on the horizon for a few months now, getting ever closer, like some giant comet heading for Earth. The last one of those that we had arrived some sixty-six million years ago and wiped out the dinosaurs. This one is turning me into even more of a dinosaur.

But I must say I don't feel any older. I can still get in and out of the bath unaided, at least I could last time I had a bath. I must look in last year's diary and see when that was. And I can still tie my own shoelaces, although there is a certain amount of grunting involved.

Before she left for work, M presented me with the parcel which had arrived earlier in the week, but which I wasn't allowed to open. And it turns out my heavy hinting has paid off! Not one, but BOTH of the power tools whose descriptions I've been printing and leaving scattered around the house, including at her side of the bed.

And the two packages I told you about yesterday turned out to be, not paint as I had feared, but some very nice malt whiskies. I'm looking forward to some serious tasting sessions over the next few days.

My hardy fuchsias arrived today, well packaged and grown in a nice plug of compost. So after a quick watering I've potted them on into three-inch pots and they can stay in the cold greenhouse until they're big enough to plant out in the shrub border. The seed company claims these fuchsias are "hardy" enough to survive without heat but I don't know whether I should trust them. They said the same thing about my winter peas, and look what happened to them.

Later we took advantage of Nicola's easing of covid restrictions to meet M Junior and Baby A in a Perthshire town halfway between both our homes. And the surprises continued down there, when we pulled into the carpark there was M Junior's car with two huge helium balloons, a "7" and a "0" anchored beside her car. So If I had ever hoped to conceal my true age, that hope was vanquished. And worse, she insisted that we should take them home and display them in our living room window so the neighbours could ridicule me as well.

And there were other gifts, including a much needed set of wireless earphones to replace my ancient ones which are attached by cable so I can't move far from the computer when I'm playing my music. With these new ones I can get all the way to the fridge for beer without interruption. They even work out in the garden, so I may wear them while cutting the grass this summer. That'll impress the neighbours.

And Farmer J sent a very smart John Deere boiler suit and baseball cap. He's hoping that a new boiler suit will get me more involved with this year's lambing, since I can longer claim: 'I've got nothing to wear'.

And the icing on the cake was, well, the cake. A superbly detailed image of me with Baby A and Dog F, with my guitar and some Gaelic sheet music and a book of bothy ballads by my side. There's even a wee telly showing Moto GP. And of course two candles in the shape of a "70" which I managed to blow out with one puff. Just.

72

❧

Day 72 – a day of more birthday revelations

Sadly, it doesn't appear to be my birthday today. I didn't realise it was only meant to last for one day, I assumed a major
milestone like this would go on for several days of feasting and
celebrating, like the Notting Hill Carnival but with a slightly
less Caribbean theme. And fewer arrests.

So today it was back to business as usual, up and out for a
walk to the stables, hang out the washing while M went shopping, read the papers and tackle the Times crossword. Just another Saturday, although these two massive golden balloons are
still floating in the living room reminding everyone who passes
that an ancient being lives here.

There are some things from yesterday that I didn't have space
to tell you about. In addition to all the gifts I described, there
was a cardboard box emblazoned with Baby A's handprints in
paint, and with the words: "Grandad's Beer, HANDS OFF".
And inside it was a selection of craft beers from a specialist shop,
none of which I have ever heard of before. So I'm looking for-

ward very much to trying a different one every day. Thanks for buying them Baby A, I don't know how you managed to pass for 18 when you're only 8 months old.

And along with that was a nice big card with a variety of photos of Baby A (and M and me), and even more painty handprints. Signed by Baby A and Dog F, such a talented family. The baby can buy beer and the dog can write.

M Junior had been very busy behind the scenes for a couple of weeks, unknown to me. She had contacted a variety of family and friends, and a couple of special guests, and got them to record short video messages for me, which she then edited and made into a 15-minute show for me. Amazingly, no-one had let the secret out even though I had spoken to several of them in the past couple of days.

And amongst the family and friend clips were special appearances. One by Gary Innes, well known Scottish musician and radio presenter, who played his accordion and sang Happy Birthday for me, and the other from the real live Harry Gow, inventor of the famed Dream Ring, who was happy that I enjoy his products and hoping they were keeping me healthy. Which is a vain hope Harry, I always opt for your most sugary treats. And I'm afraid it shows.

Another contained a specially adapted version of a famous Gaelic song called "Fear a Bhata" which was one of my party pieces when I used to sing with my backing group The Sandettes. (Yes, really, check them out on YouTube if you don't believe me!)

This particular clip features two former Sandettes singing

their own words to the song. The first verse starts: 'Sandy Thomson, from Maryburgh, happy birthday, you living legend...'. I'm afraid the remainder of the words aren't suitable for a family audience and would almost certainly result in a Facebook ban if I repeated them.

And finally, two brand new experiences for me. Firstly, I've never had a lamb named after me, but in the video Farmer J's mum is proudly holding a big sturdy pet lamb with a "70" painted on his side, and he's been named Sandy in my honour. I wonder if that makes me a kind of lamb godfather? Am I to be responsible for his moral upbringing, and hold him while the vicar baptises him? And buy him presents for Christmas and birthdays?

Secondly, I've never had a tune composed for me. But a dear friend who's a music teacher has written a superb wee tune called Sandy's Social Distance Strathspey and presented it to me in a frame so I can display it on my wall.

For non-Scots readers, a Strathspey is a dance. Not a vigorous energetic one, but a fairly slow, graceful one. I can do "fairly slow", but "graceful"? Perhaps that's stretching the imagination a little too far.

73

∽

Day 73 – a day of daydreaming

Today is Sunday. And not just any old Sunday, today is Mother's Day here in the UK. Looking back at last year's diary I see that I told you about my own mother and her one-woman defence of the UK from Hitler's Luftwaffe. Ok there might have been one or two other people involved but I'm sure she was the main reason for the fall of Nazism. 'Mein Gott Heinrich, zat Scottische voman iss invincible. Call off ze attack und pass me der white flag'.

Of course, thanks to the wonders of technology M was able to receive greetings from M Junior and Baby A. According to the photos Baby A baked a cake for her mummy, which is quite an achievement for someone who's just learning how to handle a spoon. I suspect Farmer J had a hand in the baking process, it will be a change from where he usually has his hand at lambing time.

M and I had our customary walk to Dingwall in the morning and, apart from one small shower of rain, it was a pleasant morning. So pleasant, in fact, that I've taken my wee fuchsia plants out of the greenhouse and placed them in a sunny spot so that they can get a dose of sunlight. Apparently they use the energy from sunlight to produce nutrients and help them grow. And there are some fancy words to explain how that happens, like "photosynthesis", "chlorophyll", even "xylem". Maybe if I'd listened to my Science teacher a little more attentively instead of daydreaming my way through school, I'd be able to explain it to you better.

And daydreaming is exactly what I did, through five years of secondary education. While the English teacher droned on about frontal adverbs (no, me neither) and the Maths one tried to interest me in the square on the hypotenuse of the right angle triangle (not a clue), my mind was far away. Fishing, motorbikes and girls were the main topics of my daydreams. In my perfect world I'd be taking a girl on my motorbike, on a fishing trip. Good grief, no wonder the girls avoided me. And, generally, so did the fish.

Anyway, of the nine wee plants, six of them are looking quite healthy after their long and stressful journey wrapped up in plastic. And their even more stressful experience of being potted on by me. Even though I try to handle things delicately I do fear I'm sometimes a little heavy handed. And it's the same when I'm pouring whisky, which probably explains my shaky hands.

The remaining three plants are in various stages of infirmity. If they were patients in hospital, all three would be in the Intensive Care Unit with notices above their beds: "Do Not Resuscitate". One would be receiving acute care and the other two would be receiving the last rites.

There's still a lot of birthday cake left, so M has wrapped a couple of slabs up in tin foil, inside a Tupperware container, and we've parcelled it up ready to send down to M Junior and family. In pre-covid times we could share it with neighbours and work colleagues, but of course that's not allowed any more. So I shall just have to be brave and eat a slice (or two) every day, it's a tough duty but somebody's got to do it.

74

∿

Day 74 – a day of moss and glass

And Monday comes around again, so M is away to work. And it's the Ides of March, so she'd better beware. Is this a chance for me to sit back and do nothing? Oh no, I had a long walk before breakfast. Not the full circuit because it's rather muddy in places, but to the halfway mark and back, which is all on tarmac, so I get the full mileage in without getting my boots dirty. Must keep up my smart image, you know, even though my hairstyle is anything but smart. Although I wear my woollen hat all the time (even when it's warm) my hair is now so unruly it sticks out the sides and the bottom at all angles. Like an explosion in a sofa factory.

After breakfast I drove into Dingwall to post a parcel to Baby A. As well as a wee gift for her it contained a couple of slabs of my birthday cake, for M Junior and Farmer J. I expect Dog F will get a wee taste too. And while I was in Dingwall I took my empty (beer) bottles to the glass recycling point. Isn't it funny how you automatically feel guilty recycling beer bottles on a Monday

215

morning? You imagine all the passing pedestrians are thinking to themselves: 'Aye aye, somebody's been partying hard all weekend', even though it might have taken me a whole week to produce half a dozen empties. Though I don't have many weeks as dry as that.

When I returned from the post office I was alarmed to see a man on my neighbour's roof. No, it wasn't some sort of rooftop protest nor did he appear to be fiddling. Much less excitingly, he was scraping moss off the tiles. Roof moss is a problem here, because we're surrounded by trees, and we need to get our roofs (rooves?) scraped every few years. Which inspired me to look up at my own roof and realise it's some years since we had ours done. So I went across and accosted this rooftop chap, to ask if he'd like to do mine as well. And he came across, measured my roof and arranged to come and scrape it once he's finished next door, which will be in a few days. So I'm about to add to my list of "men" I've had "in" this past year. There's been Fence Man, Roof Vent Man, Electric Man, but this is a new one – Moss Clearing Man.

And there's one more – Windscreen Man is due to come on Wednesday. Yes, I've had a broken windscreen incident. And the worst thing about it is that I was driving M's (new!) car at the time. I was overtaking a lorry on the dual carriageway near Inverness when a stone was thrown up and hit the windscreen with a heart stopping BANG. But because I had the sun visor down I didn't notice that it had actually cracked the glass, so as far as I was concerned there wasn't a problem. Not even in the underwear department.

Next day, however, when M was washing the car in the driveway I was surprised when she came to the window and summoned me outside to examine the damage. And there it was – a small round mark where the stone hat hit and an eight-inch long crack spreading towards the centre of the windscreen. A quick visit to a well-known glass replacement company's website revealed that a crack cannot be mended but the whole windscreen must be replaced. And a phone call to M's insurance company yielded the information that only emergencies can be dealt with at weekends, so the reporting would have to wait until today.

Having spent all of Sunday girding up my loins (oo-er missus) and preparing myself for a verbal battle with the insurance company, I was very surprised how efficiently my claim was dealt with. One phone call was all it took, the screen will be replaced on Wednesday, in my own driveway. And I only need to pay the policy excess and the insurance company picks up the remainder of the bill.

Sign of the times - it's easier to get a car windscreen replaced than it is to get a haircut. And you can claim it off your insurance.

75

~~

Day 75 – a day of paintwork and woodwork

The garden bear, who's been waiting patiently since Day 70, has now been completely painted and furnished with his new eyes. And he's very happy to be relocated back into his usual spot in the back garden, visible from the kitchen window, where we can keep an eye on him. To give him a decent vantage point I've raised him up on a wee wooden plant stand so that he can watch all the dog walkers passing by. He says he can see much better with these new eyes, the old ones were getting dim. And he'd rather not have to wear specs in public.

And while we're on the topic of garden ornaments, I've painted the stone frog green, sitting on a brown log, and given him wild red eyes. If anyone asks what species he is I shall say he's a Common Amazonian Angry Frog, that should deter any kids from trying to take him home. And alongside him will be the rabbit, who used to be bright orange and glowing, like a retired nuclear submarine captain. He's now been toned down considerably to a dark brown colour with the orange undercoat shining through discreetly, which looks remarkably like real rabbit fur. But any kid who tried to stroke him will soon find that he's made of stone, like his froggy neighbour. And he has a black nose and a white tail and much friendlier brown eyes. No Angry Rabbit in my garden.

Just had to have a wee play with my new power tools which M gave me for my birthday. The sander is cordless, so it went straight onto a "charging cycle" which was a new concept to me. I thought a "charging cycle" was the technical name for an electric bike, and Mr Google agrees with me. For a change.

Anyway, I had - squirrelled away in the corner of my shed - two pieces of wood which once formed shelves in M Junior's kitchen a few years ago, and which I had kept after she had her kitchen revamped. Why? Just in case, of course. I keep all sorts of wood "just in case", tiny bits, huge planks, even old fence posts, because you never know when they'll come in handy. And these two have come in very handy because I was able to use them as test pieces for my new tools. So there you go – never throw anything away.

First, the electric planer. A very scary machine, with very sharp blades revolving at high speed. The potential for serious injury is massive so for once I actually read the instructions before using it. And the most important instruction was: "keep BOTH hands in place on the machine when in use". The shelves were painted white so I planed the edges down to the bare wood, all the while keeping both hands in the appropriate position. Result – beautiful texture, woody aroma and a nice smooth finish. Just like a Speyside malt.

Then the sander, which did a great job of sanding down both sides of each shelf, removing the old paint and exposing the nice wood underneath. Also did a great job of sanding down the little finger of my left hand, exposing the neighbours to a torrent of interesting language, both in English and Gaelic. Perhaps I should have read the instructions for it too. So it was down with the tools and into the first aid kit for a sticking plaster. Not the first time I've been plastered in the shed.

And now, having done all that planning and sanding, I have two nicely finished wooden shelves. I don't know what to do with them, but I shall keep them in the shed for a few more years, "just in case..."

76

∽

Day 76 – a day of Irish celebrations. Without a drop of Guinness.

Top o' the morning to ye! Yes, today is St Patrick's Day, the one day of the year when we're all a little bit Irish. I'm not sure which little bit of me is Irish, I do have a few bits which have turned green but some of them are not particularly little. Which is borne out by my weekly visit to the bathroom scales to find that I have lost a total of NO pounds and NO ounces. I'm beginning to despair of this rigorous exercise and diet regime and feel a serious dream ring relapse coming.

And in support of that fitness regime, I walked into Dingwall before breakfast. I needed to get to the bank to withdraw some cash in readiness for paying Moss Clearing Man when he comes round to scrape my roof. He's still working next door, they have a considerably larger roof than we do and I see he's brought along a colleague to help him today. It's a pretty monotonous and soul destroying job, crouching half-bent on a 45 degree angled roof and removing moss with a wee metal scraper.

And there's always the danger that you'll forget where you are and step back, and land in the flower beds below. If he does that on my roof he'll land in the fiercely jaggy berberis bush and emerge looking like he's been in battle with a whole herd of porcupines. And came second.

My list of "men" also includes Windscreen Man, who you will remember was due to come today to replace the windscreen on M's car. Unfortunately it seems he's not coming today after all. His boss phoned to say that due to pressure of work and staffing difficulties they've fallen behind with their work and so Windscreen Man can't come until Saturday. Which is three days away, so we've effectively lost the use of M's car for a whole week. I wonder whether the insurance company will offer me any compensation? After all, I'm tied to their "approved repairer" so I can't even get a rival firm to do the job. Anyway, following the completion of the job I'm sure there will be one of those annoying "how did we do?" email surveys, which I usually ignore. But I shan't ignore this one, better get the dictionary handy for some big words.

Meantime M is using my car to get to work, which is fine because it's hardly moved since Christmas and will benefit from getting regular runs. All the spiders which have made their nests inside the exhaust pipe won't be impressed though. Can you imagine getting blown out of bed by a huge blast of foul smelling hot air? M says she can.

I had a text message purporting to be from Royal Mail, saying that a parcel is waiting to be delivered to me but I need to pay the "delivery fee" of £1.99 first. Now I know our postie, and if he has any parcels to deliver when we're not at home he knows where he can leave them, so I was immediately suspicious. And a quick visit to the real Royal Mail website confirms that this is one of those "scams", where the aim is not to get your £1.99, but to get access to your credit card details so that future frauds can follow. It was a very realistic text message though, it even had the official Royal Mail crest so it would be easy to get fooled. But I've had years of scam phone calls. Sometimes from "amazon - your ipad 7 will be delivered", or "BT - a problem with your internet" and, recently, "Her Majesty's Revenue and Customs - sending an agent round to collect your unpaid tax". And, unlike M's windscreen, I can usually see right through them.

Finally, due to lack of preparation I don't even have a can of Guinness in the house to toast our Irish cousins on their special day. But amongst the craft beers Baby A gave me for my birthday there's one called "Due South" so that will have to do. At least it's in the right direction. Slàinte!

77

～

Day 77 – a day of dental nightmares

A video appeared last night via WhatsApp – Bay A in her bath getting her teeth cleaned for the first time. Well when I say cleaned, it was only M Junior introducing her to the concept of the toothbrush. And when I say teeth, I mean the only two she has, so far. Which is nearly as many as her grandad, to be honest. I'm afraid many of my generation neglected their dental care, ignoring the benefits of Gibbs Ivory Castle (which came in a tin for goodness sake!) in favour of the much more exciting fruit gums (plenty sugar, no fruit), barley sugars (plenty sugar, no barley) and MacCowan's Highland Cow Toffee (plenty sugar, no highland cow, luckily).

Believe it or not, we even ate rhubarb rock. Which is every bit as disgusting as it sounds, but we loved it because of the addictively high sugar content. Furthermore, if it hadn't been for Love Hearts I'd never have had any chat up lines.

So it was largely hello sweeties, goodbye toothies all through our developing years. The only professional care we received was from the dreaded school dentist, who used to arrive and set up his caravan in the playground in preparation for his victims. And because the caravan walls were thin, while you were waiting for your turn you could hear the anguished screams of your predecessor as teeth were drilled and filled before they were released, bleeding and sore, with a mouth full of mercury. Ah, the good old days, eh?

Anyway, encouraged by Baby A and her early dental hygiene regime, M has purchased a special baby toothbrush, with a wide handle suitable for little hands. And today I wrapped it up in a padded envelope and posted it off to her as a wee gift. I walked to Dingwall to post it, that's two days in a row I've done that walk, I estimate it's around a four-mile round trip. Takes me an hour and a bit, anyway. And it was such a nice day, wall to wall sunshine and a temperature of fourteen Celsius, I actually walked with my jacket off. If it hadn't been for my unruly hair I might even have removed my hat but I didn't want to cause a panic in the street. 'Mum, mum, come and see – it's that Hagrid from the Harry Potter stories! And he's shorter than he looked in the movie, but just as fat'.

Froggy and rabbit from Day 75 have now been placed in their final positions outside the front window. I was aiming to give them child-friendly expressions but when I see them in the cold light of day I fear they look a little like a pair of killer beasts. I'm sure we must have learned how to do nice faces in O-Grade Art, but maybe I was absent that day.

And I've started on my next garden art project. You'll remember I told you about my Christmas board with its painting of a wee penguin. Well now I'm planning an Easter one, to amuse all the kiddies who pass by. So I found a suitable image on the internet (thanks Mr Google), copied it on to a white A4-sized board and begun painting it. So far all I've done is the sky and the grass, neither of which are particularly taxing, but the main image of a cute bunny carrying an Easter egg is a bit more challenging for someone with a 54-year old Art O' Grade and a very shaky hand.

Also, what the connection between a rabbit and an egg is, I can't fathom. Do rabbits come from eggs? Did they teach us that in Biology class? Maybe I was absent from school that day too. Or at the dentist.

78

⌇

Day 78 – a day of hand injuries

Up early and away for a (short) walk this morning, so as to be home in time to prepare for Moss Clearing Man to arrive. Moved M's car out of the drive, shifted the wheelie bins from outside the back door and relocated various plant pots so as to leave the area clear for him. When he was doing my neighbour's roof he was starting at 8am so I assumed he'd do the same for me. And while I was waiting I treated myself to that rarest of delights – a cooked breakfast! M came home from the shop this morning with a pack of cut-price bacon which she got cheap as it was nearing its sell-by date. That's what I call a bargain. Biscuits and breakfast cereals are all very well, but bacon beats them all.

And by the time she'd explained that it would have to be used up quickly I already had the frying pan out and warming up. And as I tucked into crispy bacon and a nice fresh egg (from Baby A's hens), fond memories came flooding back of the good old days pre-covid, when M and I used to go to Inverness every

Saturday for shopping and a supermarket breakfast. Now, M goes shopping on her own in Dingwall and I stay behind and eat cornflakes.

And eight o'clock came and went, and no sign of Moss Clearing Man. Maybe he thinks I'm a late starter and he's coming at nine instead, I thought. But no, nine also came and went and no sign of him. And the same at ten, and eleven. Obviously there had been some sort of mix-up. Either he'd forgotten, which is unlikely because he'll be needing his money, or I misunderstood which day he said he was coming, which is much more likely because apparently I: "...never listen to anything anyone ever says.." Which is a fair point, I wish I'd listened to the Minister 37 years ago. Only joking, dear. Keep bringing home the bacon.

Anyway, the afternoon was a reverse of the morning, car, bins and plants back to their rightful places. And I'll probably have to do it all again tomorrow.

Remember the two old shelves I sanded down the other day, along with my little finger? Well the finger has healed up so I ventured back into the shed today for more power tool adventures. Using those shelves and some old wood which Fence Man left me last year, I've made a plant stand. Quite a simple trestle-type design, but it involved many different procedures. Measuring, sawing, swearing, drilling, sanding, screwing, swearing, hammering, planning, and finally painting. And swearing.

And today's injuries list: one skinned knuckle right hand, and one skinned knuckle, left hand. For a full day's work, that's well within acceptable limits.

It seems sturdy enough, and the paint covers up all the dodgy joints, so all I need now is for the garden centres to open so I can buy some plants to display on it. Because I don't think the fuchsias are going to be worthy of displaying any time soon. I've divided them up into sections. Section A – likely to survive, Section B – sickly but might pull through, Section C – call the undertaker. There are very few candidates in Section A and, like M's favourite football team, promotion is unlikely.

And as well as my wood butchering activities, I've also finished the painting of the cute bunny and his Easter egg. It's on a plywood board and once the paint is fully dry I shall attach a stake and stick it up outside the front window, where it will share the limelight with the killer frog and angry rabbit. But I won't put it up until nearer Easter, which is a couple of weeks away. In the meantime I hope I don't forget where I've put it.

79

⧉

Day 79 – a day of spring in the air

Saturday again, so M is at home. We set off on our normal morning walk, wondering whether Roof Cleaning Man would arrive while we were gone but when we got home there was no sign of him. I don't suppose he works Saturdays anyway, so I'll just have to be patient and hope he appears one day next week. It's not as if the roof job is urgent anyway, it only gets cleaned once every ten years or so, so another week or two won't make any difference. Coincidentally that's also my policy on under-wear.

Today is the official first day of spring here in the UK, and the weather reflects that. We've had a week of sunshine and warm temperatures and the daffodils have begun appearing. Unlike the peas, which were sown into the ground on Day 54 and should have germinated within 21 days, according to the packet, confirmed by Mr Google. But there's no sign of them, so they're already four days overdue. It's a good job they're not library books.

Today's also the vernal equinox, when the sun crosses the celestial equator (no, me neither). What it means in practice is that day and night are of equal length. Twelve hours of darkness, which is nature's way of telling us to sleep, and twelve hours of daylight, which I guess is supposed to mean staying awake. But that doesn't apply to me, a man needs his naps after all.

And thirdly, today is the start of the astrological new year. Apparently we've now moved into Aries season, first sign of the zodiac, and it's an auspicious time to check your horoscope. I wouldn't say I'm a believer, but I always check mine and M's even though she has no time for such "nonsense", as she describes it. For quite a few years now Mystic Meg has been telling me that the universe is bestowing cosmic gifts on me, but they haven't arrived yet. Maybe they're coming from Amazon, along with my ipad7.

Anyway, my horoscope for the coming astrological year is both encouraging and slightly alarming at the same time: "...we're here for a good time, not a long time...a big signal to ENJOY your life". Whatever can it mean? Should I stop being Mr Grumpy and transform into Mr Happy? Doesn't sound very much like me, to be honest.

M's prediction, however, is much more accurate: "you are reviewing what needs to be left behind...you're the boss after all, and you decide what belongs in your life and what role it plays". This doesn't sound too hopeful for me.

M's car is still unusable because of the cracked windscreen, so she went shopping in my car and as soon as she had left the phone rang. And for a change it wasn't a scam call, but a genuine one from Windscreen Man, to say he'd be arriving at 1.30pm. That was fine, it gave me a couple of hours alone with The Times crossword. Which is usually enough time to solve all the easy clues and resort to Mr Google for the hard ones.

But it was not to be. Due to some super-efficient windscreen fitting on his previous call he actually arrived an hour early. And less than an hour later the new windscreen had been fitted, the insurance excess paid, and he was on his way. Very efficient. I've forgiven the company for being three days later than planned and will give them a good review after all.

I must be going soft in my old age. Or maybe my horoscope has mellowed me.

80

~⚬~

Day 80 – a day of unearthing animals. Stone ones.

Pleasant Sunday morning walk to Dingwall before breakfast, then another one to the stables after lunch. Which consisted of the last slice of birthday cake. Do I really have to wait a whole year for another one? Maybe M will share hers in August.

In between walks M was pruning out some old and overgrown clematis at the end of the house, and she came across a few more wee stone animals which we'd had for many years and quite forgotten about. Every foot of clematis clearance revealed another beast, until at last we had a grand total of five. A tortoise, a mole emerging from his burrow, two hedgehogs and a wee mouse. They've been handed over into my tender care for restoration and are currently resting in my shed, awaiting their treatment. Their treatment starts with a vigorous wire brushing, a good scrubbing and a period of drying out. Bet you're glad I'm not your doctor.

So that will keep me busy this week. All I need to do is work out what colour everything is. I'm fairly confident that light brown will be OK for the tortoise, and brown for the mouse, but what colour will I use for the hedgehogs? Apparently you get black ones, brown ones, grey ones, even white ones. Maybe I'll do a black and a white, in tribute to the two wee doggies who used to advertise Buchanan's Black and White Scotch Whisky. Back in the days when a bottle of whisky was a rare treat for Hogmanay, not a weekly supermarket purchase.

Also, before whisky began being made in every country in the world and before every man and his granny started up their own distillery. I had the skills to start one of my own, but sadly my granny wouldn't come up with the money.

In 2012 M and I were trekking in the Himalayas, and one night in a remote mountain lodge in Nepal I received an offer I couldn't refuse: 'real Scotch whisky, Sahib, very very good'. Of course I agreed, and a bottle was produced with an image of a tartan clad hero and labelled "Bagpiper Scottish Whisky". A generous dram was poured out and served up, and to describe it as "rough as a boar's rear end" would be an insult to boars everywhere. And their rear ends.

Examination of the bottle and interrogation of my host revealed that the "Scotch" whisky had in fact been made just across the border in India. And very recently, by the taste of it. I was very surprised when I awoke the next morning and found I hadn't gone mad. Or blind. Or both. In fact I was surprised that I awoke at all.

Anyway, back to my wee animals, and now that we've sorted out the hedgehogs what about the mole? According to Mr Google, a mole is black with a pink nose and front paws so that sounds straightforward enough, even for me. This particular mole is also sporting a pair of specs, so I guess I'd better look out a fine paintbrush and transform them into designer glasses. I wonder whether he'd prefer Gucci or Hugo Boss? I see there's a brand called Kate Spade, those might be most appropriate for someone who spends his life digging.

But poor Moley doesn't appear to have lenses in his glasses, so I don't suppose he'll be able to see with them, no matter what brand they are. I don't know which optician he went to, but I think he should claim a refund.

81

~

Day 81 – a day of fiddling on the roof

Round the woods for my walk this morning, I didn't want to go too far from home in case of rain. The weather presenter on the telly said it wasn't due until tomorrow, but I'd rather trust my instincts (and arthritic joints) to tell me when rain is near.

Roof Cleaning Man arrived at 9 o'clock. As I suspected, I had misunderstood which day he had planned to come. After a short chat he got his ladders out and was up on the roof in no time, scraping away at all the old moss which has gathered over the past few years. One side of the roof is fairly clean but the other side is very mossy. That's because of all the trees surrounding us on that side. They're the descendants of what was once part of the ancient Forest of Brahan, and when the builders were developing our area they left quite a few trees standing, presumably thinking that people would appreciate a tree or two in their garden. We had all of ours cut down soon after we moved in, apart from the trunk which we left to support the washing line, and which our resident woodpecker is doing his level best to decimate.

So my day was spent with the constant noise of scraping overhead, which wasn't a problem, even when the phone rang. Today's call was from a gentleman claiming to be from Microsoft who wanted to talk about a "problem" with my computer. After a few seconds of preliminary chatting, I suggested to him that perhaps he wasn't from Microsoft at all, but was simply hoping to extract from me details of my bank account. Their usual response to this is to immediately ring off, but this chappie must have been having a bad day because he treated me so some very un-gentlemanly language before hanging up. I hope he wasn't expecting to shock me, I've heard much worse on the parade ground. And in the playground.

Perhaps he was suffering from that Monday morning feeling. Or, because I suspect he was based somewhere east of Delhi, that Monday afternoon feeling.

I've made a start with the stone animals M unearthed yesterday. While Roof Cleaning Man was scraping on high, I was scraping in my shed. I've de-mossed them all, brushed all the dust off and cleaned them up ready for painting. And I've started with a first coat on three of them. Mole, mouse and hedgehog all have their bases painted – earthy brown for mole, terracotta for mouse and green for the big hedgehog. Tomorrow when that's all dry I shall progress to painting the animals themselves. The other two animals – tortoise and the wee hedgehog – don't actually have bases, so they'll be much easier. But I mustn't go too fast, I need to spin this job out for a few days in case I'm asked to tackle anything else. "Sorry dear, I can't possibly dig the garden/cut the grass/weed the borders. I'm far too busy with this painting".

And in the afternoon I left Roof Cleaning Man all on his own and set off on the 5-mile circuit walk. And just to prove me wrong the rain stayed away all day. So in future I need to pay more attention to the BBC weather report, and less to my dodgy joints.

Of course I'm talking about my ankles and knees, not any other kind of dodgy joints. Although I spent time in quite a few of those back in the day.

82

∽

Day 82 – a day of reflection

Quite cool and breezy this morning, as my pre-breakfast route took me up through Conon and down the main road. I had to hold on to my hat when crossing the bridge over the river, for fear of it blowing away and floating out to sea. There's a spot near the Cromarty Bridge, not too far downriver from here, which is a great place for spotting seals. Imagine how the tourists would react, seeing a seal lying sunbathing on a rock, wearing a John Deere baseball cap.

When I got home Roof Cleaning Man had arrived and was already up on the roof, scraping away. I would have thought it too windy for being up on the roof, but he didn't hesitate, and seemed quite confident. It amazes me to see him standing up-right on a sloping roof, if it was me up there I'd be on my hands and knees and afraid to straighten up. I don't mind heights but I do like to be on a level footing. And if I was to fall off I'd try to aim for something soft to land on, but that might be difficult here. My choices would be the berberis bush (very jaggy), the wheelie bin (very bouncy) or M's car (very divorcey).

And because Roof Cleaning Man is working at the back of the house and has the ground covered with tarpaulins, I can't easily use the back door for my usual access to the bins/shed/outdoor water tap. So that has curtailed most of my usual activities. No painting of stone ornaments today, for example, so I've had to content myself inside the house for most of the day. A good excuse for catching up with my latest box set, Deutschland 89, which is a spy thriller set around the collapse of the Berlin Wall. And it's full of intrigue, espionage, underhand dealings and betrayals as East Berlin and West Berlin stare uneasily across at each other and the threat of war is constantly in the air. Rather like North and South Korea, or India and Pakistan. Or Maryburgh and Conon.

And by late afternoon Roof Cleaning Man was finished. He's scraped off all the moss, replaced a couple of broken tiles and sprayed the roof with an anti-fungal mixture. It's looking good and hopefully will stay moss-free for quite a few years. That's the good news. The bad news is that he had to be paid, so goodbye beer money until pension day. And March is a long month so pension day is a long way away. It's lucky I still have some of Baby A's birthday beer left.

Today is a national day of reflection, organised in aid of the Marie Curie Cancer Care charity. It marks the first anniversary of lockdown and is a time for us to think of all those who have lost loved ones and to look towards a brighter future.

I, of course, misunderstood the concept, and thought that a

day of reflection was a day of looking in the mirror. Apart from daily shaving I seldom have the stomach to look at myself in the mirror. In fact it's maybe because I have too much stomach that I can't stand the sight of my own reflection. Also, my wild unkempt hairstyle is a little too reminiscent of Boris. A much older, fatter Boris.

And that's an image nobody wants to see staring back at them in the mirror.

83

Day 83 – a day of washing and woodworking

Lovely sunny morning, so up early and out to the back garden to admire my beautiful moss-free roof. Very annoyingly, a random pigeon had appeared and was perching on the very top ridge. Fearful that he might mistake my shiny roof tiles for a statue and do what pigeons do to statues (see "bears" and "woods"), I leapt into the air and clapped my hands together while emitting a high-pitched howl. It had the desired effect on the errant bird, who immediately took to the air to escape this mad shouting creature below. It had a less desirable effect on a passing lady dog walker, who hurried past with her head down, dragging poor Fido along lest he should stop for a comfort break and incur the wrath of the babbling neanderthal in the back garden.

First job today was hanging out the washing, which M had put in the machine when she got up. I take great pride in my washing hanging-out skills, everything in the correct order and facing the same way, towels on one line and underwear on the other (out of public view!). And when I meet people on my walks I always take the opportunity to say: 'Yes, I hope it stays dry, I did a washing this morning', so that they can appreciate what a good housekeeper I am. Of course the truth is that "doing a washing" involves merely shutting the washing machine door and pushing one single button. And most of the time M does that for me anyway. But I won't tell if you don't.

Then, long walk before breakfast. Five-mile circuit today, clockwise for a change to get the tarred road section out of the way first because it's hardest on the feet. The second section, on tracks through the woods, is nice and dry just now after a whole week of dry weather so my boots didn't get muddy. I'm very attached to these boots, they're handmade and bought online from a Scottish supplier. Top quality and very comfortable for long distances. Yes, I know five miles isn't really classed as long distance, but it's pretty good going for someone suffering from advanced decrepitude, short legs and a dodgy ankle.

The only issue I have with the boots is that one of the laces broke the other day. Although the boots are made by hand in the UK, I suspect the laces may have been bought in from some overseas manufacturer. Probably within the European Union. 'Alors Francois, make sure zeze inferior laces are sent oveur to zee Rosbifs. Zey told us to get knotted, letz see how zey like eet'.

Those of you with photographic memories will remember Day 72, when I told you about the box of beer Baby A gave me for my birthday. The beer was, of course, excellent, but even more special was the box. It started off life as an ordinary cardboard box but was personalised with the words "Grandad's Beer

– Hands Off!" along with Baby A's handprints in various colours. Well, having consumed all the contents I just couldn't bring myself to throw it away so I've extended its life with an insert designed to hold eight bottles of beer. I know, eight bottles isn't much, but I trust M will replenish it every time she goes shopping.

Raking about in the depths of my shed, I came across enough leftover thin plywood for the job and, using my new power tools and (dubious) woodworking skills I constructed an eight-cell bottle holder which fits perfectly inside the box. And in spite of using sharp things, heavy things and electric things I completed the whole job without injury. Amazing.

Also amazing is what you can achieve with just some scrap wood and a John Deere boiler suit.

84

∽

Day 84 – a day of activities

Busy day today, with multiple activities to cope with. Shopping, banking, housework and coffee, to mention but a few.

First the shopping and banking, both of which took place in Dingwall and which necessitated a drive because what I was buying was too heavy to carry home. A well-known supermarket of German origin, frequented by bargain hunters including M, issues a booklet every week to tell us what offers are coming up. M had spotted a sandpit which would be ideal for Baby A, which was due to go on sale today, so I was tasked with buying it. Buying it was the easy part, remembering to go on the right day was always going to be a challenge, but I got around that by leaving the leaflet, open at the appropriate page, in the middle of the sofa where I couldn't fail to see it. And because I spend a considerable amount of my time on that very sofa, the system worked.

Along with the trip to buy the sandpit, M had brought home some school fund cash which needed to be paid into the bank. Sadly, there isn't a bank anywhere near the school, in fact there isn't a bank anywhere on the Black Isle, so paying in school fund money is awkward for the staff. Dingwall is the nearest branch so M helps out by doing it for them and to save her having to visit Dingwall on her way home she asked me to take it along. A task of great responsibility, so I had to proceed very cautiously, always watching out for muggers. Although there are so few people in Dingwall High Street these days, you would see your mugger coming half a mile away.

No time for a morning walk, then. Immediately after break-fast and a quick scan of the papers off I went to carry out my two tasks. And I was glad that I went early, because the shop had only two of these sandpits left. And they're pretty heavy so I had to use a trolley, which requires a coin to release it from its com-panions. Good job I had a pound coin in my pocket, because I usually don't. And there's no point waving your contactless card at the coin slot on the trolley either. Not that I would do such a thing, you understand.

Home from Dingwall, and with an arrangement for a good friend to call round for coffee, preparations had to be made. We're still not allowed to meet indoors, so we'd have to have our coffee out on the patio. Luckily the faithful old gazebo has sur-vived the worst of the winter and is still standing, although be-ginning to look a little threadbare. Of course it hasn't got any side panels, I took those off in the autumn, leaving just the poles and the roof. And because it was a dry day but with a strong wind, I thought I should reinstall the side panels, to give us some shelter. So into the depths of the mower shed I went, found the side panels, unfolded them and found a variety of large holes with ragged edges. It appears that Mousie must have moved from M's shed into the mower shed in search of warmth, and used my panel material to make his duvet.

Anyway, it did the job and we had a nice coffee break and caught up on the gossip with the gazebo panels billowing in the wind like HMS Victory at Trafalgar, but without attack from French cannon balls. Although they would have flown straight through Mousie's holes anyway.

Mortified by my ragged gazebo, I've ordered a new one from Mr Argos, and going to collect it tomorrow. From Nairn, which is further than usual but there isn't one in stock in Inverness.

And amongst all this activity, I still managed to do vacuuming, dusting, floors and surfaces before M came home from work. So no time for a walk today, I'd better have a long one tomorrow, maybe in Nairn. Is Nairn ready for me?

85

∽

Day 85 – a day of freezing by the seaside

Cold and wet this morning, so no early morning walk. Instead, after breakfast and papers I jumped into the car and headed off to Nairn to collect my new gazebo and have a walk on the beach there. Nairn is known as "the Riviera of the North" because it has a mild climate, reputedly similar to the Mediterranean, but I suspect that that's a fable invented by the residents to attract tourists because I can't see many similarities between the south of France and the Moray Firth shore. Not in the middle of March, anyway. Topless sunbathing? You must be kidding. You need at least three layers of clothing, including a thermal vest.

I arrived in Nairn nice and early, too early to collect the gazebo. Not that the shop wasn't open, but the Argos branch is contained within the local supermarket and I had planned to do a little shopping while I was there, just for a change. And the problem with shopping too early is that alcohol sales aren't permitted until after 10am so I wouldn't be able to buy any beer.

And that would be like going to Harry Gow's and not buying a dream ring. Unthinkable. Ooh I wish I hadn't thought of that now.

So I decided I would have my walk first, and shopping second. Parked the car down at the harbour and set off along the beach, which was almost deserted. And no wonder. A freezing cold north westerly wind was blasting along the shore, and within it there were elements of sleet. It wasn't too bad at first because the wind was on my back, and I had brought my umbrella, so I got blown along the beach like Mary Poppins flying above the rooftops of London. Well, like an older, fatter, unkempt Mary Poppins. Hairy Poppins?

I don't know how long the Nairn beach is, but I walked for a full half hour and the end wasn't even in sight. And when I turned back the wind was in my face, so the return journey took twice as long. And the umbrella was uncontrollable so I took the full brunt of the sleet/hail square on my face. By the time I got back to the car my face looked like a well-fired, although somewhat wrinkly, pizza. But I'm sure my lungs benefitted from their healthy dose of Moray Firth sea air. And unlike the real Riviera there were no sunbathers to trip over, nor "looky looky" men selling fake watches and designer sunglasses. I suppose if they ever migrate to Nairn they'll be selling fake thermal vests and designer earmuffs.

Anyway, having survived the icy trek it was time to go shopping. I didn't buy much, just a few grocery items along with a couple of nice outfits for Baby A and a bottle of wine for M. Oh, and a couple of bottles of beer for my Friday night treat. Of course. And the gazebo was all ready for picking up so it's now in the back of the car, along with yesterday's sandpit. They can stay in there until I get a warm enough day to unload them.

The drive home was uneventful, although for most of the way between Nairn and Inverness I was in a queue of traffic following a farmer in his tractor. Not too slow, though, at a fairly respectable 40mph. In my day you'd be lucky if your tractor could reach 15mph. It was a relief when he turned off the main road towards the airport.

I wonder where the farmer was flying off to for his holidays. Iceland maybe, or Siberia. Either way it'll be warmer than Nairn.

86

〜

Day 86 – a day of consumer complaints

And winter is back! Temperature down to a mere one degree above freezing when M got up this morning, and only a degree or two warmer when I emerged from my cocoon. So it was woolly hat and gloves on for the morning walk, and a bowl of my special microwaved porridge when I got home. That always warms me up, and I'm sure the orange skin tone will fade eventually.

So as I settled down, glowing, with the papers, M headed off to Dingwall for the weekly shopping. And today she had a wee bonus, a voucher from that well known (German) supermarket where I bought Baby A's sandpit the other day. Last weekend M had purchased a joint of beef and cooked it for Sunday dinner. And while she was preparing it she thought it looked slightly gristly so she gave it a bit longer in the oven, but when it came out it wasn't slightly gristly any longer. It was now HORRENDOUSLY gristly. Trying to chew it was more than my few remaining teeth could handle, I don't think even Hannibal

Lecter would manage it. Even with his nice Chianti. According to Google the top ten list of tough guys includes Rocky, Rambo and Mike Tyson, but this piece of beef would have wiped the floor with all of them. Heaven knows what kind of bull it came from but I'm very glad I didn't meet it when it was alive.

Anyway, according to the supermarket's website their motto includes the words "big on quality...", and obviously they had failed to live up to that promise. So I sat down after my Sunday dinner of vegetables and gravy, and composed an email describing my disappointment. And hunger. A nice email, of course, simply pointing out the facts and suggesting that their quality control systems might benefit from a review. And I attached a photo of the label from the offending joint. If I'd had a photo of the bull I'd have attached that too, that would have scared them.

Regular readers might recall I had a similar situation some time ago, with the manufacturer of a certain (unnamed but wheaty and, erm, biscuity) breakfast cereal. I had complained about poor quality and received a phone call the next day followed soon after by a written apology and a rather nice financial compensation. I imagined that my supermarket chums would reciprocate just as fast, and just as generously. But no, it turns out that "großzügigkeit" is in the German vocabulary, but "generosity" isn't. A whole week went by, and I was just building up to another, more threatening, email, when a letter arrived today with an apology and a voucher for the exact cost of the original piece of beef. And not a pfennig more.

Oh well, no profit this time but at least M got the benefit of the refund. And she didn't spend it in the beef department.

Sadly she didn't spend it in the beer department either, but since it was her money in the first place I suppose that's fair enough.

Poor M had a disaster the other day. Just as she was sitting down to dinner she gave a sudden cry of 'Oh!' as one of the lenses fell out of her specs. Luckily, and by some miracle, I managed to retrieve it without standing on it but the tiny screw which was supposed to hold it in was lost for ever. And as it turned out she couldn't see the optician until Monday (I could make a joke here – she couldn't see the optician at all - but that would be unkind. And dangerous), so a temporary repair would have to be made. My first suggestion – stick the lens in and hold it in place with elastoplast – was not met with unbridled enthusiasm. I can't imagine why.

So since I was the only one with two good eyes it fell to me to cannibalise a screw from an old pair pf specs and use it to secure the lens. And it wasn't easy, but with one eye shut, a shaky hand and a lot of muttering I finally managed it. I learnt that routine from the school dentist in 1963.

87

‿∽

Day 87 – a day of time confusion

Last night, all over the UK, the clocks changed. But mine didn't. When I woke up this morning it was still a clock.

But in reality (I know, who wants to live there?), it was half past eight on the clock but still half past seven on my body clock so it was something of a shock when M came bouncing into the bedroom enquiring whether I was going to "lie and rot" (her words) all day! So I was obliged to drag my protesting bones out of bed and accompany her on our usual Sunday pre-breakfast walk to Dingwall. I was halfway there before I woke up.

And I was confused for the rest of the day, especially when it came to mealtimes. I was horrified to see it was well after one o'clock and I hadn't had my lunch, but of course my poor stomach was still on Greenwich Mean Time and wasn't expecting to be fed yet. But naturally it didn't complain when lunch came early, I don't suppose it will be quite so happy when the clocks go back in October.

Good news! MotoGP is back on telly after a motorbike-free

winter. This weekend's racing is from Qatar, and because of the time difference the main race was shown on British TV when we were having our Sunday dinner so I wasn't able to watch it live. Luckily I had set my Sky box to record it so that will give me something to watch tomorrow. At least I hope I've set it correctly, I'll be very angry if I settle down tomorrow and switch on to find I've accidentally recorded Call the Midwife by mistake. Although there's a lot of exciting action in both shows, including the inevitable blood, sweat and tears, there's marginally less pushing in MotoGP.

My painted stone animals are nearly finished. I applied a final coat to them today, changing the hedgehog's face from bright yellow to a more muted light brown after M's horrified reaction when she saw it for the first time. She says we can't have kids arguing with their teachers: 'But Miss, hedgehog's faces are DEFINITELY yellow, I've seen one!' All that remains to do is paint in their eyes. Brown for mouse and hedgehog, red for tortoise and gold rimmed specs for mole. I don't know what to do for the armadillo's eyes, I've never seen a real one but I suspect none of my passers-by have either, so I can choose any colour I like. Pink maybe, or bright green. That'll scare the kiddies.

For my birthday two weeks ago M Junior bought me two huge gold coloured balloons, a 7 and a 0, filled with helium. And she insisted that I should display them in my living room window to amuse the neighbours. And prevent me from lying about my age. Well, two weeks later the 0 has almost totally deflated but the 7 is still flying high and they're not in the window any longer, but brightening up a corner of the living room. I decided that the 0 should be disposed of and, rather than waste the residual helium, I did that stupid thing of inhaling it to make my voice sound squeaky. I then recorded a video for Baby A with my helium-induced Donald Duck voice, I hope it doesn't give her nightmares.

And yes, I know that's a very immature thing to do but I blame the time change. My stomach may be an hour behind the real time, but my brain still thinks I'm ten.

88

～

Day 88 – a day of mistaken iDENTity

Monday morning, and at last my digestive system is finally adjusting to Greenwich Mean Time. Stomach usually starts rumbling when I'm halfway to the stables on my morning walk, which is a good incentive to put a spurt on and get home for breakfast. Then there's a kind of hollow feeling around eleven o'clock, so that's my cue to make coffee in the pod machine and have a snack of some sort. That's followed a couple of hours later by the great hungriness which heralds the arrival of lunchtime.

And that's it, apart from a cup of tea in the afternoon (and maybe a wee biscuit or two), until M comes home at five and we have dinner. And that's my regular diet. And one of the dictionary definitions of "regular" is "frequent", so that makes it all right.

A spooky thing happened today. After all my recent talk about dentists, particularly school dentists, I had a phone call from my own dentist. That leads me to suspect I may be psychic.

Or maybe transcenDENTAL. (Ha! I made a joke! Well, very nearly.)

In common with everyone else, covid has prevented me from having a dental check-up since early 2020, so I assumed they were calling to invite me in for a routine visit. But no, it was: 'Mr Thomson, we'd like you to come in so we can complete your outstanding treatment'. This was a bit of a shock to me because as far as I knew I didn't have any treatment outstanding. Last time I was there for my check up the dentist gave me a clean bill of health and said he'd see me in six months. Boy, was he wrong about that.

So I explained to the receptionist who was phoning that I wasn't aware of any outstanding treatment and, after checking her records, she agreed with me. I suspect she had looked up someone else's record by mistake, and offered me whatever it was that that patient was due to have done. It's just as well I was alert, otherwise I might have been in the chair of doom this morning. And while I enjoy a wee scale and polish just as much as the next man, I draw the line at undergoing someone else's treatment. And it's not fair on them either, especially if they're stuck at home unable to chew, and subsisting on bread and milk.

It was very windy today, along with some nasty showers, so that was a good excuse to stay indoors and catch up with the MotoGP racing I recorded yesterday. And yes, I did manage to record the right channel, at the right time, so that was a relief. And we're heading down to the farm at the weekend to help with lambing so I'll miss next week's races, so I've already set the Sky box to record them. How organised am I? And that will give me something to watch the following week, when we come home. As long as I remember to leave the electricity on. And top up the meter.

The only time I ventured out today, apart from my morning walk, was to empty the car. As you will remember, it has been sitting with Baby A's sandpit and the new gazebo inside since late last week. We'll need it emptied for Saturday's trip down the road because every time we visit M Junior and family we always have the car loaded to the roof with such assorted items as groceries, beer, firewood, wellies, clothes, beer, boiler suits, tools, paint brushes, beer, and – if there's room – my toothbrush.

Well, I don't want to have to call the dentist, do I?

89

∾

Day 89 – a day of royal reminiscences

I was lucky to get a dry walk this morning, because by mid morning it was raining and that's the way it continued for the rest of the day. So I spent a second consecutive day under cover, either in the house or in the shed.

Finally finished painting the stone animals, it seems like I've been doing it for ever. But they've now got all their details – cute wee noses, toenails, smiling mouths and eyes in various colours. Brown for woodland animals of course, but I've given the armadillo striking blue ones since he's an exotic animal from South America and probably the only one in captivity in the Dingwall area. We just don't have a high enough population of ants to sustain them, you see.

A couple of notable events took place this day in history. Firstly, in 2002 The Queen Mother passed away at the age of 101. I met her once, in 1982 at the opening of the Kessock Bridge. We each had a role to play at the opening ceremony. Hers was relatively easy, simply stand up, cut a ribbon, say a few words, smile benevolently at the assembled dignitaries and then head off to a huge tent for tea and sandwiches. Mine was much more stressful and considerably less comfortable, thanks to the heavy and persistent rain. My job, believe it or not, was to fly the flag, and I don't mean the British Airways advert from the 1970s.

No, I was responsible for the hoisting of the Queen Mother's personal standard, which was a huge thing, twice as large as a normal flag because it was a combination of two flags. The one of her late husband King George VI, combined with her own family one (the Bowes Lyons) which featured bows and, erm, lions. Wouldn't you have thought they'd have come with something a little more original?

Anyway, this massive piece of royal canvas had come into my possession a few days earlier, I had to sign for it of course, but not in blood, thankfully. And I had been instructed by Clarence House on the protocols involved with handling it. It was important, apparently, to fly it the right way up, but even more important was that it must NEVER be allowed to touch the ground. If even a corner of the flag were to come into contact with the merest blade of grass, it was "off to the Tower" with me. 'Kneel down, sir, and put your head on this block. Yes, right there. This won't take a minute'.

And, just to compound my misery, it was heavy. And even heavier once it got wet. So there I was, rain running down my neck and out through the bottom of my kilt, with this thing draped over my arm like a huge soggy carpet, waiting for the arrival of the Royal Personage. And when she arrived in her Rolls

Royce, the Military Band struck up the national anthem and that was my cue to hoist the thing up to the top of the flagpole. And, thanks to my many rehearsals and to the Provost's obvious relief, it was the right way up!

No tea and sandwiches for me, though. The final protocol demanded that the flag remained flying as long as the Queen Mother was in the area. So while all the dignitaries were in the tent stuffing their faces with the smoked salmon vol-au-vents I had to remain on duty, beside my flagpole, in the rain, with this blooming flag dripping on me, waiting for her to leave.

And as she drove away, she acknowledged my salute with a smile and a nod of the royal head. It's a good job she didn't know what I was thinking.

And the other interesting event on this day was that in 1974 Red Rum won the Grand National for the second year running. I suppose it's just as well he was running, otherwise he'd never have won.

90

〜

Day 90 – a day of circumlocutory superfluity (no, me neither)

The last day of March, and persistently raining. I didn't get my morning walk until the afternoon so I had to have a second breakfast at 3.30pm. Just managed to finish it in time to have dinner.

Took my last multivitamin tablet of the winter today (with my first breakfast!). I've been taking one every morning since November, in an attempt to keep up my vitamin D levels. Vitamin D is the one you get from exposure to sunshine and we don't get much of that in a northern Scottish winter. Of course the tablet contains other vitamins as well, but the main one it lacks is the one I get from drinking plenty beer, vitamin P.

So it was a long, boring indoor morning. Or at least it would have been if not for the fact that M buys me The Times on a Wednesday. There's a lot of reading in The Times, and it can easily occupy two or three hours of my time. Not that there's that amount of news in it, but I have to have the dictionary beside me to look up most of the words. Some of them are almost half an inch long, for goodness sake.

I can cope with most of the terminology. "Supermajority aspiration" is a current favourite, along with "vexatious secessionism", but when I move to the financial pages and encounter "cumulative market capitalisation" I think I should maybe limit my reading to something a little less demanding. The TV Guide, perhaps.

And the crosswords take up even more time. There's the "quick cryptic" one, which is certainly cryptic but hardly ever quick. That's the one designed for senior civil servants to complete over their ten-minute coffee break. It takes me at least an hour and a half. Then there's the actual traditional Times Crossword, which is even more cryptic and probably takes the average high flying executive an hour or two. That one takes me three days.

Rain or no rain, I put out my stone animals this morning. Their paint is all dry from yesterday, but in the cold light of day some of them do look slightly less than attractive. I seem to have this knack of making the eyes look scary, no matter how soft and appealing I try to make them appear. The tortoise in particular is very nightmarish, with his red eyes and dark brown pupils. I think I'll place him at the front of the display to encourage the kids to keep their distance. Not so much a horrible hound, more like a repellent reptile.

Anyway, out they went, and I also put out my white board with its painting of a cute bunny clutching an easter egg, because I'll be away over the weekend so might as well start my

Easter display now. And I'll take it in again when I come back from the farm. According to ancient tradition the Easter season lasts for 50 days, but my bunny painting will never last that long without getting nicked/spray painted/peed upon by passing dogs.

Finally, my Zoom meeting tonight went off without a hitch, so I must have set it up correctly. This surprised me as much as anybody. It was nice catching up with some former colleagues and in an attempt to amuse them I changed my Zoom background to a picture of the Golden Gate bridge at San Francisco. Which was a nice change from my actual background, which was the smallest room in the house. Yes, that one.

Although I think they began to suspect something wasn't quite right when I hit the flush control instead of the mute button.

91

∽

Day 91 – a day of not being fooled. Much.

First of April today, and the usual batch of April Fool jokes in the papers. Some of them are pretty pathetic and easily spotted, because journalists think we won't notice if they insert a name which is an anagram of "Aprilfoolsday". One paper has a story attributed to Prof A Lilo and another has quotes from Lady Flora Pois. And Oprah Winfrey is about to interview the Queen, according to Daily Mail staff writer Olaf Pirlo and royal commentator Dr Pilaf Yosola. Just how gullible to these people think we are? Mind you, if the real Professor Lilo gets in touch I shall be mightily embarrassed.

Brrr, temperature down to freezing this morning. M had to de-ice her (new) windscreen before she could leave for work. But cold starts often herald nice days, so I hung out a washing before breakfast. And I was right to do so because the rest of the day was sunny and the washing was dried, aired in the tumble drier, brought in, folded and put away before M came home. Isn't she lucky to have me? Although, if she didn't have me there wouldn't be nearly as much washing to do. My extra-large garments take up three times as much space as her petite ones.

I had another batch of school fund money to pay into the bank so I knew I'd need to go to Dingwall at some point today. And because the money was mostly cheques, therefore nice and light, and the forecast was for a dry day, I had decided I'd walk instead of driving. So that was my excuse for not having a pre-breakfast walk and the second M was out the door I was tucking into a bowl of nuclear porridge. Or, as the Daily Mail would call it today, daily floor sap.

After breakfast I got stuck into the housework, my usual Thursday routine. Dusting, hoovering, floors and surface cleaning, all completed before my coffee break. And I had a special treat which I had been saving since yesterday. M had been in Cromarty yesterday and had brought home a mini lemon meringue pie for me, and rather than guzzle it as soon as she gave it to me, which is my default action, I used all my willpower and saved it until after housework today. And very nice it was too, along with a café latte from the pod machine. How civilised and sophisticated! And a nice change from my usual coffee break scenario - a mug of builder's tea in one hand and a Deas pie in the other. And a Harry Gow's dream ring standing by for afters.

Then, off I set to walk to the bustling metropolis of Dingwall. And it was bustling, with lots of people in the street and long queues outside Deas and Harry Gows. Which was just as well, otherwise I might have been tempted to join them. No queue at the bank though, and a nice young man took my cash and stamped my receipt while I waited outside the door. And then I visited a hardware store and bought some painting supplies for us to take down to M Junior's at the weekend. She has some old chairs she wants to upcycle and M, being an expert painter, will be happy to help refurbish them. While I stand back and issue "helpful advice", which usually results in me being sent away to "do something useful". Which I'm happy to do. Drinking beer is very useful for the brewing industry, isn't it?

And finally, some exciting news. Our shopping is about to get easier. Tesco have announced in today's newspaper that they are introducing trampoline flooring in their stores, so we can bounce up and reach the top shelves. This will be a great boon to those of us who are, erm, vertically challenged, and I'm very excited to try it out when it comes to the Dingwall store.

I must write and congratulate the journalist who broke this news. Her name? Daisy O'Farllop.

92

⌇

Day 92 – a day of packing

Friday the second of April, and Easter weekend starts here. This is "Good Friday", and as it turned out it was quite a good Friday. Firstly, it's good because M has a day off due to schools being closed for the next two weeks. Actually, she has all of next week off as well which is the reason we're able to pop down the road tomorrow to spend a few days with Baby A and Dog F. And their parents too, of course.

Secondly, it's a good day for weather – twelve degrees and some sunshine – so as soon as I struggled out of bed M whipped off the sheets and got them into the wash. That's usually a Saturday job, but because we won't be here on Saturday she brought the routine forward by twenty-four hours. If only everything could be brought forward as easily as that. I'd like to move the calendar forward ten days so that I can get my hair cut, then a further twenty so that I can have my second covid jab. Then I'd like to move it all the way back again so that I don't miss out on a Sunday dinner.

M also brought forward her weekly shopping trip to Dingwall, and while she was away in her car I began preparing to pack my one for tomorrow's journey. We always have a diverse cargo on these trips, in addition to the painting supplies I told you about yesterday I loaded up my woodworking tools, my wellies, my John Deere boiler suit, a roll of felt and several bags of firewood. We'd bought the firewood away back in December because we thought we'd be visiting in January, but Nicola stopped us from doing that so the wood has been lying in the shed ever since. It has probably been colonised by now, by ants or maybe death watch beetles. I hope they don't start "ticking" in the back of the car on the way down the road, or M will be alarmed. I shall have to reassure her that there's nothing to worry about, it's only an alarm clock in my suitcase. Or maybe a bomb.

And the most diverse piece of cargo of all is a football. Not for me, nor for Baby A, but for Dog F. She loves playing football, and eats around three balls a year, so we often take a new one down to her. It's not an easy thing to pack, so to stop it rolling around all over the car we need to jam it in somehow. Luckily there are several bags of groceries coming down with us so we'll use them. And the most important bag of groceries won't be ready until tomorrow because it will contain the bakery goodies which M will buy in the morning. Sausage rolls, dream rings and – because it's Easter – hot cross buns. Hot cross buns are all very well, but they're not terribly exciting, are they? I think it's time for a new variation, the hot cross dream ring. Are you listening, Harry Gow? Remember I thought of it first.

After lunch M took me in her car to show me one of her

favourite lunchtime walks when she's at work. It's along a disused railway line between two Black Isle villages, Avoch and Fortrose. So she parked the car at Avoch and we walked all the way to Fortrose and back, three and a half miles on a level, fairly dry surface. And very little danger of being run over by a train because the last one ran sixty years ago. And that was a goods train because passenger services were stopped away back in 1951. Obviously nobody wanted to go to Fortrose, which is hardly surprising when you consider how they used to treat people. When Kenneth Mackenzie, a psychic known as the "Brahan Seer" who could predict the future, visited Fortrose in the 16th century they burned him alive. In a barrel of tar.

You'd have thought that he, of all people, would have seen that coming. Especially when he saw the tar being delivered.

93

∾

Day 93 – a day of travel

An early start, as M heads into Dingwall for last minute shopping before we set off down the road. We always take a selection of Dingwall-based baked goodies to remind M Junior of home, because neither Harry Gow nor William Deas have shops in her corner of rural Perthshire.

While she did the shopping I tended to the manly ritual of "loading the car". Yes, I know I started it yesterday but there are always refinements to me made to ensure even distribution of weight. For example, I sit on the right hand side of the vehicle so I need to make sure that there are several bags of firewood on the left hand side to counteract my (considerable but undisclosed) weight.

And before we could leave, M had to make sure her wee plants were suitably catered for. She's been growing several flowers and vegetables from seed and was worried about leaving them all alone for a whole week while she wasn't here to adjust their temperature and make sure they didn't dry out. Her solution – leave them in the bath. Yes, a little water in the bottom of the bath to maintain moisture levels, window blinds adjusted to ensure adequate light, and door left open so the heat from the hall keeps the bathroom frost-free. And there she left them, in their containers and seed trays, while she waved them goodbye and hoped they'd still be alive next time we see them.

The journey down the A9 was reasonably uneventful. We still haven't emerged fully from lockdown so there wasn't too much traffic around. The downside is that there are no facilities open between Inverness and Perth so we can't get a cup of tea, a sandwich or – most importantly for men of a certain age – a toilet break. Driving with crossed legs is very uncomfortable, and probably illegal.

Our American cousins have a much less graphic description – "comfort break". Which doesn't happen in the toilet, but in the much more socially acceptable "rest room". Which didn't half confuse me the first time I visited the US because in Scotland the rest room is where the undertaker lays you out whilst awaiting your funeral. I was amazed that there appeared to be so many rest rooms all over town, in shopping centres, restaurants and bars. I mean, I knew Americans lived on high-fat junk food, but did they expect you to keel over during your meal and just drag you into the nearest facility? Happily, the first time I ventured into one I was delighted to find everyone else in the room appeared to be breathing. You might say I was doubly relieved.

What there is on that road, however, is an abundance of potholes. The last time we were down was on my birthday, Day 71, and several of my fillings became loose on a particularly rough stretch. That was 22 days ago so I was hoping for some improvements to have been made. And indeed they have started. The road at that point is now subject to a 20mph speed limit, the top surface of tarmac has been removed and there are savage ramps at each end of the roadworks. But there's no sign of any actual works happening, no machines operating, not a hi-viz jacket to be seen, not even a shovel nor a weary workman to lean on it.

I just hope they get it all fixed and smoothed over by the time we come back up the road at the end of the week. My fillings deserve a break and so does my bladder.

94

∽

Day 94 - a day of chicken stories

And has the day dawns here we are, on the farm. Following a safe journey yesterday we were welcomed by M Junior, Farmer J and Baby A but the most excited resident was Dog F. I could read her mind: 'Oh thank goodness HE's here. I can have a week off while he runs about pretending he's a farmer and takes over all the sheep herding'.

This morning, then, we looked out of our window and saw our neighbours. Not our usual neighbours walking their dogs, driving their cars or mowing their lawns. No, these neighbours were lounging around, idly chomping grass and occasionally rising to, erm, "fertilise" their field to encourage more grass to grow. No need for lawn mowers here.

And just like human neighbours, they spend much of their time gazing enviously at the field next door, where the grass always seems greener. And there are occasional escape attempts, as the temptations become too strong to resist and a way is found through the fence. Or under the fence, or even over the fence like a woolly Steve McQueen in the Great Escape. Luckily they don't have access to motorbikes or we'd never keep them in.

First job in the morning is to release the chickens from their coop, where they've been locked in since dusk the night before. You might expect them to have spent the long night laying their eggs, but not these chickens. Oh no, they must be released and given their breakfast, and only then do they go back inside, into their nesting boxes, and produce their daily egg. Generally we expect one egg from each hen but occasionally we find an empty nesting box, and that's an indication that one of them has found an alternative egg-laying place. And that can be anywhere around the farm. In a dusty corner of the cart shed, buried inside an old bale of last year's hay or, annoyingly, under a bush in the garden. It's most disconcerting when you're hand weeding under the bushes and you plunge your hand into a clutch of eggs which has been lurking there for six months. You certainly don't come up smelling of roses.

Today I had the pleasure of meeting my namesake for the first time. You'll remember that in honour of my "big birthday" a lamb was named after me. He was born in early March and all I'd seen of him so far was his photo, with "Sandy" painted on one side and "70" on the other.

Sandy is what's known as an "early lamb" because he arrived a month before the start of the official lambing. That's because he's the result of an unplanned liaison between a young innocent sheep and an over-amorous ram who couldn't wait until the official mating date. And he must have been the one with the motorbike because he managed to get over several fences to reach the object of his desires.

Well Sandy's now a month old and quite a chunky lad so when Farmer J's mum came and passed him into my arms I was impressed by how heavy he is. And when I asked whether he was going to be kept on to become a daddy himself in future years I was told that no, he would be "going to the market", which is the kind way of saying his future involves less marital duties and more mint sauce.

And just to add insult to injury, M Junior served up a Sunday dinner of roast lamb and all the trimmings. It was delicious, but don't tell Sandy.

95

∽

Day 95 – a day of sheep herding

Ah, awakening to life on the farm again this morning. None of the morning sounds I'm accustomed to at home – gentle birdsong, early morning dog walkers' soft footsteps, the faint thud as M pops my morning cup of tea down beside my bed. No, this morning I awoke to the roar of Farmer J's John Deere tractor (green, of course. 'If it's red, leave it in the shed', remember?) as he brought the cows their morning feed, drowned out only by the roaring of those same cows, who know what to expect when they hear the tractor approaching. I wonder if it would be a good idea for me to start roaring in the morning when I'm needing my breakfast? Would M be as attentive to me as Farmer J is to his cows? Or when I get to a certain age might she simply despatch me to the auction mart? Or have I reached that age already? Perhaps I'd better keep quiet.

And once the cows had been seen to, it was a big day for the sheep. With official lambing only a few days away, all the pregnant ewes had to be brought in from the fields to the lambing shed. This is a major annual operation involving as many human helpers as possible, which meant that M and I were enlisted as temporary sheep herders for the day. Dog F, who is supposed to be the "official" sheep dog, isn't yet fully trained so she had to be left behind while M and I carried out her duties. M did the running and I did the barking.

Of course M, who was brought up in a sheep rearing family, is much more experienced than I am. Which meant that while she was able to enjoy the actual herding element of the mission, my main duty involved standing at strategic positions, guarding gates and occasionally waving my arms about to prevent errant sheep from straying off course.

And once several hundred sheep had been herded into the farmyard and were ready to enter the lambing shed. they had to be divided up into different pens depending on whether they were expecting twins, triplets or single lambs. Farmer J was able to tell which were which because he had cleverly marked them with different colours at the time they were scanned, and so it was his job to divert them into the appropriate pen as they were driven in. And the driving in had to be done gently because some of these ewes were heavily pregnant, so that required some care.

Which is why I was, once again, left outside to guard the gate. And happily, in spite of Farmer J's refusal to issue me with a fluorescent jacket and STOP/GO sign, my gate guarding was effective, so none of them were able to carry out u-turns and escape back to the field.

Or maybe that should be ewe-turns?

Finally, they were all inside safely and settling down in their respective pens to await the arrival of their lambs. Just like a maternity ward in an NHS hospital, but with no white-coated doctor, no cot beside the bed and no cup of tea after giving birth.

And definitely no visits from Daddy.

96

～

Day 96 - a day of home improvements. For the chickens.

A bitterly cold day today, with very strong winds. But according to the TV news it's much worse at home, with heavy snowfalls and roads affected, so I'm glad we're missing it down here in rural Perthshire. Also glad that the sheep are safe and warm in the lambing shed, which has already seen some action since yesterday. Lambs have begun appearing so Farmer J's maternity ward has swung into action. And it seems that just as one sheep has her lamb, her neighbour looks across and says: 'Oh aye, that's what I should be doing' and promptly goes into labour herself. And shouting: 'Nurse! The screens!' might work for George Clooney, but sadly not for Farmer J.

And so with Farmer J being fully occupied, I've taken over the household maintenance and DIY duties. And the first house to be in need of DIY isn't M Junior's farmhouse, but her henhouse. She has half a dozen chickens who live in their own wooden house. It was bought a year ago and had begun suffering from the ravages of twelve months outdoors in all weathers so

M Junior was concerned that the chickies might be vulnerable to leaks. And damp chickens means no eggs, and no eggs means Baby A can't have omelette for breakfast, so some serious refurbishment was in order.

The outer shell (sorry!) of the henhouse needed to be painted with wood preserver, and M Junior had already done that before I arrived. But she hadn't just painted it with one colour. Oh no, she used a variety of different shades of paint with the result that the henhouse was looking nice and colourful with horizontal stripes. In pastel shades. Like Cinderella's palace at Walt Disney World but with sawdust and hay on the floor instead of plush carpets. And no bored American teenagers spending their gap year dressed up in a Mickey Mouse costume to entertain visiting kiddies.

Also, although the hennies are treated as farmyard royalty, no handsome prince either. Unless you count me. What? No, didn't think so.

So with the walls taken care of, the only job left for me was to waterproof the roof. You'll remember back on Day 92 that I packed a roll of felt in the car. Well, now you know what it was for. Although to be honest it didn't exactly qualify for the title of "roll". It was just some offcuts I had left over from a shed re-roofing project at home a couple of years ago, and thanks to my policy of "never throwing anything away" its time had come to be useful.

Anyway, I'd brought my hammer and some felt nails and soon had the hen's roof nicely covered up, so it's now completely waterproof. Although the felt was three feet wide and the henhouse three metres wide, so my O'Grade arithmetic came in handy. I'm sure the inmates will be suitably grateful and the daily supply of eggs will continue uninterrupted, so Baby A's eggy breakfasts are safe for the foreseeable future. And Dog F will also be thankful, because a few scraps of omelette always get dropped from the high chair. And it would be a shame to waste them.

Knowing my luck, now that I've used up all my spare felt my shed at home will inevitably spring a few leaks and I shall be forced to buy some more. And I don't suppose there's any point sending the bill to the chickens – I can hear their response already: 'Hard luck Chuck. Cluck Cluck.'

97

∽

Day 97 – a day of home improvements. Not for the chickens.

Hard frost this morning, as I got up early to fetch M a cup of tea in bed. And while waiting for the kettle to boil I popped outside and released the hens from their multi coloured (and weatherproof) house. They seemed quite happy but, as usual, no eggs have been laid until they've had their breakfast.

This is our second last day before going home, so I had to squeeze in as many DIY jobs as possible. First of these was the installation of a toilet roll holder. Where else, but in the toilet, of course. M Junior had procured one from a well-known online supplier who's name I had better not reveal but there's a river in South America with the same name. However, I can reveal that it wasn't the Orinoco, which of course is famous in the world of wombling. American readers may wish to Google "wombling" and watch the YouTube video. If you always thought that we Brits were a little eccentric, there's your final confirmation.

Anyway, after a few verses of the wombling song I got

around to fitting the toilet roll holder. Drills in the wall – done. Rawlplugs inserted – done. Mounting bracket screwed into rawlplugs – done. It was all going so well, something had to go wrong. And it did.

The actual holder is fixed on to the mounting bracket by a very small grub screw with an allen key head, and as I was turning this screw I couldn't understand why it was never getting any tighter. So I kept on turning and turning until it dawned on me that the turning of the screw was actually pulling the rawlplugs OUT of the plasterboard. So now I had two beautiful (and perfectly positioned) holes in the plasterboard which were slightly too large for the rawlplugs. Result – a wobbly toilet roll holder. And no-one wants anything wobbly in the toilet, do they?

So what does the average handyperson do when things go wrong? Easy, he refers to the instructions which came with the device. Which he should have done before even starting the job. And there it was, the stark warning: "take care not to over-tighten the screw".

But all is not lost. I immediately asked Mr Google for advice and he referred me to that same South American river website to purchase a rescue kit for just such an occasion. So I've ordered it but of course it won't be delivered until after I'm back at home so Farmer J will just have to put up with a shaky toilet roll holder until my next visit. It should be ok until then. As long as he doesn't lean on it.

Also on the list was the fitting of a draught excluder on one of M Junior's internal doors, to save Baby A from getting a chill from the freezing wind whistling underneath the door. One of the troubles with being a baby is that you're nearer the floor than anyone else so much more susceptible to draughts. There are benefits too, though. As you crawl around the floor you can often spot tiny objects that your parents have missed, and pop them in your mouth before they notice. And when your father's a farmer all sorts of interesting things come in, on the soles of his boots.

Happily, the fitting of the draught excluder went pretty smoothly. A few holes along the bottom of the door and on it went. No rawlplugs involved this time, thankfully, and nothing wobbly or unstable. Except for my increasingly creaky knees.

98

~~

Day 98 – a day of number confusion

Another hard frost this morning, just to remind us that we're still in the grip of winter even though the calendar claims it's spring. Thankfully the sheep are all indoors, nice and cosy with their lambs, but they're about to get a rude awakening because it's time for some of the older lambs and their mothers to be discharged from the maternity ward and adapt to outdoor living once again. But don't worry about the wee lambs getting cold and wet, Farmer J fits each of them with a plastic coat to help keep them warm and dry. Very similar to the ponchos you get at Walt Disney World but considerably cheaper. And no mousey logo.

And of course the coats need to be made of clear plastic so that the lambs' individual numbers can be seen through the material. Not that sheep can read, you understand, but it helps Farmer J reunite stray lambs with their brothers/sisters/mothers when they wander off. The transfer of these sheep and lambs takes place using a livestock trailer towed behind the tractor, because the hill fields are too far away for little lambs to walk. And inevitably in the confusion mothers and babies get separated so Farmer J needs someone to help him sort them out when they get to the other end. That's far too much responsibility for me, so M was chosen as official "lamb sorter-outer". That's an un-official title, of course, but it won't half look impressive on her CV.

On the hill, the first load arrived and the pairing commenced. The mother sheep were so excited to be seeing real grass again af-ter a couple of weeks in the lambing shed that they forgot they had lambs and immediately wandered off and began chomping. M's task was to reunite the bleating lambs with their (uncaring) mothers and so that's where the clear plastic came in handy. Suc-cessfully paired – ewe 33 with her twins, ewe 45 with her single lamb, ewe 48 with twins. But wait! There's still an unmatched lamb with number 33 – how can this be?

Farmer J confirmed that none of today's sheep had borne triplets so how could there be a third number 33? Then, in the top corner of the field, M spotted a lone ewe, merrily grazing, with a 33 painted on her side, no lamb and not a care in the world. Mystery solved – somehow TWO sheep had been num-bered 33. Farmer J's explanation? Let's put it down to an "ad-ministrative error".

Meanwhile, far from the chills of the hill park and sheltered from the elements, my job today was cleaning out the fireplace. A simple enough task, you may think, but as usual there was an element of surprise in it for me. When the farmhouse was built, a clever design feature was a hatch on the outside wall giving access to the base of the fireplace, so that you can remove the ashes from outside the house. Having done that, I left the hatch open while I went inside to give the fireplace a final clean out. Of course I'd neglected to take into account the fierce wind that was blowing, with the result that as I bent down facing the fireplace a gust blew all the residual ash right into my face.

A look in the mirror saw a grey wrinkly face staring back with red eyes. Now I know how the elephant man felt.

And that was our last full day on the farm, home tomorrow to a world with no sheep, no chickens and - luckily – no fire to clean out.

99

~

Day 99 - a day of travel (uneventful) and a homecoming (eventful)

The end of our short break, and time to face the journey up the A9 once more. The car is considerably lighter on the way home now that we've lost all the firewood, felt and bakery produce that we took down with us. The heaviest thing in the car on this trip is probably, erm, me.

I expect fuel consumption to be much more economical because not only is the car lighter but – contrarily – there are more downhills than uphills between south and north. Yes, I know, I wouldn't have believed it either but Dunkeld is 660 metres above sea level while Maryburgh is a mere 36 metres.

The journey (up/down?) north was uneventful, apart from the potholes, which are just as bad on the way home as they were on the way there. Although of course this time we were driving on the opposite side of the road so we encountered some new ones we hadn't noticed five days ago. Managed not to break any springs though, and most of my fillings are still intact.

No toilet breaks, of course, so the final twenty miles were achieved with legs crossed. Which made the driving quite interesting, if a little challenging. Come on Nicola, please allow our roadside services to open again. M needs her coffee breaks and I need my toilet breaks.

Anyway, the journey passed without disaster. I was only joking about driving with legs crossed, honest, constable! On the other hand, we arrived home to not one, but two disasters. Firstly, as soon as we get home from anywhere M's first action is to put the kettle on so she headed straight for the kitchen. And while waiting for the kettle to boil she ran the hot tap to get some nice hot water for the cups. And she ran the hot tap some more. And some more. And eventually realised that no matter how long she ran it for, there was no hot water coming through. A quick visit to the hall cupboard and a feel of the tank confirmed that it was stone cold.

Faulty thermostat? Or heating element? Either way I don't suppose it will be a cheap fix so I've left a voice message with my local friendly electrician asking him to come round and have a look. But because it's Friday night I don't expect him to come until Monday so it looks like we'll be having a few days of cold baths. Brrrr.

The other disaster involved the long-standing gazebo in the back garden, which has remained standing throughout the worst weather the winter could throw at it. Until now. Yes, it seems that while we were away in wind-free Perthshire there were howling gales here, so the last of the tent pegs were uprooted and the gazebo went flying across the garden. No great loss, you may say, because it was several years old and due to be replaced this year anyway. Fair enough, but out of spite it had aimed itself at the greenhouse and shattered a couple of panes of glass.

So now I have a garden full of broken glass which I'll need to clear up tomorrow. And I can't even have a hot bath to cheer myself up.

100

∽

Day 100 – a day of recycling

It's Saturday, and we're at home, in that great area known as "Up North". Although to the good folks of Caithness and Orkney we're actually "Down South". And as far as the residents of Shetland are concerned, we live in a completely different country. Scotland.

Isn't it funny how we always refer to going from south to north as going UP? There are exceptions, of course. In some of the more far-flung parts of the Western Isles they talk about going "up south". So presumably they go "down north". I can't imagine how they cope with stairs. That may explain how the 1947 Snakes and Ladders World Championship ended in chaos. Who thought it was a good idea to host it in Benbecula?

Anyway, today I was forced to go up (or maybe down) to Inverness to buy some replacement greenhouse panels following yesterday's shock demolition of the greenhouse by a flying gazebo. I decided that perhaps it's a little dangerous to replace it with real glass, given my gazebo-anchoring skills, so I've bought polycarbonate sheets. They're light, strong and unbreakable, and easy to cut to size, perfect for an amateur glazier. And they come in packs of two, so I can afford to make a pig's ear of cutting the first one.

What a strange expression. Anyone would think a pig's ear was a bad thing, whereas it's actually a very good thing indeed. And especially important if you're a pig.

Luckily, no pig's ears were made today and the sheets were cut to the correct size and fitted. And I gathered up all the broken glass, both inside and outside the greenhouse, wrapped it up in newspaper and bagged it up ready to go to the recycling centre. Or, as it's universally known, the dump.

Also ready for the dump was the remains of the gazebo. Metal poles separated, and the fabric rolled up. The metal can be melted down and made into something else, but I don't think the fabric is any use for anything, it's very brittle and full of holes after a few summers (and, this year, a winter) outdoors.

And so it was with a sense of sadness that I packed all the elements of my much loved gazebo into the car and drove to Dingwall to dump – I mean recycle – them. I've had many happy hours in that gazebo over the years, barbecuing burgers, drinking beer, writing my diaries and sometimes just snoozing in the sun. But only when M wasn't looking, of course.

And finally for today, as usual after a break away from home we returned to a mountain – well, a small hill – of mail. Mostly junk of course – trashy catalogues, adverts for double glazing, and of course the ever persistent funeral planners. They're determined that I'm going soon, and they want my money up front.

But in amongst the mail was one brown envelope addressed to me, from "MyCSP", which is an abbreviation used by the Civil Service Pensions Agency in an effort to appear less boring. 'Ooh, exciting', I thought as I ripped it open. And as it turned out, it was quite exciting – my pension is to be increased from the 11th of May.

By how much, I hear you ask? A thundering £11.74. A day? A week? No, actually £11.74 a year, which works out at a slightly less thundering 22 ½ pence a week. So, sorry darling, there'll be no Christmas this year, and no birthday presents. And no new gazebo until 2031.

101

～

Day 101 – a day of endings. And beginnings.

And here we are, dear reader, at the end of another hundred and one days of, if not actual lockdown, at least social restrictions. It's been a bit of a roller coaster three and a half months, Covid restrictions have been redefined by the Scottish Government on almost a weekly basis so that by now nobody knows whether we're allowed to meet three people from two households, four people from three households or ten people from nine households. Luckily I don't know ten people so that last one isn't going to be a problem.

I don't know whether I'm allowed to go to England, or Northern Ireland, or Wales. And if I do go to one of those, how many people am I allowed to meet with? I don't even know whether I'm allowed to go to the Western Isles, as it seems the ferries are reserved for residents only, even when they're immobilised. The ferries, that is, not the residents. Mind you, having been to one or two Stornoway Mòds I've witnessed quite a number of immobilised residents, especially on the Saturday morning.

Today's Sunday papers are, predictably, packed with tributes to the Duke of Edinburgh, who passed away on Friday at the age of 99. I only met him once, at a military event in 1986 when he was introduced to me and my fellow members of the grandly titled "Warrant Officers and Sergeants Mess". 'Aha,' he declared, 'what a bunch of crooks!'. I think he was joking, but then you never could tell for sure.

I still have the group photograph from that day, Philip seated in the middle at the front and me standing right behind him, gazing into his left ear in what I hoped was a suitably deferential manner. Well, you wouldn't want me to be sent to the Tower for disrespecting the Royal lughole, would you?

And so to the new beginnings. Firstly, whilst I'm not beginning to erect the new gazebo I'm certainly beginning to think about it. Bravely, I've even opened the box to see what it looks like, so progress is definitely being made. It's a different design from the old one, which was a simple metal frame and pole design. This one appears to have some sort of trellis arrangement which unfolds into something resembling a miniature Forth Bridge, although I fear it may not last as long. The real Forth Bridge was opened in 1890 but I don't expect my gazebo to survive beyond the winter gales of 2021.

And the other new beginning I'm hoping for is the restoration of my hot water supply. We've had two nights of cold baths, and another one to look forward to tonight. And yes, I know, cold baths are good for toughening me up, and also for burning calories, but when a man gets to a "certain age" he needs a little mollycoddling.

So all that remains is to thank you for your support, and for buying the book. At least I hope you bought it, and didn't steal it from the Public Library.

And as usual I shall leave you with some wise words from my favourite philosopher, the 95-year old Winnie the Pooh:

"Goodbye..? Oh no, please. Can't we go back to page one and do it all over again?"

Perhaps we shall, friends, perhaps we shall.

Dear reader

Thank you so much for buying my book, I hope you've enjoyed sharing my daily diaries.

And if you haven't already, please buy my first book "Sandy's Daily Diaries", available to order from Amazon or through your local book shop. ISBN 9 781838 326807

I'm always happy to hear your comments and thoughts, you can reach me by email at sandy_thomson3@hotmail.co.uk

Sandy Thomson

2021

02/ 23

BOEING-BOEING

A Comedy
by Marc Camoletti

Translated by
Beverley Cross and Francis Evans

samuelfrench.co.uk

FOR AMATEUR PRODUCTION ENQUIRIES

UNITED KINGDOM AND WORLD
EXCLUDING NORTH AMERICA
plays@samuelfrench.co.uk
020 7255 4302/01

Each title is subject to availability from Samuel French,
depending upon country of performance.

THINKING ABOUT PERFORMING A SHOW?

There are thousands of plays and musicals available to perform from Samuel French right now, and applying for a licence is easier and more affordable than you might think

---

From classic plays to brand new musicals, from monologues to epic dramas, there are shows for everyone.

Plays and musicals are protected by copyright law, so if you want to perform them, the first thing you'll need is a licence. This simple process helps support the playwright by ensuring they get paid for their work and means that you'll have the documents you need to stage the show in public.

Not all our shows are available to perform all the time, so it's important to check and apply for a licence before you start rehearsals or commit to doing the show.

LEARN MORE & FIND THOUSANDS OF SHOWS

Browse our full range of plays and musicals, and find out more about how to license a show

www.samuelfrench.co.uk/perform

Talk to the friendly experts in our Licensing team for advice on choosing a show and help with licensing

plays@samuelfrench.co.uk   020 7387 9373

Acting Editions

BORN TO PERFORM

**Playscripts designed from the ground up
to work the way you do in rehearsal,
performance and study**

Larger, clearer text for easier reading

Wider margins for notes

Performance features such as character and props
lists, sound and lighting cues, and more

+ CHOOSE A SIZE AND STYLE TO SUIT YOU

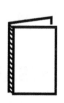

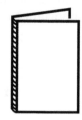

STANDARD EDITION

Our regular
paperback book at
our regular size

SPIRAL-BOUND EDITION

The same size
as the Standard
Edition, but with a
sturdy, easy-to-fold,
easy-to-hold
spiral-bound spine

LARGE EDITION

A4 size and spiral
bound, with larger text
and a blank page for
notes opposite every
page of text – perfect
for technical and
directing use

LEARN MORE | **samuelfrench.co.uk/actingeditions**

ABOUT THE AUTHOR

Marc Camoletti was a man of many and varied talents, from architect to acclaimed artist to global success as a playwright with over 40 produced plays to his credit. He was also a highly respected theatre director in Paris, responsible for a host of hit productions.

A French citizen, born in Geneva in 1923 with Italian family origins, Marc Camoletti initially trained as an architect. He continued to develop his early talent as an artist which led to five major exhibitions of his paintings in Paris and the provinces, many of his works selling to important private collectors.

Playwriting took over when in 1958 his theatre career got off to a flying start with three plays being presented simultaneously in Paris, the first *La Bonne Anna* running for 1300 performances and going on to play throughout the world.

Marc Camoletti's first great British success was *Boeing Boeing* which, following its recent West End triumph, also enjoyed a smash hit revival on Broadway. The original 1962 London production ran for seven years at the Apollo and Duchess Theatres, notching up over 2000 performances. The Paramount film version starred Jerry Lewis, Tony Curtis and Thelma Ritter. In 1991, it was listed in the Guinness Book of Records as the most performed French play throughout the world. The latest Paris revival enjoyed a five year success at the Theatre Michel.

Don't Dress for Dinner, the English language version of the established Paris hit *Pyjama Pour Six*, also enjoyed a seven year run in the West End opening at the Apollo Theatre and transferring to the Duchess. It was recently revived at the Roundabout Theatre on Broadway. The play has also been performed throughout the United States, as well as in Canada, Australia, New Zealand and South Africa and in different languages throughout the world, always to great acclaim.

His last play, *Sexe et Jalousie*, now titled *Ding Dong* in its English version had a successful Paris production and was the tenth Camoletti play to be shown on television.

In a long theatrical career, Marc Camoletti gained worldwide acclaim through the multitude of productions of his plays in numerous languages in fifty five countries. In Paris alone 18 of his plays have enjoyed more than 20,000 performances in all.

An Associate of the Societe Nationale des Beaux Arts, Marc Camoletti became a Chevalier de la Legion d'Honeur – one of France's highest honours. He died in 2003.

MUSIC USE NOTE

Licensees are solely responsible for obtaining formal written permission from copyright owners to use copyrighted music in the performance of this play and are strongly cautioned to do so. If no such permission is obtained by the licensee, then the licensee must use only original music that the licensee owns and controls. Licensees are solely responsible and liable for all music clearances and shall indemnify the copyright owners of the play(s) and their licensing agent, Samuel French, against any costs, expenses, losses and liabilities arising from the use of music by licensees. Please contact the appropriate music licensing authority in your territory for the rights to any incidental music.

IMPORTANT BILLING AND CREDIT REQUIREMENTS

If you have obtained performance rights to this title, please refer to your licensing agreement for important billing and credit requirements.

All producers of *Boeing-Boeing* must give credit to the Author of the Play in all programmes distributed in connection with performances of the Play, and in all instances in which the title of the Play appears for the purposes of advertising, publicizing or otherwise exploiting the Play and/or a production. The name of the Author must appear on a separate line on which no other name appears, immediately following the title, and must appear in size of type not less than fifty per cent of the size of the title type. In addition the following credit must be given in all programmes and publicity information distributed in association with this piece:

BOEING-BOEING

By Marc Camoletti

Translated by Beverley Cross and Francis Evans

The translators' names to be no greater than 75% of the size afforded the author.

BOEING-BOEING

Original version presented at the Apollo Theatre, London, on February 20th, 1962, by John Gale in association with Jack Minister, with the following cast:

JANET	Carole Shelley
BERNARD	Patrick Cargill
BERTHA	Carmel McSharry
ROBERT	David Tomlinson
JACQUELINE	Andrée Melly
JUDITH	Jane Downs

Directed by Jack Minster
Designed by Hutchinson Scott
Costumes by Joan Littlewood
Production Stage Manager: Grimmond Henderson

This version presented at the Comedy Theatre on February 15th, 2007, by Sonia Friedman Productions, ACT Productions, Matthew Byam Shaw, Robert G. Bartner, and Bob Boyett, with the following cast:

GLORIA	Tamzin Outhwaite
BERNARD	Roger Allam
BERTHA	Frances de la Tour
ROBERT	Mark Rylance
GABRIELLA	Daisy Beaumont
GRETCHEN	Michelle Gomez

Directed by Matthew Warchus
Designed by Rob Howell
Lighting designed by Hugh Vanstone
Sound designed by Simon Baker
Original music by Claire van Kampen
Production Stage Manager: Patrick Molony

CHARACTERS

GLORIA, an American air hostess
BERNARD, a Parisian bachelor
BERTHA, Bernard's housekeeper
ROBERT, a friend of Bernard's
GABRIELLA, an Italian air hostess
GRETCHEN, a German air hostess

SYNOPSIS OF SCENES

The action of the play takes place in Bernard's flat, near Orly Airport, in Paris.

ACT I   Morning
ACT II   Afternoon
ACT III   Evening

Time—1960s

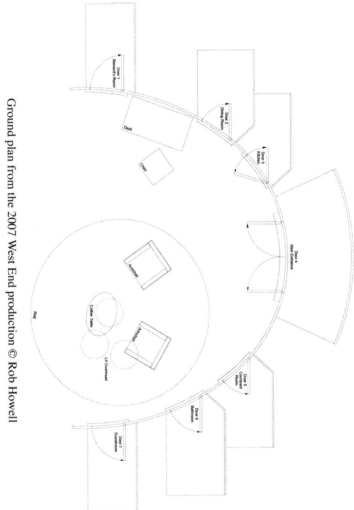

Ground plan from the 2007 West End production © Rob Howell

Door 1
Bernard's Room

Door 2
Dining Room

Door 3
Kitchen

Door 4
Main Entrance

Door 5
Courtyard Room

Door 6
Bathroom

Door 7
Guestroom

Desk

Chair

Armchair

Armchair

Coffee Table

LX Overhead

Rug

ACT I

BERNARD's *flat, morning.*

There are two armchairs, a coffee table, a desk with a globe on it and a chair at the desk.

BERNARD *and* GLORIA *are breakfasting.* GLORIA *has an American accent.*

GLORIA Bernard, darling, do you think I've time to eat another pancake?

BERNARD *(looking at his watch)* I should think so – if you hurry. *(He goes to door 3 and calls)* Bertha!

GLORIA I adore pancakes for breakfast, don't you?

BERNARD Not especially.

GLORIA But back home, all our dieticians agree that a big breakfast prevents day-long neurosis.

BERTHA *enters from door 3.*

BERTHA Did you call, monsieur?

BERNARD Another pancake, Bertha.

BERTHA For mademoiselle?

GLORIA Please, Bertie.

BERTHA And more of that "black stuff" to pour over it?

GLORIA Yes, please. But it's not "black stuff," it's molasses – very good for the complexion.

BERTHA Well, I don't know what it's for, but I suppose it's all right. I don't like the look of it myself, but then I'm not here to reform the world.

BERNARD Well, that's a relief. So, just get busy on the pancake.

BERTHA Right. But don't blame me if it makes her ill.

BERNARD Are you going to eat it?

BERTHA No.

BERNARD So, there's no need to argue about it. Just hurry up– Mademoiselle Gloria hasn't got much time.

GLORIA Please, Bertie, do hurry. I shall miss my plane.

BERTHA All right. I'm going. But it isn't easy, you know.

BERNARD What? What? What is it now?

BERTHA Nothing...nothing...

  BERTHA *exits, door 3.*

GLORIA That woman's always in such a bad mood.

BERNARD Is she?

GLORIA It's getting annoying.

BERNARD No. It's just her way. Don't worry about it.

GLORIA I *do* worry. If it goes on like this we'll just have to get rid of her, honey.

BERNARD Whatever for?

GLORIA I don't think she likes me.

BERNARD Now, darling, of course she likes you. It's just all this food you eat. It seems to upset her. It gives her a kind of indirect indigestion.

GLORIA What time is it, darling?

BERNARD Between twenty and a quarter to ten.

GLORIA I don't know – when I'm with you it just whistles by.

BERNARD It's sweet of you to say so.

GLORIA It's true. Is it the same for you?

BERNARD Of course.

GLORIA And does it drag when I'm away?

BERNARD Terribly. Never-ending.

BERTHA *enters with a pancake and molasses.*

BERTHA Mademoiselle's pancake and black stuff.

GLORIA How marvellous. Thank you, Bertie.

BERTHA And is that the lot?

BERNARD No. Some more coffee for me, please, Bertha, and another orange juice for you, darling?

GLORIA No, darling. Truly. I've had enough.

BERTHA Well, thank the Lord for that!

BERTHA *exits, door 3.*

GLORIA You see – she doesn't like me.

BERNARD Darling!

GLORIA She doesn't. Whenever I get home she's always on edge. While I'm here, she's kind of OK. But when it's time to go, she's downright hostile.

BERNARD Well, she's sad you're going.

GLORIA Because I'm your fiancée?

BERNARD Of course.

GLORIA Oh. And if I was here all the time, she'd be all right?

BERNARD Absolutely! Then we'd all be happy.

GLORIA I'd better get dressed quickly, or I'll miss the plane.

BERNARD That would never do.

GLORIA No, it would be terrible.

BERNARD Terrible. Tell me, darling, when do you get back?

GLORIA Well – it's Saturday today. I'll be in New York at 17:08, then San Francisco – but straight there and straight back.

BERNARD And when will you be back here in Paris?

GLORIA We arrive back in Paris Monday evening. And off again on Wednesday.

BERNARD Monday. Monday. Monday. *(Taking out a notebook and pen)* What time on Monday, darling?

GLORIA 18:30 local time.

BERNARD Excellent. So whatever happens in San Francisco, you'll be back in Paris on Monday?

GLORIA That's right.

BERNARD Good. Good. Good. Good. Good.

GLORIA It's so sweet how you always have to write it down.

BERNARD So I don't get it mixed up.

GLORIA Get what mixed up?

BERNARD My arrangements. My business arrangements. I'm a busy man. I've got work to do. I want to make sure that it's all done by the time you get back here so I can spend Monday to Wednesday with you.

GLORIA You're a genius.

BERNARD I know – it's lovely, isn't it? Now hadn't you better rush?

GLORIA You want to get rid of me?

BERNARD Darling, of course I hate to see you go. But time passes. Planes take off.

   BERTHA *enters with coffee.*

BERTHA Here's your coffee.

BERNARD Thank you, Bertha.

GLORIA Bertie, dear? Will you do me a favour?

BERTHA Depends.

GLORIA It's Mr Bernard. Will you take good care of him till I get back on Monday?

BERTHA I'll do my best. But he's a big boy now, you know.

GLORIA Yes, but they're all just kids at heart.

BERTHA I don't know about that. There aren't too many like monsieur. He's in a class of his own.

BERNARD Yes. Yes. Very good. That'll do, Bertha.

GLORIA See how much she appreciates you, darling?

BERTHA Oh, I spend my life appreciating monsieur.

BERNARD Well, could you appreciate me somewhere else?

BERTHA She asked me a question and I answered it.

BERNARD And we're all very grateful.

GLORIA Well, don't appreciate him too much. You could end up falling in love with him, and I'll be very jealous.

BERTHA I doubt it'll come to that.

BERNARD Mercifully. And you'd better hurry, darling.

GLORIA I'll go and get dressed.

GLORIA *exits, door 1.*

BERNARD What's for lunch?

BERTHA The American's flying out?

BERNARD Yes. Well?

BERTHA I'm waiting for my orders. Monsieur has his timetables. And the menus change according to the timetables. All the time! They change. They change round all the time.

BERNARD All right. Take it easy. Now then, Mademoiselle Gabriella will be here for lunch.

BERTHA Ah! Well, that's all right then. Think I can cope with that one. But it isn't easy you know. I find it very difficult to keep track of them all. I don't know how you manage it. It isn't easy.

BERNARD I know it isn't easy. You don't have to keep reminding me.

BERTHA Well, as long as you appreciate me. That's all I ask, just a little appreciation. So what do you want for lunch?

BERNARD You're the cook. You please yourself.

BERTHA Mademoiselle Gabriella? What about saltimbocca alla romana?

BERNARD We had a saltimbocca last Saturday.

BERTHA Of course we did. Mademoiselle Gabriella was here last Saturday. She liked it. She told me so.

BERNARD All right, you win. Saltimbocca alla romana.

BERTHA And what about dinner? A nice roast? Lamb, perhaps?

BERNARD Roast lamb? Yes, excellent.

BERTHA With olives?

BERNARD *(getting his notebook out)* Yes – er, no, no, wait a minute. Can't be done.

BERTHA No olives?

BERNARD No. No roast lamb either. Near thing that, Bertha. You see it's Mademoiselle Gabriella for lunch, but it's Mademoiselle Gretchen for dinner. She arrives at 19.06.

BERTHA I see. No need to say any more. No roast lamb. Back to sauerkraut and frankfurters.

BERNARD I'm afraid so. Sorry about that.

BERTHA Just one thing after another. I don't know.

> **BERTHA** *exits, door 3.*

> **GLORIA** *enters in her TWA uniform.*

GLORIA Darling, is the clock in our room right?

BERNARD I don't know, darling – but it's almost ten o'clock.

GLORIA Then I've just time to do my nails.

BERNARD Do your nails! But you have to be at the airport by eleven, darling.

GLORIA I can spare two minutes.

BERNARD Don't blame me if the traffic's thick and the lift gets stuck. I really think you ought to hurry.

GLORIA *takes out a nail file from her shoulder bag.*

GLORIA Oh, stop fussing. Darling, I can't tell you how happy I am right now.

BERNARD Why, because you're going?

GLORIA No. Don't be silly. No, I'm happy because they're going to transfer me to a new aircraft.

BERNARD Really?

GLORIA Brand new. The Super-Boeing. It's just fantastic. Delta wings and four Rolls-Royce turbo-jets. And do you know, darling, each jet has a thrust of nineteen thousand pounds.

BERNARD Oh, that's interesting.

GLORIA You bet it's interesting, and especially for us.

BERNARD Darling, I know you take your work seriously, but I can't see what a thrust of nineteen thousand pounds has to do with me.

GLORIA But it'll make the journey so much faster, darling. So, I'll be here more often and we can spend more time together.

BERNARD I see.

GLORIA You don't seem very pleased.

BERNARD Oh! But of course I'm pleased, darling. Very pleased. No point in getting too excited. I mean, you're not transferring tomorrow, are you?

GLORIA Not tomorrow. But soon, very soon.

BERNARD Good.

There's a ring at the front door, door 4.

BERTHA *enters, door 3.*

Good. Excellent, and if I wanted to be sure of that transfer, I'd make certain of catching this plane. And if you want to get to Orly by eleven, you'll have to go now.

BERTHA He's quite right, you know. Better safe than sorry, eh, monsieur?

BERNARD Absolutely.

GLORIA I'm off across the world. Leaving my little French home behind me. All ready to welcome me when I come back.

BERNARD You'll find nothing changed, darling.

GLORIA I hope not.

BERTHA There's a Monsieur Castin to see you, monsieur.

BERNARD Castin? Castin? I don't know anyone called Castin. Oh! Robert. But of course! Robert Castin. Show him in!

BERTHA *exits, door 4.*

Why, we are old friends! We were at school together. Dear old Robert. Haven't seen him for ages.

BERTHA *enters with* **ROBERT.**

Robert, my dear fellow!

ROBERT *laughs.*

You! Here in Paris. I can hardly believe it. How are you?

ROBERT I'm fine, how are you?

BERNARD I'm fine. How are you?

ROBERT I'm fine. How are you?

BERNARD Bloody Robert!

ROBERT Bloody Bernard!

BERTHA Bloody marvellous!

    BERTHA *exits, door 3.*

ROBERT I say, I'm not interrupting anything, am I?

BERNARD Of course not. An old friend like you. And it must be ten years or more since we met.

ROBERT Eleven years, eight months.

BERNARD Whatever it was, it was much too long. It's good to see you.

ROBERT Me too. Much too long.

GLORIA Bernard!

BERNARD Oh, sorry. An old friend of mine. Robert Castin.

GLORIA How do you do?

ROBERT Delighted.

BERNARD Gloria Hawkins. American by birth, and air hostess by profession.

ROBERT My congratulations, Miss Hawkins.

BERNARD TWA, as you can see.

ROBERT And to TWA.

GLORIA But Bernard, darling, you've forgotten the most important bit.

BERNARD Oh really? What bit?

GLORIA That we're engaged, honey.

BERNARD Of course. Robert – this is my fiancée.

ROBERT Congratulations all round then. Especially you, Bernard. You're a lucky fellow.

BERNARD Isn't she gorgeous?

ROBERT Gorgeous.

GLORIA And your friend, Bernard, is sweet. So we're all lovely. Are you engaged, Robert?

ROBERT No. No, not yet. I come from Aix, you see, and in the provinces things are much quieter, much quieter.

BERNARD Much.

GLORIA But there are a lot of pretty girls in the South.

ROBERT Oh yes. Of course. But I haven't found one yet. So I will have to fall back on a Parisian. But, anyway, you can't be interested in the story of my life. I'm in the way. I'll come back another time.

GLORIA Not at all. Besides, I'm just off.

BERNARD And about time too, darling.

ROBERT Are you sure? You're not going just because of me?

GLORIA Of course not. But it's such a pity. You're the first friend of Bernard's I've ever met. He's such a secretive man. He hides them all away somewhere.

BERNARD Not at all. The fellow lives in Aix. It's not next door, you know.

GLORIA Are you going to stay in Paris?

ROBERT I have to. I'm up here on business, you see.

GLORIA Wonderful! Then we're bound to meet again.

ROBERT I shall look forward to that.

GLORIA And you can look after Bernard for me while I'm away.

ROBERT If you say so.

BERNARD Darling, if you don't go soon you won't get back anywhere!

GLORIA Don't rush me. Besides, I've got to give you just one more kiss.

BERNARD *(to* **ROBERT***)* Excuse us.

ROBERT Please. Go ahead. Don't mind me. *(He turns to the mirror)*

GLORIA *and* **BERNARD** *embrace.*

GLORIA I adore you.

BERNARD Me too.

GLORIA Goodbye, Mr Castin.

ROBERT Goodbye.

GLORIA You're a darling. An absolute darling.

BERNARD You too.

GLORIA See you Monday.

BERNARD 18:30 – local time.

GLORIA 'Bye now.

GLORIA *blows* **BERNARD** *a kiss and exits, door 4.*

ROBERT You rascal! I must say you've done yourself very well. That's a marvellous girl – lovely!

BERNARD Yes. She's pretty good, isn't she?

ROBERT Much better than that. If I can find myself something half as good I'll be a happy man.

BERNARD Well, let's have a quick drink shall we? Whisky?

ROBERT Anything you like. What a lovely girl. And what a fantastic view you've got from up here, Bernard. You can see all Paris. *(He approaches the forestage and surveys the auditorium)*

BERNARD It's all right.

ROBERT Are you still in the architect business?

BERNARD Still at it – you know. It's good to see you again, Robert, it really is. So, what brings you to Paris?

ROBERT Well, you always said, "Come and see me when I'm fixed up in Paris," and here you are, all fixed up. And here am I.

BERNARD Dear old Robert.

ROBERT And if you give me the address of your estate agent, I'm going to fix myself up too, Bernard – I want a flat just like this. Same layout, same wonderful view. I need a flat because I'm going to get married.

BERNARD You're not!

ROBERT I am.

BERNARD Who are you engaged to?

ROBERT No one, not yet. But I know a girl, well, we're vaguely acquainted, you see. A charming girl. I haven't actually asked her yet, but I should think it'll be all right. I'd like to get married; I can't go on living alone much longer.

BERNARD You look perfectly all right to me.

ROBERT Of course I'm all right. So are you for that matter.

BERNARD You're still young.

ROBERT Well, so are you. You're in good shape, you're young, and you're going to get married.

BERNARD I certainly am not.

ROBERT Not? But I thought – well, this charming American girl, just now – she said you were engaged. Wait a minute, you agreed with her. I heard you.

BERNARD Well, if you want to be technical I suppose you could say we were engaged. Yes.

ROBERT Then you're going to get married.

BERNARD No.

ROBERT Bernard, you're always doing this to me. Look. If you're engaged, you're going to get married. It's not only technical, it's logical! Isn't it?

BERNARD It is not. And anyway, why do you want to get married? Do you love this girl?

ROBERT I don't know. I'm not raving mad about her. I don't write poems or refuse to eat or any of that sort of thing. But it would be nice. I mean, think of the social advantages. They're not to be sneezed at, are they?

BERNARD I can't think of *one*. Still if you must get married, get married my way.

ROBERT Your way?

BERNARD Polygamy.

ROBERT Polygamy?

BERNARD It's the ideal life – pleasure, variety...it's fabulous. You ought to try it!

ROBERT Polygamy? You mean lots of wives?

BERNARD Not wives, fiancées. You have all the advantages of married life with none of the drawbacks. Fiancées are much more friendly than wives. And you don't need all that many. I do very well with three.

ROBERT Three?

BERNARD Three is the ideal number. Less than three would be monotonous. More than three would be terribly tiring. Three is the dream.

ROBERT But it's immoral.

BERNARD Immoral? But my dear Robert, they all think they're the only one. *They* don't think it's immoral, so why should I? You've all the pleasures of the harem, but right here in the middle of Paris.

ROBERT They say you have your hands full with one woman, but three!

BERNARD Not me.

ROBERT Three fiancées?

BERNARD The whole secret is order. I am organized – beautifully organized.

ROBERT But, Bernard – isn't it incredibly complicated?

BERNARD Not in the least. All you need is a timetable.

ROBERT A timetable?

BERNARD A special kind of timetable. An airline timetable.

ROBERT What, to get out in a hurry?

BERNARD Not at all. Look – here it is. *(He produces a book of timetables)* The timetables of all the major routes – all in one volume.

ROBERT One volume.

BERNARD You understand?

ROBERT Yes.

BERNARD You don't really, do you?

ROBERT No.

BERNARD But it's so simple, a child could see it. Someone just had to think of it. My three fiancées are all air hostesses.

ROBERT All three?

BERNARD Yes.

ROBERT Air hostesses?

BERNARD All three.

ROBERT Don't be barmy! Three air hostesses?

BERNARD That's the trick. And they're all fantastic girls.

ROBERT Fantastic? If TWA was anything to go by, they're devastating.

BERNARD And the other two are just as good. Of course they are. You see, they're all tried and tested.

ROBERT They've been what?

BERNARD They're hand-picked through the admissions procedures of the different companies. In every respect! Physical, moral, intellectual. So, all the work's done for me. I'm choosing from a pool which has already been super-sifted. Not bad, is it?

ROBERT Yes. Yes. Not bad.

BERNARD The only thing is that I have to pick them from different airlines and with different routes – so they don't meet, you see.

ROBERT Ah, yes. All right. It all seems very well in theory, but I'd be curious to see how it works out in practice.

BERNARD And you will, couldn't be simpler. Gloria, my American, the one you've seen... Well, she takes off in ten minutes...and in a quarter of an hour Gabriella lands.

ROBERT Gabriella?

BERNARD My Italian. A beautiful kitten – she'll be here for lunch.

ROBERT Lunch? That's cutting it a bit close, isn't it? I mean the other one was only just here for breakfast.

BERNARD Yes, it is a bit touch and go today. But today's an exception. Gabriella is in transit. Normally it's perfectly straightforward. Two days Gloria, two days Gabriella, and two days Gretchen.

ROBERT Gretchen?

BERNARD That's my German.

ROBERT That's your German. It's an international harem.

BERNARD Exactly. Look. *(Indicating the globe)* Gretchen gets in from Stuttgart this evening; at the same time, Gabriella will be on her way to Caracas, and Gloria will be in San Francisco – you see the beauty of it?

ROBERT Perpetual motion.

BERNARD Pure mathematics. Everything designed, organized, regulated and working to the precise second. The earth revolves on its axis and my fiancées wheel above the earth. One this way. One that. One towards the sun. One towards the moon. And eventually they all, in turn, come home to me. It's geometrical, my dear Robert. So precise as to be almost poetic. And here I live in the middle of a perfect example of polygamous family life. I don't just change women, I change my diet as well. It's like living in a restaurant. So there's no chance of ever getting bored. Either in the dining room or the bedroom. It's perfect.

ROBERT Remarkable! Quite remarkable.

BERNARD Things are going a bit awry with Gloria. She does eat the most extraordinary things. Apart from that, though, flawless. I tell you, it's a dream.

ROBERT But Bernard, how do you find them?

BERNARD I've a friend who works in the travel agency at Orly Airport and he knows all the air hostesses. They talk to him. They tell him their secrets – and if he thinks they might be lonely, well, he introduces them to me.

ROBERT Does he really?

BERNARD He might help you. After all he's a friend of mine, I'm a friend of yours. I'll give him a ring.

ROBERT Oh no! This sort of thing's not for me. No. I'm not the type. It's all right for you. You've got the talent, the flair.

BERNARD That's got nothing to do with it. The timetables are the timetables. You just have to follow them.

ROBERT No! No! Not now – I'll have to think about it for a couple of years. But what happens if they get switched to a different route?

BERNARD Impossible. It's all been worked out. It's all on a schedule. Mathematical – marvellous!

BERTHA *enters, door 3.*

BERTHA *(indicating* ROBERT*)* Will your friend be here for lunch?

ROBERT No. No.

BERNARD Yes.

ROBERT I don't want to upset your arrangements.

BERNARD You're going to eat with us, and you are going to stay – till you've found yourself a flat in Paris.

BERTHA He's going to stay?

ROBERT I'm going to stay.

BERNARD He is.

BERTHA And where?

BERNARD Where do you think? Here of course.

BERTHA Which room?

BERNARD Whichever he likes.

BERTHA Oh, great, whichever he likes.

BERTHA *exits, door 3.*

BERNARD Where's your luggage?

ROBERT I left it at the station.

BERNARD Well, you can trot along and fetch it later.

BERTHA *enters.*

BERTHA What time do you want to eat?

BERNARD As soon as Gabriella gets here.

BERTHA That's a lot of help!

BERNARD What difference does it make to you?

BERTHA You don't just rub two sticks together, you know.

BERNARD I'll let you know.

BERTHA Mind you do. We can't all make it up as we go along.

BERNARD All right, Bertha. Thank you, thank you, thank you.

> **BERTHA** *goes to the door and turns.*

BERTHA *(taking a letter from her pocket)* Yes. And there's a letter for the American. From America.

BERNARD Oh really? Give it to me.

> **BERTHA** *gives him the letter.*

BERTHA She won't be able to read it till she gets back, obviously.

BERNARD Obviously.

BERTHA So you'll let me know.

BERNARD What?

BERTHA What time you want to eat?

BERNARD Yes of course I'll tell you, but I'm sure Gabriella won't be long. She must be touching down about now, especially if she had the wind behind her.

BERTHA Right, let's hope Mademoiselle Gabriella has the wind behind her, then. Lunch is on its way.

> **BERTHA** *exits, door 3.*

BERNARD That woman!

ROBERT Is she always like this?

BERNARD Yes, she is, yes, to be honest, when I took the flat she was already here so I kept her on, she's fine. It's all this coming and going. She has to keep changing her style of cooking, and I think it upsets her.

ROBERT Well, I can understand that. It's enough to rattle anybody. All this traffic. One taking off, one landing, one already airborne. Isn't it at all possible that two of your fiancées might find themselves wanting to spend the night in Paris at the same time?

BERNARD No, impossible – because of the timetables. And even if it did happen that one girl landed when another who was supposed to be taking off didn't take off, well I'd stay with the one who wasn't taking off and spend the night in Saint-Germain-en-Laye or somewhere like that.

ROBERT Yes, right, but meanwhile, what would be happening with the one who'd landed?

BERNARD She'd come here.

ROBERT She'd come back here.

BERNARD Yes, even if Bertha is out, she has her own key.

ROBERT She has her own key?

BERNARD Yes. They all have their own keys.

ROBERT They all have their own keys.

BERNARD Oh yes, and Bertha would tell her I've had to go out of town on business. Next morning, I take Saint-Germain to the airport, see her aboard a plane, wave my handkerchief, and hurry back here into the arms of the other. No panic. No problem.

ROBERT No panic, no problem. But the whole thing's a bit – well. Don't you love any of them?

BERNARD But I adore them. I can't be without any of them! I love them so much that if one asks me for something – a tiny present, say – well, I go out and buy three tiny presents! I can't bear to spoil one without spoiling the other two!

ROBERT Yes, that's very kind of you but I'm not convinced. I'll settle for a quiet little marriage with just one woman.

Everything ordinary but everything calm, with all the social advantages.

BERNARD You're wrong, you know. It's the perfect life. Oh! Just one detail – my three fiancées have the same initial for their Christian names. "G" for Gabriella, Gretchen, Gloria. It's not essential, but it does help. Initials on presents, slips of the tongue – all that sort of thing.

BERTHA *enters.*

What do you want now?

BERTHA I don't want anything. I'm just doing my job, that's all. But now America's gone, I've got to change the room for Italy.

ROBERT She thinks of everything!

BERTHA That's why I'm here, monsieur. That's my function, you see. Without me, I don't know what would happen to Monsieur Bernard – with all his complications. If Mademoiselle Gabriella is only in transit, monsieur; I mean, perhaps I needn't clear up too thoroughly.

BERNARD No. Just tidy up and change the photographs.

BERTHA And I'll make up the room properly after she's gone, before Germany gets here.

BERNARD Fine, thank you, Bertha. Perfect.

BERTHA If you say so. It's just one chore after another, if you ask me.

BERTHA *exits, door 1.*

ROBERT Change the photographs. She must be invaluable.

BERNARD Yes she's always complaining but she does know the routine.

BERTHA *enters.*

BERTHA Done.

BERNARD Thank you. And you haven't forgotten anything?

BERTHA I don't think so.

BERNARD She'll be here in a matter of seconds.

ROBERT That's cutting it a bit fine.

BERTHA Yes, today's a bit touch and go.

BERNARD Precision is the key.

BERTHA Precisely. All I know, monsieur, is that every time one of the ladies is in transit, then everything gets faster.

BERTHA exits, door 3.

GABRIELLA enters, door 4, wearing the Alitalia uniform.

See what I mean?

GABRIELLA Darling!

BERNARD Gabriella! Darling!

They kiss.

Darling, an old friend, Robert Castin.

GABRIELLA Oh, *ciao.*

ROBERT From Aix.

BERNARD We were at school together.

GABRIELLA How do you do, Robert?

ROBERT How do you do?

BERNARD He's just got in.

ROBERT I just dropped in to see Bernard's photographs. I mean, we're old friends and we haven't met at the same time for ages. He told me you were next, you were coming, that he was waiting for you – you're sure I'm not in the way?

GABRIELLA Of course not. I'm delighted – really I am. You're the first friend of Bernard's I've ever met. He never introduces me to anybody. He's such an old hermit.

ROBERT A hermit. Yes. I suppose he is.

GABRIELLA Bernard, darling, fix me a drink, will you?

BERNARD Yes, of course.

GABRIELLA I'm worn out. You've no idea how good it is to see the sun – it was ghastly over there. You know we were held up in Helsinki?

BERNARD Really?

GABRIELLA The Met people forecast a storm, but it was more like a hurricane! Miserable visibility, wind all over the place, and the cloud ceiling was right down to four hundred feet. Imagine it! And fog, and so cold! It only cleared over the Channel – but anyway, I'm back and that's the main thing. Have you behaved yourself, darling?

BERNARD Me? What do you think?

GABRIELLA There's a good boy. Has he told you that we're going to be married?

ROBERT No. Yes. He did say you were engaged.

BERNARD And I also told him you were beautiful. Isn't that what I told you, Robert?

ROBERT Yes, you did. Perpetual motion, pure mathematics. Like a beautiful German! A beautiful kitten! He said so many complimentary things...

GABRIELLA And are you disappointed?

ROBERT Yes. No. On the contrary. He wasn't anywhere near the truth.

GABRIELLA I like your friend, Bernard darling. He must join us for lunch.

BERNARD I've already invited him.

GABRIELLA Wonderful.

ROBERT I couldn't do that.

GABRIELLA Now, not a word. You must do as you're told.

BERNARD And I've also asked him to stay here till he finds himself a flat in Paris.

GABRIELLA Well done. You'll be company for him. He's always telling me he's so lonely and complaining that I abandon him for too long.

BERNARD You're so right, darling. I'm absolutely lost! When you're not here, I'm all alone.

ROBERT You poor chap!

BERNARD That's love for you.

GABRIELLA You're marvellous. I'll just clean up and then we'll eat. I've just three hours before we take off for Caracas! And that reminds me. It's on.

BERNARD What is?

GABRIELLA They're putting the Super-Caravelli on our route. She's so fast, I'll be able to see you more often.

BERNARD Oh good. That's great. Really great. You must remember to let me have the new timetables.

GABRIELLA Of course, darling. *Uno minuto.*

GABRIELLA *goes into the bathroom, door 6.*

ROBERT If these planes are going to go faster and faster, your mathematics aren't going to add up.

BERNARD Oh! These things take time. They won't all happen at once.

ROBERT I must congratulate you, Bernard. I was trying to work out which is the prettier, but I can't decide.

BERNARD Fortunately, it doesn't concern you. They're both engaged.

ROBERT They're both engaged!

The telephone rings. **BERNARD** *picks it up.*

BERNARD Hello – yes? Yes, I'll hold. *(He whispers to* **ROBERT***)* It's Gretchen – my German.

ROBERT But you've got one in there.

BERNARD *(on the phone)* Hello darling! ...You are going to be back at 23:00 instead of 19:00. What a shame... Yes, I've got that... You'll do what? And you'll eat on the plane... Yes, of course, darling. That's great... 23:00 hours then.

BERTHA *enters.*

BERTHA Monsieur Bernard.

BERNARD *(on the telephone)* Yes, darling. Love you...yes. *(He replaces the telephone)* Ah, Bertha. Cancel the frankfurters.

BERTHA Germany's delayed?

BERNARD Stuck in Stuttgart.

BERTHA But I've bought the sauerkraut.

BERNARD Too bad.

BERTHA Oh, good God! This is no life for a maid. *(She starts to go out and then comes back)* And another thing—

BERNARD Well?

BERTHA There's something I have to tell you.

BERNARD Out with it then.

BERTHA I've forgotten what it is now. It's all this coming and going.

BERNARD It'll come back to you.

BERTHA Then I'll come back.

BERTHA *exits, door 3.*

BERNARD Yes. That's right.

GABRIELLA *enters.*

GABRIELLA Was that the telephone?

BERNARD Yes, darling.

GABRIELLA It wasn't for me?

BERNARD No – why? Were you expecting someone?

GABRIELLA They may make a change in the flights – because of the weather.

ROBERT Change in the flight?

GABRIELLA Yes, they've already cancelled the VC 10 to Beirut.

ROBERT It's fascinating to hear how all this aeronautics works.

BERNARD Yes. They won't change your flight, will they darling?

GABRIELLA No. Instead of leaving at 15:00, we'll take off at 16:00.

BERNARD Oh good.

GABRIELLA Why do you say "oh good"?

BERNARD Did I say "oh good"?

ROBERT Yes, you definitely said "oh good."

BERNARD Well, I said "oh good" – because I instantly realized it would mean an extra hour with you.

GABRIELLA Oh! *Sei bello!* So who was it, then?

BERNARD Who was who?

GABRIELLA On the telephone. It wasn't another woman?

BERNARD How on earth could it be another woman? You know I adore you. Don't I, Robert?

ROBERT Of course you do.

GABRIELLA Cross your heart?

BERNARD But Gabriella! No, really, you mustn't be so silly. It upsets me.

GABRIELLA All right. So you can tell me.

BERNARD Tell you what?

GABRIELLA Who it was.

BERNARD Who was what?

GABRIELLA On the telephone.

BERNARD Oh. On the telephone! It was a wrong number.

ROBERT Yes, that's it. A wrong number.

   GABRIELLA *sees the letter.*

GABRIELLA And what's this?

BERNARD What's what?

GABRIELLA This letter. It's addressed to Miss Gloria Hawkins.

BERNARD Letter? I don't know anything about a letter.

GABRIELLA It's here. On your desk.

BERNARD Nothing to do with me, darling. I've been talking to Robert.

ROBERT I only just got here. I only just arrived.

BERNARD All the time.

GABRIELLA And it just appeared from nowhere?

   BERTHA *enters.*

BERTHA I've just remembered what it was.

GABRIELLA Morning, Bertha, how are you?

BERTHA Much the same, mademoiselle.

BERNARD What is it you've just remembered, Bertha?

BERTHA Lunch is ready.

GABRIELLA *Grazie.* Oh, Bertha! What's this? *(She holds up the letter)*

BERTHA A letter.

GABRIELLA I can see that. But it's addressed to a Miss Gloria Hawkins. Do you know her?

BERTHA Never heard of her.

GABRIELLA Well, what's it doing here?

BERNARD Well, Bertha?

BERTHA Ah! Yes! I've just remembered. The old fool downstairs – the concierge – he muttered something about me taking a letter belonging to someone else in the block. By mistake, you see.

BERNARD There. Quite simple, really. Everything sorted out.

ROBERT Yes. Everything explained – really well, too.

BERTHA My mistake all along. I'm sorry about that, mademoiselle. Sorry, monsieur.

BERNARD We all make mistakes, Bertha.

BERTHA If you'd like to give it back to me, mademoiselle, I'll slip it downstairs after lunch. Well, it's all ready when you want it. Lunch, that is.

GABRIELLA *Grazie*, Bertha. You're a marvel. You run the flat as if it were your own.

BERTHA That's exactly right, mademoiselle. But it isn't easy.

BERTHA *exits, door 3.*

BERNARD It isn't easy, my darling, but we do our best. You arrive, you wash your hands, have a drink, and – hey presto! – lunch is ready. All you have to do is to sit down and enjoy it.

ROBERT Family life. It's a wonderful thing.

GABRIELLA You're right, Robert dear. You ought to try it. Copy Bernard. Find yourself a fiancée.

ROBERT Yes, as a matter of fact – I've been thinking about it – quite seriously.

GABRIELLA *Mio dio.* It's already twenty-five to. We must hurry. Let's have lunch.

GABRIELLA *exits, door 2.*

BERNARD So, you see how it's done?

ROBERT Yes, yes wonderful.

BERNARD Yes, right, come and eat, Italian cuisine today.

ROBERT Bernard, these air hostess uniforms. You know, they're so beautifully cut. They're really very handsome.

BERNARD Handsome? They're dazzling! Irresistible!

ROBERT Bloody Bernard!

BERNARD Bloody Robert!

BERNARD *and* ROBERT *exit laughing after* GABRIELLA.

Curtain.

ACT II

Afternoon.

The telephone rings.

BERTHA *enters and answers the phone.*

BERTHA Hello. Yes, that's right. No, he isn't here at the moment. It's Bertha. Oh! It's you, Mademoiselle Gretchen! You're in Paris? Already! Oh you are early. Yes, oh I see, right, right. Well, then, see you later. *(She hangs up)*

The doorbell rings.

Oh good God alive, who can that be? All this coming and going. It's no life for a maid, no life for anyone.

BERTHA *exits to answer door 4.*

ROBERT *(offstage)* It's only me.

BERTHA *(offstage)* Oh. It's you, monsieur.

BERTHA *enters.*

ROBERT *enters with cases.*

ROBERT Could you?

BERTHA No, I couldn't.

ROBERT There was a queue a mile long at the station. You do wonder why there are so many people in Paris. It's much more peaceful back at home in Aix.

BERTHA It wouldn't be so crowded in Paris if the people from the provinces didn't keep piling in.

ROBERT No, I suppose not.

BERTHA And what do you want with all these bags? I thought you were only here on business.

ROBERT I always believe in being prepared.

BERTHA I hope you're not going to stay too long.

ROBERT Goodness me! You're not very welcoming to your master's friends, are you?

BERTHA I'm only telling you for your own good. Just you wait and see, people coming and going all the time. You'd have been better off at the station and there'd have been more room for your bags!

ROBERT I'm a guest. I have been invited, you know.

BERTHA It's not a hotel.

ROBERT Everything seems beautifully organized to me.

BERTHA Organized. That's just it. It's too organized. Shall I tell you what I think?

ROBERT Well – I don't know.

BERTHA It's not human! That's what I think. It's all very well for Monsieur Bernard giving out invitations left, right, and centre, but I have to do all the work. What with you and your luggage and now Germany.

ROBERT What about Germany?

BERTHA She's just rung to say she's on her way.

ROBERT Well, that's all right, isn't it? Mademoiselle Gabriella has just taken off.

BERTHA I know, but Germany wants to stay for three days. She just said it to me, thinking it'll be a nice surprise for monsieur.

ROBERT For me?

BERTHA No. For monsieur. My monsieur.

ROBERT You have a monsieur?

BERTHA Of course I have a monsieur.

ROBERT Oh, I see.

BERTHA My boss, I mean.

ROBERT Oh. Right. So, what does it matter if she stays three days?

BERTHA There may be friction... Well, it's nothing to do with me, of course. But Mademoiselle Gloria – that's the American—

ROBERT Yes, I know. I've seen that one.

BERTHA Well, she's due back on Monday.

ROBERT Yes. Well, not to worry. It's only Saturday. Bernard will have plenty of time to work something out. Where shall I put my bags?

BERTHA You put them where you like.

ROBERT crosses to door 7.

Not there, there won't be enough room there.

ROBERT crosses to door 1.

No, not that one. That's monsieur and his wives' bedroom. So, not that one. Over there if you like. *(She indicates door)* It's quieter there on the courtyard. Oh, just make yourself at home.

ROBERT Thank you very much indeed, Bertha. That's very kind of you. *(He crosses to go out door 5)*

BERTHA No, it's not. I'm just doing what I'm told. I've got enough to do, thank you very much, without being kind to all monsieur's guests.

ROBERT If you don't like it here, why don't you change your job?

BERTHA No! New job. New problems. What's the point?

ROBERT Well that's an optimistic view.

BERTHA Look monsieur, I'm a cheerful soul at heart. I like a bit of fun, but this place goes too far. But what can you expect if you're in domestic service? I mean there's no dignity in being a maid.

ROBERT *(carrying a case to door 5)* Right. Well, if you'll excuse me, I'll get settled in.

BERTHA Stick your bags in there. They're in the way here. I'd help you with them myself but when I was a little girl the doctor told my mother – "She's a great trier, your daughter, but not very strong, she must be very careful not to lift anything."

ROBERT Not to lift anything.

    ROBERT *takes the cases off stage, door 5.*

BERTHA So I try to be careful. And when you think about it, the body's not much of a thing, is it? Very feeble. It gets tired. It wears out.

    ROBERT *enters.*

ROBERT That's absolutely true, Bertha.

BERTHA So I let other people wear themselves out.

ROBERT I see what you mean. You are quite a cheerful person at heart, aren't you Bertha?

BERTHA Thank you. You don't often meet people who appreciate a maid's personality, do you?

ROBERT Quite, quite! Right, well, see you later.

BERTHA Oh, has sir had enough of me?

ROBERT No, no. Not at all!

BERTHA Oh yes. You've had enough of me. When people say, "See you later," especially to a maid, it always means they've had enough.

ROBERT No, I assure you.

BERTHA I'm getting on your nerves.

ROBERT Nonsense.

BERTHA Yes. I'm getting on your nerves.

ROBERT You are not getting on my nerves, look...

BERTHA Oh yes. Oh yes. Monsieur Bernard's exactly the same. Always brushing me off. Never wants to talk. But, you know monsieur, conversation is the only thing that separates humans from beasts. If human beings didn't speak they'd be beasts.

ROBERT Uh, yes. Yes, that's right. Beasts.

BERTHA It must be awful to be a beast.

ROBERT Huh!

BERTHA Don't you think?

ROBERT Yes, yes, I suppose. I don't know anything about it.

BERTHA Well, I don't know anything about it, but I'm guessing... I sense it! A beast! What is a beast? Even less than a maid. That just about says it all! It's lucky I'm an optimist. That's what keeps me going.

ROBERT Could I have a bit of ice?

BERTHA No!

ROBERT Why?

BERTHA I'm defrosting the fridge.

ROBERT Oh. Right.

BERTHA So, there's no ice.

ROBERT I'll do without.

BERTHA Well, you'll have to. Is monsieur in business?

ROBERT Yes.

BERTHA Same business as Monsieur Bernard?

ROBERT No.

BERTHA Ah. There are so many different businesses but it's all business, isn't it?

ROBERT That's right.

BERTHA Are you married?

ROBERT No.

BERTHA Perhaps you should be.

ROBERT Why?

BERTHA You're still quite nice.

ROBERT Thank you.

BERTHA But old age is fast approaching.

ROBERT I've got a few good years ahead of me!

BERTHA That's what they all say. You take my advice. You get married while you're still worth it.

ROBERT I intend to, but now I've seen Bernard's set-up, I think I'll wait a bit.

BERTHA That's a mistake. This isn't the life for you, you're not the type. You have to have your wits about you. You have to be in your physical prime.

ROBERT Who says I'm not?

BERTHA Oh no, sir. Oh no! It's obvious, sir, if I may say so, it's obvious to the naked eye.

ROBERT For God's sake! Give me some peace!

BERTHA Very good, monsieur.

ROBERT Honestly! It's too much!

BERTHA Very good, monsieur.

ROBERT Goodbye, Bertha.

BERTHA Goodbye, monsieur.

ROBERT Goodbye!

BERTHA Goodbye.

ROBERT Well. I think I'd better go into the other room.

BERTHA You do what you want.

ROBERT I think I'll have a little rest.

> **ROBERT** *exits, door 5.*

BERTHA They pitch up from the provinces, totally out of their depth.

> **GRETCHEN** *enters. She is in her Lufthansa uniform.*

GRETCHEN Bernard *liebling!* Bertha!

BERTHA Ah, hello Mademoiselle Gretchen. You're here already.

GRETCHEN *Ja.* I came as fast as I could. If you only knew how happy I am to be home.

BERTHA I can see that.

GRETCHEN Herr Bernard isn't in?

BERTHA No, no. He's gone out – on business.

GRETCHEN Oh!

BERTHA But he'll be back in a minute.

GRETCHEN Are you sure?

BERTHA Oh yes. It's nothing very serious. He went out just before you telephoned.

GRETCHEN And is he happy?

BERTHA He's marvellously happy. You know how he looks forward to seeing you.

GRETCHEN Do you think he loves me as much as I love him?

BERTHA Well, now, that I don't know. I mean, how could I know a thing like that?

GRETCHEN Doesn't he talk about me when I'm not here?

BERTHA Oh, yes, he never stops talking about you, but I can't tell you if he loves you as much as you love him, if I don't know how much you love him.

GRETCHEN But Bertha, darling, you know I adore him.

BERTHA Well, that's all right, then. He adores you too.

GRETCHEN And I've got three whole days this time. Isn't that *wunderbar*?

BERTHA *Wunderbar.*

GRETCHEN Herr Bernard will be pleased.

BERTHA I can't wait to see his face.

GRETCHEN You can't realize how marvellous it is to be back. It seems ages since I've seen him. Though I think of him all the time. In Melbourne. In Ankara, in Colombo. I am always dreaming of our little flat, and my little Bernard sitting here all alone thinking of me.

BERTHA It's beautiful.

GRETCHEN And when we're up about nineteen or twenty thousand feet, roaring away at six hundred miles an hour, and if I've nothing special to do, do you know I creep back into the luggage hold.

BERTHA Good heavens above.

GRETCHEN I'm all alone there, you see. And I look out of the porthole and stare at the stars dancing and the moon out there in the sky. And I say to myself that my Bernard is looking at them too. And I feel as though we are looking into each other's eyes across the layers of planets and meteorites and the nebulae. I'm madly romantic, you see.

BERTHA I can see you are. Madly.

GRETCHEN And does he do that too?

BERTHA Do what?

GRETCHEN Stare at the moon while I'm away.

BERTHA Oh, I'm sure he gives it a glance now and then. Mind you I'm not always there when he's doing it.

GRETCHEN No. I suppose he prefers to keep it a secret.

BERTHA And I should hope so. I mean life's complicated enough without dragging in the nebulae.

GRETCHEN But you understand these things, don't you, Bertha? I always like talking to you. You know about life. You're a woman.

BERTHA Well, thank you very much, mademoiselle. I'm more than that, I'm a domestic servant. And believe me, Mademoiselle Gretchen, we domestic servants get to know a great deal. And what we know we keep to ourselves – we never say anything. Mind you, very few people ever ask us.

GRETCHEN Oh, but you're something very special, Bertha.

BERTHA Do you think so?

GRETCHEN I am certain. You're the virgin in the legend of the Grail in the story of the Nibelungen.

BERTHA Well, I've been called worse.

GRETCHEN You're a guardian. You keep me alive in Bernard's thoughts. You keep the flame of love burning in his heart!

BERTHA I do?

GRETCHEN You're like me – capable of great passion.

BERTHA It's very nice of you to say so.

GRETCHEN I love him so much! Every time I come home, I seem to love him more, and every time I go it just tears me to tiny pieces.

BERTHA You're very intense, aren't you?

GRETCHEN I'm worse than that – I'm passion itself.

BERTHA Don't get yourself into a state. Save your passions for Monsieur Bernard. He'll be back soon.

GRETCHEN *Ja. Ja.* You're right. Oh, I have forgotten to buy cigarettes. Would you, could you, would you?

BERTHA Straight away. I'll be back in five minutes.

GRETCHEN You're a darling, Bertha. I'll get settled in while I'm waiting. I'm mad with happiness, Bertha, mad with happiness!

BERTHA And so am I, mademoiselle, so am I!

GRETCHEN goes out through door 1, taking her bag, and closes the door as BERTHA goes out through door 4.

ROBERT enters through door 5.

He goes into the bathroom, door 6, and washes his face. Then he enters with a towel round his shoulders and impersonates BERNARD.

He tries some of BERNARD's aftershave which he accidentally sprays in his eyes. He sits down with the towel over his head to remove the aftershave.

GRETCHEN comes out of door 1 and, not recognizing ROBERT, throws herself at him.

GRETCHEN My love! My darling lover!

ROBERT Oh God!

GRETCHEN Excuse me. Sorry, sorry.

ROBERT No, really. Don't mention it.

GRETCHEN But, oh monsieur, I'm so sorry.

ROBERT No harm done, mademoiselle, on the contrary.

GRETCHEN What are you doing in my flat?

ROBERT Your flat? Don't you mean Bernard's flat?

GRETCHEN If you like. But it's still mine – mine or Bernard's, it's the same thing.

ROBERT I'm an old friend of Bernard's. An old school friend.

GRETCHEN Oh?

ROBERT My name's Robert – I've forgotten my own name. Robert Castin.

GRETCHEN How do you do?

ROBERT How do you do? And you must be Gretchen?

GRETCHEN He's told you about me?

ROBERT Told me! My dear girl, it's Gretchen this, Gretchen that; here a Gretchen, there a Gretchen. It's Gretchen – Gretchen – everywhere.

GRETCHEN How divine!

ROBERT He hardly mentions anybody else.

GRETCHEN But how come you are here when he's not?

ROBERT Well – Bernard's just gone out.

GRETCHEN On business.

ROBERT That's it! Yes – on business. And he told me to wait for him. I just arrived – this morning – you see – from Aix.

GRETCHEN From Aix!

ROBERT Yes.

GRETCHEN It's not true!

ROBERT Oh! Yes, it's true – this afternoon on a train – from Aix.

GRETCHEN But that's marvellous.

ROBERT Yes, I like trains.

GRETCHEN My mother lives in Aix.

ROBERT No really.

GRETCHEN She's lived there for years. Whereabouts do you live in Aix?

ROBERT Near the station. Number twenty-seven.

GRETCHEN It's not true! The Bahnhofstrasse!

ROBERT The Bahnhof what?

GRETCHEN The Bahnhofstrasse.

ROBERT Oh! You mean the station.

GRETCHEN You must know my mother's house. It's on the corner of the Friedenstrasse.

ROBERT The Frieden – what?

GRETCHEN The Friedenstrasse.

ROBERT I don't think I know that one.

GRETCHEN But you must. It's the next street down from the Bahnhofstrasse.

ROBERT Is it?

GRETCHEN Come on! You know it.

ROBERT Know it! I can't even pronounce it.

GRETCHEN Well, you know the corner? Where Napoleon is?

ROBERT The grocer?

GRETCHEN You're not trying. No – Napoleon, the chap on a horse. A statue.

ROBERT A large statue?

GRETCHEN Enormous.

ROBERT I don't know it. No, I assure you. I've lived in Aix all my life. I can show you my papers, I can show you my credentials. My grandfather made olive and sunflower oil, my father did almond oil and I do walnut. Walnut oil I mean. In short, my family have oiled the whole of Provence!

GRETCHEN Provence?

ROBERT Yes. Aix is in Provence, isn't it?

GRETCHEN But I was talking about Aix-la-Chapelle.

ROBERT I was talking about Aix-en-Provence.

GRETCHEN Obviously.

ROBERT So we are both from Aix, but not the same Aix.

GRETCHEN I suppose so. I really am very sorry.

ROBERT It's too disappointing. You would have made a marvellous neighbour.

GRETCHEN You're very kind.

ROBERT Not at all, Mademoiselle—

GRETCHEN Gretchen. You may call me Gretchen, since you're a friend of Bernard's.

ROBERT And I'm Robert Castin.

GRETCHEN I shall call you Robert.

ROBERT Good Gretchen. How do you do?

GRETCHEN How do you do? You won't say anything to Bernard about me kissing you, will you?

ROBERT Only by mistake, unfortunately.

GRETCHEN A mistake yes...but a kiss all the same.

ROBERT Don't worry. I won't say a word. But even if it hadn't been a mistake, I wouldn't have told him anything.

GRETCHEN Thank you, you're a gentleman... But if there hadn't been a mistake I wouldn't have kissed you, so...

ROBERT Yes, and anyway, a mistake like that, well, it doesn't really count, you know. It was so sudden. I've forgotten about it already.

GRETCHEN Didn't it mean anything then?

ROBERT You didn't give me much time. And there was no anticipation and I think that's very important, don't you? So—

GRETCHEN So—?

ROBERT So to ensure my complete silence and my absolute discretion, perhaps you'd better give me another one.

GRETCHEN Another one?

ROBERT Another kiss. I quite liked the first one.

GRETCHEN Because you weren't expecting it... It's the element of surprise.

ROBERT Hmm... Yes...but it could have been a nasty surprise... whereas it was a nice one and I wasn't able to get the full benefit, you see, completely... That's why, if you wouldn't mind doing it again...

GRETCHEN Again?

ROBERT Just once.

GRETCHEN But it would be awful of me to do it again! I'd have no excuse for my mistake this time and I'd regret it for the rest of my life.

ROBERT Let's not exaggerate.

GRETCHEN I see you do not know the German soul.

ROBERT Uh, no...not very well.

GRETCHEN That's why you don't know what the knowledge of good and evil is like.

ROBERT Evil? But when you get married you'll have to kiss all of Bernard's friends.

GRETCHEN Not on the mouth! And anyway, when the bride kisses the friends of the groom, it's in front of her husband. He's there watching.

ROBERT I've never thought that quite fair, have you? There are particular circumstances. Ours, for example.

GRETCHEN I don't see that our case is so special. In fact, I think we should both feel very guilty. We are all alone in my fiancé's flat—

ROBERT Please don't make a tragedy out of it. It's not enormously important.

GRETCHEN Then why are you insisting?

ROBERT Because we're from Aix.

GRETCHEN But not the same Aix. Not the same Aix at all! Aix-la-Chapelle.

ROBERT Aix – Aix – Aix. All you can talk about is Aix. Can't you allow yourself one innocent kiss?

GRETCHEN It would be the second.

ROBERT I didn't count the first. That was just my way of saying hello.

GRETCHEN You really are very incorrigible.

ROBERT You really are very beautiful.

GRETCHEN But I am engaged to Bernard.

ROBERT Exactly. You won't get another chance. And nor will I. If we lived in America we could kiss each other at the drop of a hat, and if it wouldn't be wrong in America, why should it be wrong here? After all, America's a great country.

GRETCHEN So is Germany. (*She kisses him abruptly and breaks off*) You see? We're a great country too.

ROBERT You crept up on me again. I wasn't expecting it. Where are you going?

GRETCHEN I'm just leaving you; otherwise you'll end up persuading me that American fiancées always kiss their fiancé's best friends twenty-five times on the mouth, and I'm sure that's not true!

ROBERT Well, now I've heard cases where—

GRETCHEN No! Shut up! What you're doing isn't right!

ROBERT You're just afraid that I'll manage to convince you...

GRETCHEN No...but you do have advantages. You're charming and quite funny so I need to be careful... And I love Bernard. There... *Auf wiedersehen.*

ROBERT Gretchen.

> **GRETCHEN** *exits door 1 and shuts the door just as* **BERTHA** *comes in, door 4, with cigarettes.*

BERTHA Here we are.

ROBERT Who? Who?

BERTHA No. The cigarettes for Mademoiselle Gretchen. She's arrived, you know. The German.

ROBERT I know. I've seen her.

BERTHA Oh really? Is she in the bedroom, then?

ROBERT Yes. She is.

BERTHA Fine. *(She goes towards door 1)*

ROBERT No, it's all right. I'll give them to her, Bertha.

BERTHA You?

ROBERT Yes me?

BERTHA You've introduced yourselves then, have you?

ROBERT Yes. We have.

BERTHA Then I suppose it's all right if you give her the cigarettes. *(She gives him the cigarettes)*

ROBERT Of course it's all right, Bertha.

> **BERTHA** *does not move.*

Thanks Bertha, I can manage. Bertha, haven't you got anything to do?

BERTHA Well, as a matter of fact, at this particular minute, I haven't.

ROBERT Well, off you go.

BERTHA Does monsieur wish me out of the way?

ROBERT No. No. You see—

BERTHA I see very well. I see you want me to go away.

ROBERT No. I don't care what you do. But there's nothing to do here.

BERTHA No. Nor anywhere else.

ROBERT Well, find something. What are you waiting for, Bertha?

BERTHA Nothing.

ROBERT Nothing.

BERTHA Nothing.

BERTHA *exits, door 3.*

ROBERT *crosses to door 1 and knocks.*

GRETCHEN *(offstage)* What is it?

ROBERT It's me, Robert.

GRETCHEN *(offstage)* NO... I'm resting... Leave me alone!

ROBERT I've got cigarettes for you.

GRETCHEN *(offstage)* Oh, good...come in.

ROBERT Here we are, here we are, here we are!

ROBERT *goes into the bedroom, door 1.*

A short pause.

GRETCHEN *(offstage)* Oh no...no! You're not starting that again!

ROBERT *(offstage)* But really...

GRETCHEN *(offstage)* You should die of shame!

ROBERT *is shoved back onstage.*

ROBERT But...

The bedroom door slams closed.

At the same time, **BERNARD** *enters with* **GABRIELLA** *who carries her Alitalia shoulder bag.*

GABRIELLA *Ciao*!

BERNARD We've come back...

GABRIELLA Yes, here I am again!

ROBERT You?

GABRIELLA *Si.* They've transferred me to the Super-Caravelli, and she's so fast now, with the new engines, we can fly non-stop. So, I don't need to leave until tomorrow.

ROBERT Oh, good.

GABRIELLA Fab, eh?

ROBERT Fab, yes. Really fab.

BERNARD So, we've come back.

ROBERT Yes. So, I see.

BERNARD So what's the matter?

ROBERT The matter?

BERNARD Yes, you look worried.

ROBERT Worried? I'm not worried. Are you worried?

BERNARD No.

GABRIELLA Aren't you pleased to see me again?

ROBERT Yes. Of course I am. I am delighted to see you.

GABRIELLA We can spend the evening together. And I'll have the whole night with my darling Bernard.

BERNARD As a matter of fact, I've been thinking. I thought it might be fun to go away for the night – to Saint-Germain-en-Laye, or somewhere.

ROBERT That's an outstanding idea. An absolutely marvellous idea. Saint-Germain-en-Laye.

GABRIELLA But why Saint-Germain?

BERNARD Well, Saint-Germain, or somewhere else. It would make a nice change for you.

GABRIELLA But I'm perfectly happy here at home.

ROBERT Yes. Yes, of course you are. But think of the country. The air's so good at Saint-Germain – you can really breathe there, into your lungs.

GABRIELLA No! It would be awfully mean to leave you here all alone on your first day in Paris.

ROBERT Oh, don't worry about me. You go. I'm used to being on my own. I'm used to it. So, why don't you go straight off into the country right now?

BERNARD Right now? No, we'll go later, after dinner at about 23:00 hours, eleven o'clock.

ROBERT Oh no!

BERNARD Oh no? What do you mean, "Oh no?" There's no hurry.

ROBERT Oh, yes!

GABRIELLA What do you mean, "Oh yes?"

ROBERT Oh yes! Oh yes! I mean, dinner in the country, oh yes, under a tree, surrounded by flowers, little rabbits, at this time of year…it'll be idyllic! Absolutely not to be missed!

GABRIELLA Yes – but I really would prefer to stay here. I'm not home so often.

BERNARD I'll tell you what, my darling. We'll have dinner here, and then have the night in the country. It will do us good. We'll get there at about eleven.

ROBERT You MUST go there for dinner! NOW! Bernard, don't be like that. That'll do you even more good. An amazing amount of good! More good than you can possibly imagine! And frankly, you're looking a bit pale.

GABRIELLA Me?

ROBERT Yes, you. You are definitely looking pale.

GABRIELLA It's nothing. I'll go redo my make-up. *(She goes towards door 1)*

    ROBERT *rushes across to fling himself in front of door 1.*

ROBERT No! No!

BERNARD What? What is it?

ROBERT There's no need for her to redo her make-up. She was just sitting in a bad light... Now I can see you properly and you're looking really good.

GABRIELLA Even so – perhaps a little touch of powder. *(She starts towards the door again)*

ROBERT *(defending the door)* No, no. I assure you. Don't touch a thing. I forbid it. You are perfect as you are. Lovely!

GABRIELLA Isn't he a darling?

BERNARD Well, he's a good bloke, aren't you?

ROBERT More than you think.

GABRIELLA But don't you know, Roberto, it's a woman's right to make up her face before dinner?

ROBERT Yes. Other women perhaps, but not you. You're superb, sensational. An absolute miracle.

GABRIELLA Whoa! What's this? A declaration of love?

BERNARD Yes. You're getting in a bit of a state. Calm down.

ROBERT I'm extremely calm. I'm just saying you both look as if you should have dinner and spend the night in the country.

BERNARD He's right, you know.

ROBERT Thank you, thank you.

BERNARD About the night, anyway...we'll go around eleven...

GABRIELLA I don't know what's got into you all of a sudden; you can't stand the countryside.

BERNARD Yes. That's true. Usually I hate it there, but—

ROBERT But you're so wrong.

BERNARD Yes, it is wrong of me. That's why every now and again when there's an opportunity...

ROBERT A perfect opportunity...

GABRIELLA You know what? You're making me think you don't want me to sleep here tonight.

ROBERT No. No. What on earth do you mean?

BERNARD Yes. What on earth do you mean? He's only thinking of you.

ROBERT That's right. I'm only thinking of you. And you.

BERNARD Come to think of it, I suppose it might do us both good – sleeping with the window open, listening to the wind in the chestnut trees...

ROBERT Oh, dear me, yes! So good!

BERNARD Yes. Yes. We'll leave at about eleven o'clock.

ROBERT Now! Now! Go now! Don't waste a second. Every second of greenery does you good and a single second missed could be fatal...for your health, you could die!

BERNARD You can tell you've just come from the provinces, you know. You're so enthusiastic!

ROBERT I'm saying all this for you. It's nothing to do with me.

GABRIELLA Right! Anyway, I'm going to redo my make-up.
(She goes towards door 1 again)

ROBERT No!

GABRIELLA What?

BERNARD Let her if she wants to. You should never contradict a woman.

ROBERT Yes! You should.

BERNARD Why?

GABRIELLA Yes, why?

ROBERT Why? You're making this difficult. You should really try and understand.

BERNARD Understand what?

GABRIELLA Yes, I don't understand.

ROBERT Look, when I arrived, you said to me, "How are you? It's nice to see you." Now you said that didn't you?

BERNARD Yes, I did, I did and it's true.

ROBERT Good. Then you said, "Go to the station, get your bags and when you get back, Robert, you can have that room." *(He points to door 1)*

GABRIELLA Our bedroom?

BERNARD Did I say that?

ROBERT You did. You said, "It's really my room."

BERNARD No, but wait a minute, what I said was—

ROBERT Bernard!

BERNARD What I said was—

ROBERT Bernard! Would I lie to you, Bernard? Sorry, sorry.

BERNARD No, you must be confused. That's our room, Gabriella's and mine.

ROBERT But that was the whole point. You said, "You can have our room so you'll feel perfectly at home. Settle in."

BERNARD I don't remember.

ROBERT Then you've got a short memory.

BERNARD Right. Well, possibly, but it's different now. Gabriella has come back. So you'll have to give us back our room.

ROBERT No.

BERNARD What?

GABRIELLA Why not?

ROBERT I'm just getting settled in... I've unpacked one of my bags...all my little personal things are all over the place. It's embarrassing—

GABRIELLA I wouldn't look at them.

ROBERT Maybe, but I'm embarrassed. Put yourself in my position. I've unpacked one of my bags. Actually, I've opened all my cases. Everything's all over the place – shoe trees, dental floss, sister's photograph...and to see you so ravishing, coming into my bedroom like that...you see? I'm a young man. I was brought up by the Holy Fathers.

GABRIELLA All right, all right, if that's how you feel. I'll go into the guestroom. Really, Bernardo, you have the most extraordinary friends.

GABRIELLA *takes her bag and goes out through door 7.*

BERNARD Are you out of your mind? What's wrong with you?

ROBERT And Gretchen? Your German? Have you forgotten her?

BERNARD Of course not. But she won't be here until after eleven.

ROBERT Oh, that's what you think, is it?

BERNARD Don't you remember? She rang to say she was going to be late?

ROBERT Yes. And while you were out she rang back to say she was going to be early.

BERNARD Really? How early?

ROBERT How early? She's here! *(He points to door 1)* In there.

BERNARD Oh my god! Why didn't you say so, you cretin?

ROBERT Cretin? Where? When? How? In front of the other one? I've spent ten minutes, trying, struggling to get you to go out for dinner. But you, oh no, you had to economize. You had to eat here!

BERNARD Well, how was I supposed to know?

ROBERT You could start by listening to me when I'm talking! Really it's too much, this!

BERNARD Yes. OK. OK. OK. OK.

ROBERT Never mind "OK, OK, OK." You might be grateful for my efforts to save you. But instead you shout at me.

BERNARD No. No.

ROBERT Oh yes. It's too much. You turned on me.

BERNARD Never, never.

ROBERT You did. You turned on me.

BERNARD Well, I didn't understand.

ROBERT No, really. I've had enough. You're on your own. I'm off. I'm finished. I'm going to a hotel, I'll send for my trunk and you can fend for yourself, with your international harem.

BERNARD Calm down. Calm down. We mustn't get so worked up.

ROBERT I'm not getting worked up. I'm perfectly calm and I know what I'm doing. I'm going.

BERNARD You wouldn't do that.

ROBERT Yes, I would.

BERNARD You wouldn't be such a bastard.

ROBERT So I'm a bastard, am I?

BERNARD No, I didn't mean that.

ROBERT You did.

BERNARD Well, I'm sorry. Robert. Robbie. Bobby. Bob. Forgive me.

ROBERT You apologise?

BERNARD I apologise.

ROBERT Sincerely?

BERNARD Sincerely.

ROBERT All right, then, I'll stay.

BERNARD Thank you. Thank you. Thank you. Thank you.

ROBERT Don't mention it.

BERNARD What do we do? What do we do? Nothing like this has ever happened before. Never. Never.

ROBERT Well, I'm amazed. But keep calm, Bernard. Let's try to sort it out. Right, I know! You get out of here with Gabriella, before Gretchen comes out of there. I'll tell Gretchen you've been called away on business.

BERNARD That's it! You look after her, and I'll take Gabriella to Saint-Germain. Tomorrow morning she'll fly off and everything will be back to normal.

ROBERT As long as she really does fly off this time, because Gretchen's staying for three days.

GRETCHEN *comes out of the bedroom, door 1.*

GRETCHEN Bernard *liebling*! You've come back.

BERNARD Well, yes – I have – just now.

GRETCHEN I am so happy.

BERNARD So am I. But now, I'm afraid, I have got to go out again.

GRETCHEN No.

BERNARD Afraid so.

GRETCHEN Then I'll come with you.

BERNARD Can't be done.

ROBERT Can't be done.

GRETCHEN What?

ROBERT Can't be done.

GRETCHEN Look, do you mind?

BERNARD You two have met, then?

GRETCHEN Yes...yes... So I can't come with you?

BERNARD No, it's business.

ROBERT You know what it's like...

GRETCHEN Leave us alone, can't you?

ROBERT Me?

GRETCHEN Yes. Go to your room.

ROBERT My room?

GRETCHEN Yes.

ROBERT Certainly.

BERNARD Oh, he can stay – he won't be in the way.

GRETCHEN He will.

BERNARD But he's a friend, and I've got to go out.

> **BERTHA** *enters, door 3.*

BERTHA Ah. You've come back, monsieur.

BERNARD Apparently.

BERTHA Mademoiselle Gretchen gave you quite a surprise, I expect.

BERNARD Yes. Yes.

BERTHA Will you be eating at home, sir?

BERNARD No, no. I can't make it. But my friend will be eating with Mademoiselle Gretchen, if that's all right, darling?

GRETCHEN Without you?

BERNARD But I'll be back straight away...well, as soon as I can.

GRETCHEN Then I don't want any dinner. I'll just have a bath and wait for you in bed.

BERNARD If you like.

GRETCHEN I adore you. And did you know that I've got three whole days this time?

BERNARD That is good news.

ROBERT Oh yes, indeed. It is very good news.

GRETCHEN What's it got to do with you?

ROBERT I'm so happy for everybody.

BERNARD Isn't that's nice of him? He's participating.

BERTHA He certainly is.

BERNARD Now you go and have your bath, darling... I'll give you a kiss before I go.

GRETCHEN I'll have a little one on account now, please.

ROBERT Quick, quick!

GRETCHEN Quick, quick? What do you mean, quick?

BERNARD He's right. Got to get going. There. Have a nice bath! *(He semi-pushes her toward the bathroom)* Have a nice bath!

GRETCHEN I won't be long.

> GRETCHEN *goes into the bathroom, door 6, and the door shuts at the moment* GABRIELLA *comes in from the bedroom, door 7.*

GABRIELLA I knew I was right – I looked an absolute fright.

BERTHA Oh! Oh! Mademoiselle is still here.

GABRIELLA Yes, Bertha... As you see... I don't take off until tomorrow.

BERTHA Tomorrow? Oh! Monsieur...mademoiselle is here too? *(She gestures towards the bathroom)*

BERNARD Well spotted.

GABRIELLA Too? Why "too"?

BERTHA I mean...with monsieur and monsieur...you know... too... Oh, monsieur...

BERNARD Yes, what? What is it? Is something wrong?

BERTHA Oh no! I'm not well, monsieur.

ROBERT Give her a cognac!

GABRIELLA She looks as though she's had a shock.

BERNARD No. No. No.

ROBERT Here. Drink this.

> **ROBERT** *gives* **BERTHA** *a glass. She drinks.*

BERTHA Thank you, monsieur.

ROBERT *(to* **BERNARD**, *taking charge)* Go on, get going! Go on!

BERNARD Eh? Oh, yes! Let's go!

GABRIELLA Go where?

BERNARD To dinner, *al fresco.*

ROBERT Yes...under a tree.

GABRIELLA No, I'd rather stay here. I've told you.

BERNARD But what for? I'd like to take you out. I need the fresh air.

GABRIELLA Then you go and get it. Your friend can keep me company.

ROBERT What, me and you? Out of the question.

GABRIELLA What do you mean me and you? Out of the question?

ROBERT I've got to go out too! And I've got a terrible headache.

GABRIELLA Well, you'd better go and get some fresh air with Bernard. I'm staying here.

BERNARD Darling, don't you ever want to do anything else but sit at home and slop around in slippers?

GABRIELLA Look, I cover three hundred thousand miles a year. It's a change to slip around in sloppers. I like it. You—

BERNARD This is no time—

GABRIELLA Don't muddle me.

ROBERT Think of all that lovely fresh air.

GABRIELLA We fly at twenty thousand feet. I get enough fresh air. For once I've got a night at home and this is where I'm going to stay.

BERNARD But, darling—

GABRIELLA No, I won't listen to another word. I've made up my mind. Feeling better, Bertha?

BERTHA A little better. It's all this coming and going. I'm overworked, probably.

GABRIELLA Do you feel strong enough to cook dinner?

BERTHA You want to eat here?

ROBERT No, no.

GABRIELLA Yes.

ROBERT No.

GABRIELLA Yes, yes!

BERNARD We're going out.

ROBERT I'm going out too! We're going out. Everyone's going out!

BERTHA But monsieur just told me you'd be dining here.

ROBERT I've changed my mind. I'm allowed, aren't I?

BERNARD Yes. He's changed his mind. He's allowed isn't he?

BERTHA Fine, right!

GABRIELLA So, what's for dinner?

BERTHA Frankfurters.

GABRIELLA What?

BERTHA It's nothing to do with me. I don't make up the menus. I just carry out orders.

GABRIELLA Did you ask for frankfurters?

BERNARD Yes – no – it was Robert.

ROBERT Me?

BERNARD Yes. Don't you remember, after you went there – you said you'd never eat anything else?

ROBERT Went where?

BERNARD Frankfurt!

ROBERT Oh yes. Frankfurters.

GABRIELLA But haven't you got anything else, Bertha?

BERTHA Sauerkraut.

GABRIELLA But I detest sauerkraut.

ROBERT So off you go to Saint-Germain.

BERNARD Yes, come on...

ROBERT Ah, the countryside...there's nothing like it...

GABRIELLA All right, no need to go into all that – you win. We'll go out to Saint-Germain and come back here after dinner.

BERNARD We'll see...we'll see... Come on then... Let's get going... I'm starving hungry and by the time we get there...

GABRIELLA Aren't you coming with us?

ROBERT Yes!

BERNARD No! He's staying here.

ROBERT I am?

BERNARD Yes you are!

GABRIELLA So, you're not going out now?

ROBERT Well, no...no... I'm not going out now... I'm feeling much better, I'm staying here, I am!

BERNARD You see? Right, let's go!

GABRIELLA Oh, my bag!

> **GABRIELLA** *exits through door 7 and shuts the door.*

BERNARD Oh, my God!

> **GRETCHEN** *comes out of the bathroom, door 6.*

GRETCHEN I can't find my loofah!

ROBERT Shh!

GRETCHEN What?

ROBERT Keep your voice down. He's got a headache.

BERNARD What?

ROBERT You've got a headache.

BERNARD I've got a headache.

GRETCHEN My poor darling – I know what you need... I'll get you an aspirin.

BERTHA Get me a couple, too.

GRETCHEN I think there's some in the spare room. *(She goes towards door 7)*

BERNARD No. No.

ROBERT No. No. I know, what about a bath?

BERNARD She's only just had one, you fool.

ROBERT Have another one.

GRETCHEN I've not had one yet. The water's too hot.

ROBERT Get back quickly – before it gets too cold.

BERNARD Yes, it gets cold very quickly in this flat.

GRETCHEN You won't go away?

BERNARD No, no – later – later— *(He pushes her towards the bathroom)*

> **GRETCHEN** *goes into the bathroom at the moment* **GABRIELLA** *comes back through door 7 with her bag.*

> **BERNARD** *continues, but in song.*

Later – we're going to the country.

BERTHA Monsieur, do you mind if I help myself? *(She helps herself from the cognac bottle)*

BERNARD No. Go ahead.

ROBERT I'll have one as well, Bertha.

GABRIELLA Are you feeling ill again?

ROBERT I'm a bit dizzy.

BERTHA *(handing* **ROBERT** *a drink)* Probably a storm coming.

ROBERT Any minute now.

GABRIELLA Well, if there's going to be a storm, we're not going out.

BERNARD Oh, yes we are. A storm in the countryside. You don't want to miss that.

GABRIELLA *Mio dio.* All right. See you later.

> **GABRIELLA** *exits, door 4.*

ROBERT That's right. That's right.

BERNARD I'm right behind you.

ROBERT And for heaven's sake keep her at Saint-Germain.

BERNARD Don't worry. She gets back here over my dead body. What a mess. I think I'm having a panic attack.

ROBERT Whatever you do, don't panic. *Bon appetit.*

BERNARD Thanks. Same to you.

GABRIELLA *enters.*

GABRIELLA Bernard. Come now – or I won't go.

GABRIELLA *goes out again as* **GRETCHEN** *enters from the bathroom, door 6.*

GRETCHEN It's still too hot.

BERNARD What is?

GRETCHEN My bath.

BERNARD Well, blow on it!

GRETCHEN You're going now?

BERNARD I'll be back. But he's staying here. He's charming.

GRETCHEN ⎫ *(together)* See you soon.
BERNARD ⎭

BERNARD *exits door 4 and* **GRETCHEN** *goes back into the bathroom.*

BERTHA Well done, sir. I'd go a long way to see something like that again. Congratulations! Cheers.

ROBERT Cheers.

BERTHA We've earned this.

ROBERT We certainly have.

The telephone rings. **BERTHA** *answers it.*

BERTHA Hello. Yes, I'll take it. A message from a Mademoiselle Gloria Hawkins? Storm over the North Atlantic. Stop. Turning back stop. Will be in Paris at twenty-two hundred hours... Do you mean tonight? Anything else? ...Love and kisses, Gloria. *(She hangs up)* Did you hear that?

ROBERT Every word.

BERTHA Drink up. We're in for a stormy night.

ROBERT Could be.

BERTHA Now, you must admit monsieur, it's no life for a maid here.

ROBERT Not for a maid no, but for a man. A real one. It seems pretty sensational.

Curtain.

ACT III

Evening.

GRETCHEN *comes out of the dining room, door 2, followed by* **ROBERT**.

ROBERT Yes, yes...well, say what you like. It's just my opinion. Sauerkraut has to be heavy on the digestion.

GRETCHEN Absolutely not!

BERTHA *enters behind them.*

BERTHA Don't suppose you'll be requiring coffee will you?

GRETCHEN No, Bertha. You know very well, not for me...never in the evening.

BERTHA Very well, mademoiselle.

ROBERT Yes, I'll have some, Bertha. Otherwise that sauerkraut will give me nightmares.

BERTHA It's nearly twenty-two hundred hours.

ROBERT Yes, yes, hurry up, hurry up.

BERTHA *exits, door 3.*

GRETCHEN If you're trying to annoy me by denigrating German food, I might as well tell you that it's pointless. You're wasting your time.

ROBERT I'm not denigrating anything. It's just that pickled cabbage weighs me down a bit.

GRETCHEN Nobody seems to get nightmares in Germany.

ROBERT I expect you're used to it. But me, not having any German origins, I think I'll have some trouble.

GRETCHEN You don't know what you're talking about. Sauerkraut is an outstanding dish. In fact we eat it throughout the country. That proves people like it...

ROBERT But I'm not saying people don't like it. I'm saying, "It's heavy." That's all.

GRETCHEN When it's nicely prepared and served with chilled wine, it's delicious.

ROBERT It is delicious, but heavy! It sends all the blood to my head, don't you find?

GRETCHEN No.

> **BERTHA** *enters with a cup of coffee on a tray.*

BERTHA Here we are, monsieur. And if you want my advice, you'll drink it while it's hot because sauerkraut *(she mimes physical heaviness)*.

ROBERT Thanks, Bertha.

GRETCHEN Bertha?

BERTHA Mademoiselle?

GRETCHEN When did Bernard say he'd be back?

BERTHA Uhh...

ROBERT He had things to do and he—

GRETCHEN I wasn't asking you! I was speaking to Bertha. Well?

BERTHA Well, I know when Monsieur Bernard went out. But I won't know when he'll be back until he's back.

GRETCHEN Thank you, Bertha.

BERTHA I mean, he doesn't tell me everything.

GRETCHEN Well, he might have told me.

BERTHA Well, yes...but it all happened so suddenly – something unforeseen. Isn't that so, monsieur?

ROBERT Yes. That's right, Bertha. That's how the unforeseen happens – it's something you just don't foresee.

BERTHA Of course not, as it's unforeseen – you see.

ROBERT Because if we'd been able to foresee it, it wouldn't have been unforeseen. It would have been – what would it have been, Bertha?

BERTHA Different.

ROBERT That's it – different.

BERTHA You see.

GRETCHEN Yes. Thank you, Bertha. I do see. Thank you.

BERTHA Don't mention it, mademoiselle. Don't mention it.

BERTHA *does a physical reminder of* **GLORIA***'s imminent arrival and goes out through door 3.*

ROBERT If it hadn't been for that sauerkraut, I would have enjoyed myself very much tonight.

GRETCHEN Why?

ROBERT Well, Bernard wasn't here, it was very nice – just the two of us.

GRETCHEN Oh please don't waste your efforts.

ROBERT Oh, don't get angry. Come on, give me a little smile. You know you're really very pretty for a—

GRETCHEN For a German girl? Is that it? Is that what you were going to say?

ROBERT No, no, not at all! You've misinterpreted me.

GRETCHEN Do you really think I can't see what you're up to? All through dinner you never stopped winking at me...and those bizarre and cryptic little smiles...

ROBERT Not at all!

GRETCHEN Don't deny it! You're wooing me scandalously! You're hanging round me like...a caveman round his fire...

ROBERT I can't help it if I like you so much.

GRETCHEN That's no reason. And even if you do like me so much, I don't like you...so good-night.

ROBERT Wait! Wait... Let's be sensible. Let's be really grown up about this. I know what we should do.

GRETCHEN Oh, really? What?

ROBERT We should go out together.

GRETCHEN At this time?

ROBERT It's not late.

GRETCHEN It's dark. You can't see a thing.

ROBERT Who needs to see...? It's just for a breather... Everything absolutely above board, of course...

GRETCHEN Of course!

ROBERT There's no risk. You're big enough. I mean, capable enough – to look after yourself, if you really think I'll make a pass at you.

GRETCHEN I forbid you to make a pass at me!

ROBERT But it's only a bit of fun...

GRETCHEN Yes, but I know all about French fun. It's a dangerous kind of fun.

ROBERT Dangerous? Not for you. You have Bernard.

GRETCHEN Right! I have Bernard. But even if it's not dangerous, in the first place it doesn't appeal to me, and in the second, I think it's dishonest.

ROBERT When you kissed me—

GRETCHEN By mistake!

ROBERT You kissed me twice.

GRETCHEN The first time by mistake and the second because of your despicable, insufferable, detestable, deplorable blackmail! But I won't be blackmailed anymore!

ROBERT *is doubling up with pain.*

Are you in some sort of grip of an obsession?

ROBERT No, I think it's that sauerkraut. But, yes yes, I am obsessed with you, romantically obsessed.

GRETCHEN Romantic! I must say you look romantic – lying there all red and congested!

ROBERT That's just why I'd like to go out. To get some fresh air.

GRETCHEN I'm not stopping you.

ROBERT But not without you... Oh go on. Be an angel.

GRETCHEN You won't make a pass?

ROBERT I promise. I swear. How could I with this wind? Word of honour.

GRETCHEN All right, we'll just pop out for an hour then straight back.

ROBERT Oh! Thank you!... Thank you! *(He flings himself on her)*

GRETCHEN Put me down – word of honour indeed! My mother warned me about men like you!

ROBERT Please. I got carried away. Forgive me. I was just thrilled you agreed with me for once.

GRETCHEN Yes. When we were out in the country, in the dark, in your car, I suppose you'd get carried away again. You'd pounce on me.

ROBERT Pounce on you in my car? Impossible!

GRETCHEN I don't believe you any more!

ROBERT I haven't got a car. We'll take a taxi and there will be a driver. I could say to him "This lady's rather nervous so would you mind coming and sitting in the back with us."

GRETCHEN I'm not going. I've had enough. You come in here like some dreadful—. Think up all sorts of devilish plots, try and get me away from my fiancé and up some pitch-black country lane – well, you want me to go out?

ROBERT Yes.

GRETCHEN Right! I'll go fetch my jacket and go... On my own!

ROBERT Listen! *Liebchen*!

GRETCHEN Don't you *Liebchen* me.

ROBERT Let me *Liebchen* you.

GRETCHEN How dare you be so familiar!

ROBERT *(singing)* Liebchen. Liebchen.

    BERTHA *enters.*

BERTHA Can I take the coffee away?

ROBERT Yes. Gretchen. Gretchen. Listen, listen to me.

GRETCHEN I will not listen to you. I shall never listen to you again – you vandal!

She exits door 1, slamming the door and leaving her bag.

BERTHA A bit upset, is she?

ROBERT Yes, a bit. She's a lovely person, though.

BERTHA Oh yes...she is nice, I suppose. Is she going out or not?

ROBERT Yes.

BERTHA Oh, good. Are you going with her?

ROBERT No. She won't let me.

BERTHA Oh dear. My poor monsieur. It looks like you'll have to deal with the American then.

ROBERT Me? Oh, no!

BERTHA What else can you do, monsieur?

ROBERT Yes, that's right, I can desert Bernard.

GLORIA *enters, door 4, in uniform.*

GLORIA Hi!

ROBERT Hi!

BERTHA Good-evening, mademoiselle.

GLORIA Good-evening, my dear little Bertie. Oh, it's so nice to be home again!

BERTHA So what happened with the flight, mademoiselle?

GLORIA There was a terrible storm over the North Atlantic and we had to turn back. Isn't that marvellous! Another whole night at home! Where's Bernard?

ROBERT He had to go out.

BERTHA On business.

GLORIA Not for long, I hope.

BERTHA Oh no, not for long.

GLORIA *(putting her bag on the chair)* And how have you got on since I left this morning?

ROBERT It's been quite dull, really.

GLORIA Cosy here, isn't it? Home sweet home. Everything's so calm.

ROBERT Calm, isn't it? Really calm, Bertha?

BERTHA Calm as calm can be.

GLORIA *goes towards door 1.* ROBERT *dashes and stops her.*

GLORIA I'm famished.

ROBERT Where are you going?

GLORIA I want to get out of this uniform.

ROBERT Opposite! Opposite!

GLORIA What do you mean, "opposite"?

ROBERT Go in the room, opposite.

GLORIA Me?

ROBERT Yes.

GLORIA What for?

ROBERT To get out of your uniform.

GLORIA But my room – Bernard's and mine – is this one.

ROBERT Yes, I know, I know... But he's given it to me.

GLORIA What?

ROBERT Yes, he said...

BERTHA Yes, that's true.

ROBERT He said, "Since Gloria's in America, and you're my best friend, you can have my room."

GLORIA Oh!

BERTHA Yes, he's right. That's what he said.

ROBERT So I've moved in there, you see?

GLORIA Well, move out again because I'm back!

ROBERT Can't be done.

BERTHA That's right. Can't be done.

GLORIA What a way to behave! Listen! I'm back. Give me back my room!

ROBERT I have to wait till Bernard gets back!

BERTHA Yes. Monsieur Bernard gave orders. It wouldn't do to cross him.

ROBERT No. It wouldn't.

GLORIA This is unbelievable! Is it the man or the woman who gives orders in the home?

BERTHA
ROBERT } *(together)* It's the man

GLORIA No it's not! It's the woman!

ROBERT Oh, come on!

GLORIA And I happen to be the mistress of this house.

ROBERT No comment.

GLORIA In America, the woman of the house gives the orders. And the man keeps his mouth shut. He obeys with no argument.

ROBERT No argument?

GLORIA No argument! The man makes the money and the woman is the brains. That's how it is in America, so let me go into my bedroom and you go in the one opposite!

ROBERT Yes. Yes, but we happen to be in France here, aren't we, Bertha?

BERTHA Yes. We most certainly are.

ROBERT Well, in France, it's the man who gives the orders. Sorry about that.

GLORIA You're wrong. Look, I'm starving. But as soon as I've had a coffee and something to eat you and I are going to have a little talk, and I'll bet you fifty dollars to a franc that you're going to agree with me before you're very much older.

ROBERT We'll see. We'll see.

GLORIA What have you got to eat, Bertie?

BERTHA Frankfurters. Prime quality.

ROBERT And sauerkraut.

GLORIA Any whipped cream?

BERTHA Yes. For pudding.

GLORIA No, to eat with the frankfurters and sauerkraut.

BERTHA Oh you eat want you want.

GLORIA Lay a place in here.

ROBERT No! No! Can't be done. Can it, Bertha?

BERTHA No. It can't. Come into the kitchen with me, mademoiselle, and we'll sort it out together.

GLORIA OK. You stay right there, we're going to have a little talk.

GLORIA exits, door 7, just as **GRETCHEN** *enters through door 1 in uniform.*

BERTHA Sauerkraut and whipped cream coming up.

ROBERT Oh yes, please, Bertha. I'd love some more sauerkraut and whipped cream.

BERTHA exits, door 3.

GRETCHEN Right. I'm off.

ROBERT Me too.

GRETCHEN Oh no. Leave me alone. I don't trust you at all any more.

ROBERT Where are you going?

GRETCHEN Out. Is that clear?

ROBERT What shall I tell Bernard?

GRETCHEN Tell him I've gone out.

ROBERT But he told me to look after you...

GRETCHEN Yes! You've a curious way of looking after me, and a curious look in your wicked chestnut eyes...

ROBERT Hazel! They're hazel! It says so on my passport. Come and look at them and you'll see they're hazel.

GRETCHEN No thank you. I can see you well enough from here.

GRETCHEN *suddenly sees the TWA bag on the chair.*

What's this TWA bag doing here?

ROBERT *(seizing it)* It's mine.

GRETCHEN Yours? Funny sort of bag for a man to have.

ROBERT I keep little things in it—

GRETCHEN If you were patriotic, you'd keep your little things in an Air France bag.

ROBERT I never thought of that.

GRETCHEN You're all the same. Insensitive, unthinking, and unpatriotic!

GRETCHEN *exits, door 4, just as* GLORIA *returns.*

GLORIA Is it normal in France for men to go through ladies' handbags?

ROBERT What?

GLORIA Why are you going through my bag?

ROBERT Me?

GLORIA Yes, you.

ROBERT Why on earth would you ask me that?

GLORIA Because I see you clutching it.

ROBERT Me? So I am. I'm clutching it.

GLORIA There's no money in it. I pay everything by cheque. There's a Parker pen, a lipstick and a few little personal things for the night, that's all. You can believe me.

ROBERT But of course I believe you.

GLORIA Well, then, let it go.

ROBERT What? Oh of course. I'm still clutching it. You'd left it on the chair and I just came along and picked it up as I sat down. I mean, I didn't want to sit on top of it. Here I was clutching it – it's stupid, really. You don't really think I was going through your bag, do you?

GLORIA No. Just kidding. Drink?

ROBERT OK.

GLORIA Scotch?

ROBERT Thanks.

GLORIA Have you thought about it?

ROBERT About what?

GLORIA What I was just saying...about American women... giving the orders.

ROBERT Oh yes, yes... I agree.

GLORIA So you've changed your mind?

ROBERT Have I?

GLORIA For things to go smoothly, the woman has to give the orders...and Bernard agrees.

ROBERT Well, there we are then...everything's perfect.

GLORIA And so, if I wanted to make myself at home in my bedroom, I would make myself at home.

ROBERT Yes, yes...right away...why not?

GLORIA And without waiting for Bernard to get back.

ROBERT No. Make yourself at home.

> **GLORIA** *goes out door 1, slamming the door. She returns almost at once, holding the Lufthansa handbag.*

GLORIA What's this Lufthansa bag doing here?

ROBERT That bag? It's mine! It's mine!

GLORIA Oh?

ROBERT I keep my little things for the night in it – my pyjamas
– my toothbrush – spare pair of socks, toothpaste, shaving
brush, you know...

GLORIA Whose are these? (*She removes some women's underwear*)

ROBERT Those are mine.

GLORIA Yours?

ROBERT Yes, those are mine.

GLORIA Oh, oh I see. You're a very interesting kinda guy. I can
see you're all settled in my room, and Bernard did give it
to you, so I'll let you stay there.

ROBERT Oh, that's not necessary.

GLORIA You know, I'll even give you a TWA bag to put your
things in.

ROBERT That's very kind of you, Gloria, but mine will do me
for a while yet.

GLORIA There's no way you're having a bag from a German
company! Look at ours, there's a little pocket inside with
a zipper. It's really handy.

ROBERT I see. I see.

GLORIA What's yours like inside? (*She tries to open the bag
that* **ROBERT** *is holding*)

ROBERT Oh mine's got some pockets...this sort of pocket...
that sort of pocket...and those sorts of pockets...it's full of
pockets...stuffed with pockets...it's made of pockets! It's a
pocket bag.

GLORIA My dear Robert. It would make me very happy if you
accept my bag as a gift.

ROBERT Well, if it'll make you happy.

GLORIA That's right. A man mustn't refuse a present from an
American woman!

ROBERT Oh really? Why's that?

GLORIA It's very rare for an American woman to give presents! But you said, "No!" when I wanted to go into my own bedroom! So you're not a baby. It takes a man to say, "No!"

ROBERT Oh. I see. I understand. Yes, well...a man...yes, I think...

GLORIA You know, people wonder why America is such a great country.

ROBERT Yes, people do wonder.

GLORIA Well, it's quite simply because American men stay babies all their lives.

ROBERT As long as that?

GLORIA The Kinsey report proved it.

ROBERT Did it?

GLORIA In my country the woman is stronger than the man because he always says yes to her. And so by demanding more every day, she can make the man work his way to total exhaustion.

ROBERT They don't mind?

GLORIA Oh, they mind. But one little mutiny and we're off to Reno. You can get a divorce in six weeks – for mental cruelty. And that means alimony.

ROBERT What happens if they don't pay it?

GLORIA Jail.

ROBERT Jail?

GLORIA So to avoid going to jail, they pay up and to pay up, they have to work. They have to produce. This ensures a stable economy. And that's why America is such a great country.

ROBERT Although he could produce, while in jail, baskets, espadrilles, little rubber-like things... Poor Bernard.

GLORIA Why?

ROBERT You're going to marry him.

GLORIA Never.

ROBERT Why not?

GLORIA He's a Frenchman. He's grown up. He might argue with me, and I couldn't take that. I shall just have to find an American. But I shall always love Bernard.

ROBERT So you'll marry an American but you won't necessarily love him?

GLORIA How could I? How can you love someone who spends his whole time working?

ROBERT It's not impossible.

GLORIA Oh! Say that again.

ROBERT What?

GLORIA "It's not impossible."

ROBERT Why?

GLORIA Your lips are just so cute when you say that.

ROBERT Really?

GLORIA Truly... Say it again.

ROBERT What was it again?

GLORIA It's not impossible.

ROBERT It's not impossible.

GLORIA Oh, your mouth really is a gorgeous shape. *(She comes closer)*

ROBERT Really?

GLORIA Yes...say it again!

ROBERT Again?

GLORIA Yes, please. For me.

ROBERT It's not impossible.

GLORIA There they go again. It's like a tiny flower opening.

ROBERT You're embarrassing me.

GLORIA No, no, honestly... Say, have you ever kissed an American woman?

ROBERT No! No, in Aix the chance never really came up.

GLORIA That's a great shame. We Americans are like the French, really. Very rational about love.

ROBERT Really?

GLORIA Oh yes. *(She kisses him)* Well?

ROBERT Well what?

GLORIA What do you think?

ROBERT Um, it's hard to say.

GLORIA Staggered by my astonishing technique?

ROBERT No. No. I wouldn't go that far. It's difficult to say when you're not expecting it.

GLORIA Oh right. So, you're expecting it now?

ROBERT Why? Are you going to do it again?

GLORIA I want you to tell me what you think of my technique.

ROBERT Oh, well. You know, I'm no expert.

GLORIA That's why it's interesting.

ROBERT But we're not going to kiss just like that, are we? For no reason?

GLORIA Are you crazy?

ROBERT Why?

GLORIA Well, I don't love you...

ROBERT I see.

GLORIA I just love your mouth.

ROBERT Oh, right.

GLORIA And there's nothing between the two of us, is there?

ROBERT Well, no. Nothing at all.

GLORIA No emotion.

ROBERT Not one!

GLORIA So we can kiss technically...to formulate an opinion...a technical opinion. Right are you ready?

ROBERT Yes...yes... Go for it!

GLORIA Right... *(She kisses him)*

The doorbell rings.

Well?

ROBERT Oh, definitely better than the first time.

GLORIA You think?

ROBERT Yes...and I was expecting it too! It didn't even have the benefit of the element of surprise!

GLORIA And how did you find it technically?

ROBERT Was that the classic American technique?

GLORIA Yes.

ROBERT It's really very impressive. It actually made my ears ring a bit.

GLORIA Really? How about this? *(She kisses him again)*

The doorbell rings again.

BERTHA *enters, door 3, and crosses to answer it.*

BERTHA That's a very depressing sight...

BERTHA *exits, door 4.*

GLORIA Well?

ROBERT Oh now that, that was really good! Congratulations... That made my ears ring even louder, I even heard voices!

GLORIA Well, I'm so glad you liked it, so glad! Say it again.

ROBERT It's NOT impossible.

GLORIA I can't resist it. *(She kisses him again)*

ROBERT Gloria, can't you see all this technique will end up by giving me ideas.

GLORIA Oh, but you mustn't get any ideas.

ROBERT No ideas.

GLORIA No. The technique of the kiss is based on not having any ideas.

ROBERT Not having any ideas.

GLORIA No.

ROBERT But what's the point of it, then?

GLORIA It helps to pass the time.

ROBERT It helps to pass the time.

GLORIA When you're with people you don't much care for – you can't always be playing gin-rummy.

ROBERT I can't play gin-rummy at all.

GLORIA So when you come across someone with such a cute little mouth like yours – well, it's a good chance to get in some practice – right, are you ready?

ROBERT Ready.

> **GLORIA** *kisses him.*

> *At the same time,* **BERNARD** *enters, door 4.*

BERNARD I forgot my keys. *(He sees* **GLORIA***)* You! You...you-hoo! ...You shouldn't be here!

GLORIA You-hoo. Yes, here I am. Hello, Bernard, darling.

BERNARD Bertha didn't tell me you were back.

BERTHA *enters from door 4 and heads towards 3.*

GLORIA But I rang and you'd gone out... There was a snowstorm. We had to turn back.

BERNARD Yes, right.

BERTHA Yes, stroke of luck, wasn't it – a snowstorm.

BERNARD Thank you, Bertha.

BERTHA *exits through door 3.*

GLORIA Where were you?

BERNARD Out...held up by business.

GLORIA You seem on edge.

BERNARD No. No. Everything all right?

ROBERT Splendid!

BERNARD Ah, good, so no slip-ups...from a business point of view?

ROBERT Not for the moment.

GLORIA In fact, your friend and I were just having a fascinating chat.

ROBERT Chat. Yes, just having a chat while we waited for you to get back.

BERNARD Well, I'm back now.

ROBERT Lovely to see you.

BERNARD And I'm going to interrupt your little chat so you can come away with me and spend the night at Saint-Germain.

ROBERT Me?

BERNARD No, you fool, Gloria.

GLORIA Why?

BERNARD A sudden inspiration.

ROBERT A very good idea.

BERNARD Yes. It'll be fun. It'll make a change.

GLORIA It's awfully sweet of you, darling, but I'm much too tired. Let's stay here. I'll have a bath and then we can go to bed. And we'll have enough change of scene as it is, and as you've given our room to your friend, we could try this room over here. *(She crosses to door 7)*

ROBERT No! No! I remember something. You can't use that room.

GLORIA Why not?

BERNARD Yes, why not?

ROBERT You told Bertha she could sleep in there.

BERNARD I did?

ROBERT Yes. Don't you remember?

GLORIA Instead of sleeping in her own room? Why?

BERNARD Why?

ROBERT Why? It's perfectly reasonable.

BERNARD Yes...yes...that's it... You're right, I remember now. Bertha fancied a bit of a change too.

ROBERT That's right. It's natural.

BERNARD You're travelling all the time. You don't realize!

ROBERT That's right. And she gets jealous.

BERNARD So she decided she wanted to travel too...across the flat.

GLORIA Where would you have slept if I hadn't come back?

BERNARD Me? Over there – *(Indicating door #5)* in that one.

GLORIA That little courtyard room?

BERNARD Yes, that's right. There's less noise in there...and since I find noise stressful, I was very glad to have a change as well. So, let's go to Saint-Germain!

GLORIA Oh no, darling, it's late. Let's stay here. I'll have a bath and we'll go to bed...in the little courtyard room. It's so exciting, don't you think?

BERNARD No. It's not.

ROBERT Oh no. Absolutely not.

BERTHA *enters, door 3.*

BERTHA Will that be all, monsieur?

BERNARD Yes, that's fine. Thank you.

GLORIA Is the bed made up in the little courtyard room?

BERTHA No, mademoiselle.

GLORIA Well, if Bernard's friend is having our room, where are we going to sleep?

BERTHA Oh, yes? Monsieur's given... Right. Well! Over there, I suppose.

BERNARD ⎫
ROBERT ⎬ *(together)* No!

GLORIA You don't imagine we're all going to tuck in with you, Bertha?

BERTHA With me?

ROBERT Well, you are sleeping in there.

BERTHA Me?

BERNARD Of course, you! You asked me yourself!

BERTHA Did I?

BERNARD Yes! For a change of scenery.

BERTHA Me?

ROBERT Yes! Because you were jealous.

BERNARD Yes! Clear?

BERTHA No.

BERNARD Yes!

BERTHA Right!

BERNARD So go and make up the courtyard room.

BERTHA Very good, monsieur.

GLORIA Come on. I'll help you, Bertha.

BERTHA That's very kind, I'm a bit bewildered at the moment...

GLORIA Oh, I know...if I were here all the time things would be different!

> **GLORIA** *and* **BERTHA** *exit, door 5.*

BERNARD Where is she?

ROBERT Who?

BERNARD Gabriella.

ROBERT How should I know? Didn't you take her to Saint-Germain?

BERNARD I tried, but it just couldn't be done... She made a scene in the restaurant! ...Right in the middle of the meal she upped and walked out on me... By the time I got into the street she'd vanished.

ROBERT Oh. Right.

BERNARD Where's Gretchen?

ROBERT Gone out for a walk.

BERNARD Well, that's all right then. Now all I've got to do is get Gloria out to the country, trees, chestnut, the birds, until tomorrow.

ROBERT You want to watch that, Bernard. People will think you're a rural maniac.

BERNARD What else can I do? Now, if Gabriella comes back, I can't be here! And you know nothing about it.

ROBERT What happens if Gretchen comes back too? What do I say?

BERNARD You say...you say...you say...whatever you like?

ROBERT Easy for you to say. I'm the one who'll have to do all the talking.

BERNARD I'm sorry – but I'm having a nervous breakdown. How about you?

ROBERT No, no. I'm fine. It's a bit of a change from Aix, obviously. But it's quite interesting. Sometimes thrilling, always varied and exciting! I've met lots of interesting new people. Of course there are risks, but if there's no risk there's no pleasure – and you wanted pleasure.

GLORIA *returns with* BERTHA.

GLORIA It's a sweet little room! So calm and tranquil. Much better than the country.

BERNARD No, darling – the chestnut trees – the wind—

A door slams offstage.

What was that?

ROBERT The wind.

BERTHA The front door.

BERTHA *exits, door 3.*

ROBERT The front door.

BERNARD The front door – I've just realized, darling. I've never seen inside this sweet little room.

BERNARD *pushes* GLORIA *ahead of him into the room, door 5, and shuts the door behind them at the moment that* GABRIELLA *bursts on to the stage, door 4.*

GABRIELLA Where is he?

ROBERT Who?

GABRIELLA Where is Bernard?

ROBERT I thought he was with you. At Saint-Germain.

GABRIELLA What is it with this countryside craze? All through the journey, all through the meal, all Bernard would do was babble about fresh air and chestnut trees. He went on and on just as if he was trying to hide something.

ROBERT Really? What could he have to hide, do you think?

GABRIELLA That's just it! I know he has nothing to hide. I know him... But this insistence is infuriating. The more people tell me to do something the less I want to do it. That's how I am. It's my nature!

ROBERT Yes, of course.

GABRIELLA wanders towards door 1.

That's my room.

GABRIELLA What?

ROBERT My room.

GABRIELLA Oh, of course, I'm sorry. I don't know where I am any more. I'm so annoyed.

ROBERT Now, you mustn't be...

GABRIELLA He got on my nerves so much, I didn't even finish dinner! I went out for some air and when I went back into the restaurant he'd gone! Don't you think that's outrageous?

ROBERT Yes, yes, absolutely! Well, perhaps he fancied some air too. And perhaps after you left he went back. Perhaps he's upset too. He loves you...

GABRIELLA But I love him too! Anyway, we wouldn't have these problems if we were together all the time. I know he's here, all alone, when I'm at the other end of the world... I wonder what he's doing, I worry...

ROBERT But he worries too. I'm sure that's why...why he was so keen to take you off to the country, to sort out all the worrying!

GABRIELLA It would all be so simple if only he'd marry me!

ROBERT Simple, yes, absolutely!

GABRIELLA I mean it's really too stupid to spend all that time apart.

ROBERT Stupid.

GABRIELLA Never mind, when we're married it'll all change. Right, well, good-night, little Robert... *(She finds the Lufthansa handbag)* What's that Lufthansa bag doing there?

ROBERT It's mine. It's MINE. *(He clutches the bag)*

GABRIELLA Yours?

ROBERT Yes, I use it to keep my little things for the night in – my pyjamas, socks – spare pair of toothbrushes—

GABRIELLA How weird!

ROBERT It's not illegal, is it?

GABRIELLA No, no, of course not, but it's a woman's bag; so seeing you holding it like that, it looks funny! Look. I hope you don't mind, but I'm going to bed.

ROBERT Off you go.

GABRIELLA And when Bernard gets here, tell him to come and say sorry...and tell him he's made me very unhappy.

ROBERT I'll tell him...if I see him.

GABRIELLA Thanks...good-night, little Robert.

   GABRIELLA *exits through door 7.*

ROBERT Good-night.

   Hearing **GLORIA** *coming back* **ROBERT** *puts* **GRETCHEN**'s *bag back in the bedroom, door 1.*

*GLORIA comes out of the bedroom, door 5, with **BERNARD**. She's in a towel with her shower cap in her hand.*

GLORIA Let me go! No, darling, I see absolutely no point in taking off to the countryside when we're so cosy here. Robert, don't you think it's ridiculous?

ROBERT Oh, me, you know... I don't have a view.

GLORIA He agrees with me, of course!

BERNARD But it would be so much nicer...

GLORIA No! I adore that sweet little bedroom. And now I'm going to have a bath.

GLORIA goes off through door 6.

BERNARD Sheer stubbornness... Honestly, you can't make them do anything!

ROBERT Gabriella.

BERNARD Gabriella?

ROBERT At the front door. We had a choice between Gretchen or Gabriella. It was Gabriella. *(He points to door 7)*

BERNARD Oh my God! What are we going to do? It can't go on like this! It's going to fall apart at any moment!

ROBERT You must take hold of yourself, Bernard. This is no time for panic. This is the time for resource, resilience, aggression. You must put on a strong aggressive front. Just remember, Gloria and Gabriella are just behind these doors *(indicating the doors)* and any minute now Gretchen will return. It's Gabriella.

GABRIELLA enters, door 7, in her night clothes.

GABRIELLA So you've come back, have you? How dare you?

BERNARD Come back?

GABRIELLA After leaving me in the middle of dinner.

BERNARD But you left me.

GABRIELLA I went back into the restaurant and you'd gone.

BERNARD Now darling, just because we all got a little hysterical—

GABRIELLA We got hysterical? You got hysterical! Really it's not enough to have a place of our own, a flat like this. We have to go tramping off into the country to sleep, just as though we were hiding away to make love.

BERNARD Shush! Don't get so worked up.

GABRIELLA Never mind "Shh"! I don't want to hide away to make love.

ROBERT }
BERNARD } *(together)* Shush!

GABRIELLA You do, I suppose. Because you're ashamed of not marrying me!

BERNARD Look, it's very embarrassing having this scene in front of Robert.

GABRIELLA I'm sure he agrees with me, don't you?

ROBERT Oh you know me... I keep out of love stories...

GABRIELLA There! He said the word! Love! We ought to be proud of it. Tell everybody about it! Tell the whole world.

BERNARD I agree. I absolutely agree, but not so loud.

GLORIA *(offstage)* Bernard.

ROBERT Bernard. Not so loud.

BERNARD Yes, all right, all right. Please calm down.

GABRIELLA *(going to the bathroom door, door 6)* OK. Fine. I'm going to calm down, by having a bath.

BERNARD *(blocking the bathroom door)* No, no! You can't!

GABRIELLA Why not?

BERNARD Because he's going to have one.

ROBERT Am I?

> **BERNARD** *pushes* **ROBERT** *to the door.*

BERNARD Yes.

GABRIELLA Surely he can have one after me.

ROBERT No.

GABRIELLA What?

ROBERT I said no!

GABRIELLA Well, really.

BERNARD He's our guest. He said "No!"

GABRIELLA But surely you can let me go first.

ROBERT No. Everybody must take their turn in the queue.

GABRIELLA Well, I must say your friend is terribly considerate.
A gentleman, quite overpoweringly polite—

BERNARD Gabriella, darling—

GABRIELLA And you stand there and let him insult me!

ROBERT
BERNARD } *(together)* Shush!

> **GABRIELLA** *marches into her bedroom, door 7, and slams
> the door behind her, just as* **GLORIA** *enters from the
> bathroom, door 6.*

GLORIA I really feel much better. Coming, darling?

BERNARD In a minute, darling...

ROBERT Yes. In a minute, darling—

GLORIA Don't keep me waiting too long, or I'll fall asleep.

BERNARD No, no!

GLORIA I've had a very tiring day, you know.

BERNARD Me too.

ROBERT And it's not over yet.

GLORIA Do you have much more to do?

BERNARD No. No. A few little things with Robert.

GLORIA Not for too long, I hope.

BERNARD No, no!

GLORIA Good-night, Robert dear.

BERNARD ⎫
ROBERT ⎭ *(together)* Good-night.

GLORIA I'll be waiting for you.

BERNARD Hmm mm...

> **GLORIA** *goes out through door 5.*

ROBERT You know – I've never seen a girl freshly bathed before – it's quite something.

BERNARD Gloria's very special.

ROBERT Yes, but Gretchen's not bad either.

BERNARD Yes. Personally, I prefer Gabriella.

ROBERT She's irresistible too. It's a difficult choice. But you know, Bernard, I don't think we've got the time to grade them right now. In fact, hang on. Now I think of it...the coast is clear now... Gabriella can have her bath... Go on. Tell her. I'd hate for her to think that I wouldn't let her have her bath before mine.

BERNARD No, you tell her. I'll check there's nothing left lying about.

> **BERNARD** *goes into the bathroom, door 6.*

> **ROBERT** *knocks on door 7.*

GABRIELLA *(offstage)* What is it?

ROBERT It's me, Robert.

GABRIELLA (*offstage*) What do you want?

ROBERT You can have my turn in the bathroom.

GABRIELLA (*offstage*) Forget it!

BERNARD OK. All clear.

ROBERT OK. All clear. (*Catching himself*) Come on, Gabriella.

GABRIELLA *enters, dressed for bed.*

GABRIELLA You are a very rude, unpleasant man!

ROBERT Me?

BERNARD No, no. Listen, it was a joke. I got him to say he wanted a bath to see how you'd react.

GABRIELLA Well. You saw!

BERNARD I did... I adore you...there, happy now?

ROBERT I mean, if you can't have a laugh any more...

GABRIELLA You should have told me it was a joke, then I'd have understood...

ROBERT Yes...yes... But that wouldn't have been funny for us, you see, because you wouldn't have got really, really really annoyed!

GABRIELLA It amuses you, does it? To see me getting really really really annoyed?

BERNARD Yes – no. It amuses me to see Robert being amused because—

GABRIELLA Because I'm annoyed.

BERNARD No. That can't be right.

ROBERT I really am terribly sorry.

BERNARD And so am I. Please, Gabriella. (*He kisses her*)

GABRIELLA Well, all right, darling. Bernard, you really should marry me, you know.

BERNARD But of course I will marry you. Of course I will... sooner or later.

GABRIELLA Don't you think he ought to?

ROBERT Oh yes, absolutely! You're marvellous and he doesn't deserve you.

GABRIELLA If you were in his place, wouldn't you marry me at once?

ROBERT At once, I wouldn't have waited this long.

GABRIELLA There, you see? Your friend would have already married me!

BERNARD Would you keep out of this?

ROBERT What? She asked my opinion; I answered. I'm entitled to an opinion, aren't I?

GABRIELLA Because, I'm telling you Bernard, you're made for marriage.

BERNARD Me?

GABRIELLA Yes! You're an old-fashioned stay-at-home. You like things to be nice and smooth. You hate complications. You're too nervy for them!

ROBERT It's true...that's you to a T.

BERNARD You think?

ROBERT Don't you?

BERNARD Yes, yes...maybe...

GABRIELLA You see! You admit it to yourself! Oh, I know you so well! You're a classic one-woman man! You're the prototype perfect husband!

ROBERT Let's not get carried away.

BERNARD Yes, that's perhaps a little strong.

GABRIELLA Not at all! And I'll tell you why you hesitate to marry me.

BERNARD Oh really?

GABRIELLA Yes! Because you're honest and scrupulous! You want to be absolutely sure you can make me happy. There! Isn't that it?

BERNARD Ah! ...that's spot on...psychologically speaking.

ROBERT Yes, I'd say you've hit the nail on the head.

GABRIELLA I'm not an Italian woman for nothing. So when then?

BERNARD When what?

GABRIELLA When are we getting married?

BERNARD Er, well, soon, soon! Let's just wait a little longer...

GABRIELLA You see? What did I say? *(She kisses him)* Adorably scrupulous! You see how happy we'll be...

BERNARD But we already are!

GABRIELLA Once we're married, it'll be completely different, you'll see!

GABRIELLA *exits to the bathroom, door 6.*

ROBERT Completely different.

BERNARD Another day like this will kill me. How do you keep so calm about it all...it's unnatural.

ROBERT No. It's the sign of a good nervous system, that's all. But of course, in your case Bernard, to get you out of this situation you're in now you need more than nerves boyo, you'd probably need a miracle or some kind of divine intervention.

GRETCHEN *enters, door 4.*

GRETCHEN Right!

BERNARD Who are you? I mean, how are you? Darling, it's so lovely so see you.

GRETCHEN Bernard, I want to talk to you.

BERNARD Of course. But what's the matter? You don't look yourself.

ROBERT Are you all right?

GRETCHEN As a matter of fact, I'm not.

BERNARD Darling, what is it?

ROBERT She's probably tired. Why don't you go and lie down?

BERNARD Good idea. In here?

ROBERT No.

BERNARD In here?

ROBERT No.

BERNARD In here?

ROBERT Yes.

GRETCHEN No. Leave me be. I'm dishonest!

BERNARD You? Dishonest? What on earth do you mean? No one's more honest than you.

ROBERT That's true.

GRETCHEN You keep out of it!

ROBERT Me?

GRETCHEN Yes, you! It's because of you I'm dishonest!

ROBERT Because of me?

BERNARD Because of him?

GRETCHEN Yes. I like your friend.

ROBERT Me?

BERNARD Him?

GRETCHEN Yes, you!

BERNARD Well, that's great! I like him too! He's a really good friend.

GRETCHEN Yes, but I like him in a different way from the way you do...

BERNARD A different way? What do you mean?

GRETCHEN I like him more than I like you...now.

ROBERT But I'm absolutely—

GRETCHEN Shut up! ...You know nothing!

BERNARD Yes, shut up! Keep out of this!

ROBERT Well it seems to concern me rather...

GRETCHEN Yes! I kissed him!

BERNARD *(to* ROBERT*)* You kissed her?

ROBERT Well, that's to say—

GRETCHEN Because I thought it was you!

BERNARD Me?

GRETCHEN Yes, from behind.

BERNARD I see?! From behind.

GRETCHEN And then he wanted to... And I liked it. I love him, Bernard.

ROBERT Me? You love me?

GRETCHEN Yes! ...So now I can't be your little fiancée *from beyond the Rhine* any more... You understand don't you?

BERNARD Well, it's a bit sudden! *(To* ROBERT*)* Pushing it a bit, aren't you?

ROBERT It's not my fault!

BERNARD What about you? Do you love her?

ROBERT Well, I really, really, really like her...

BERNARD Given the circumstances... I won't stand in your way!

They both fall on **BERNARD**'s *neck.*

ROBERT ⎫
GRETCHEN ⎭ *(together)*   Oh, thank you, Bernard! Thank you!
                    Thank you! Thank you!

BERNARD Don't mention it.

GRETCHEN You're not too upset?

BERNARD Yes, of course... But what can you do? Please, kiss!
It'll make me feel better...

GRETCHEN Robert, darling.

ROBERT *Liebchen.*

GABRIELLA *enters from the bathroom, door 6.*

GABRIELLA There! ...Oh, excuse me! ...Who's this?

BERNARD Uh oh!

GRETCHEN *(to* **ROBERT***)* Who's this?

ROBERT Who's this?

GABRIELLA *(to* **BERNARD***)* Who's this?

BERNARD Who's this? Who's this? Who's this? Well now...
I... I... Let me introduce Robert's fiancée...this is Robert's
fiancée...isn't it?

ROBERT Yes. Yes, Robert's fiancée. Who's Robert?

GRETCHEN Robert! Darling!

GABRIELLA Congratulations.

GRETCHEN If only you knew how happy I am—

GABRIELLA Yes. I'm sure you are – and I see you fly as well.

GRETCHEN *Ja.* Lufthansa.

GABRIELLA *Si.* Alitalia.

ROBERT What a coincidence.

GABRIELLA Yes! We're sisters of a kind...

BERNARD Yes...of a kind.

ROBERT Of a kind...

GRETCHEN I'm delighted to meet you.

GABRIELLA Me too. You're on stopover?

GRETCHEN Yes, stopover. You too?

GABRIELLA Yes, me too. So what brings you here at this time of night?

GRETCHEN Well, you see – I came to see—

ROBERT *kisses her to silence her.*

I came here—

ROBERT *kisses her again.*

I came—

ROBERT *kisses her.*

ROBERT That's what she came for.

BERNARD That's exactly right!

GRETCHEN Well no, not exactly...

BERNARD Yes, yes...well...apart from a couple of details...not important!

GABRIELLA But why didn't you tell me you were engaged?

ROBERT Hmm...me?

GABRIELLA You're a sly one!

GRETCHEN Because it's only just happened.

ROBERT That's right...just this second!

GABRIELLA You were quick. I go into the bathroom, have a bath, and whoosh! There you are, engaged.

BERNARD That's it, you see? ...Whoosh!

ROBERT Whoosh! Yes...that's right.

BERNARD He's a seducer.

GABRIELLA *(to* GRETCHEN*)* And where did you meet this seducer?

GRETCHEN Here.

GABRIELLA Here? So to sum up, you came here to see your fiancé, in the middle of the night, not knowing he'd be here because you didn't actually know him; is that right?

GRETCHEN Not exactly right! It's because of a mistaken kiss.

BERNARD Yes, right, well, you can tell us your life story another time! The way I see it one thing is clear: these two love each other. Let's not go trying to explain it! There'd be no end to it!

GABRIELLA Very well. My best wishes once more.

GRETCHEN Thank you. I hope *you* will find someone so—

GABRIELLA Easily?

GRETCHEN No – so sweet as my Robert.

GABRIELLA Oh! But I have, haven't I, Bernard, darling?

BERNARD Er yes, yes.

GRETCHEN What?

BERNARD Well, it's difficult to explain.

ROBERT Yes, and it's already late!

GRETCHEN Are you engaged to Bernard?

GABRIELLA Of course I am.

ROBERT Oh dear oh dear, we don't want to be bothered talking about that...

BERNARD No! Because...actually... I was going to tell you, as soon as I saw you two together... I said to myself, those two are together. They're made for each other.

GRETCHEN But you couldn't have known!

GABRIELLA Anyway what's it got to do with you, whether they liked each other or not?

ROBERT He's always interfering!

GRETCHEN I'm very sorry but that's not quite accurate. I was Bernard 's fiancée before...

GABRIELLA What?

BERNARD Wait! Let me explain. I was engaged to her before I was engaged to you.

GABRIELLA Oh really? And?

BERNARD And? ...And? ...And? ...And? Then I had a feeling she was really in love with Robert.

ROBERT You see?

GRETCHEN But I didn't know him before. It's only *after* that I—

BERNARD There's no such thing as "before" and "after"...the past is the past! ...There's one fact...just one... You love him! ...And I saw that, you see? ...So I got engaged to her... To Gabriella, I mean... I mean, to you...so as not to be ditched by you... I mean, by her!

GABRIELLA I don't understand.

BERNARD Even so, it is clear.

ROBERT Crystal clear.

GRETCHEN And to think I felt guilty. And here you are, engaged all the time!

GABRIELLA But of course he is. We've been engaged for ages... Or are you a liar?

BERNARD Me? Me? A liar? *(To* **ROBERT***)* All right. Robert, you tell her.

ROBERT Tell her what?

BERNARD Ha! There you are, you see? My dearest and oldest friend speaking up for me. And he knows me. He really knows—

GABRIELLA I don't understand any of this!

BERNARD But it's so simple.

GRETCHEN Then explain it.

BERNARD But there's nothing really to explain. Just answer "yes" or "no". *(To* **GRETCHEN***)* Are you engaged to Robert?

GRETCHEN Yes.

BERNARD Good. *(To* **ROBERT***)* Robert, are you engaged to Gretchen?

ROBERT Well – I suppose – the point is—

BERNARD Yes or no?

ROBERT Yes.

BERNARD Great! So, who's left? *(To* **GABRIELLA***)* Oh yes, are you engaged to me?

GABRIELLA Yes! ...No?

BERNARD Yes! Of course! So what more do you want? *(He indicates himself)* I'm engaged. *(To* **GABRIELLA***)* You're engaged. We're engaged. *(Indicating* **ROBERT** *and* **GRETCHEN***)* They're engaged. And that's all there is to it.

BERTHA *enters from the kitchen.*

BERTHA I have to speak to you.

BERNARD I'm engaged. Speak to me tomorrow.

BERTHA No! Right now!

BERNARD Tomorrow!

BERTHA Oh! *(Realizing the situation, she looks from* **GABRIELLA** *to* **GRETCHEN** *and from* **GRETCHEN** *to* **GABRIELLA***)* Do these young ladies know each other?

BERNARD As you see, they're getting to know each other. (*Indicating* **GRETCHEN***)* Let me introduce my friend Robert's fiancée. That's HIS fiancée.

ROBERT Yes, she's MY fiancée!

BERTHA Oh really? Congratulations, monsieur.

ROBERT Thank you.

BERNARD (*indicating* **GABRIELLA***)* And now, let me introduce—

BERTHA I know – I know.

    BERTHA *exits, door 3, in disgust.*

GABRIELLA (*going to door 7*) Now do come along, Bernard – I'm exhausted.

GRETCHEN Me too, I'm pooped.

BERNARD Yes, right away.

GRETCHEN You'll come and say good-night, won't you, my fiancé?

ROBERT Yes. Yes, I certainly will.

GABRIELLA See you in the morning.

GRETCHEN *Ja,* see you in the morning.

    GABRIELLA *exits door 7.*

    GRETCHEN *exits door 1.*

    ROBERT *and* **BERNARD** *sit and look at each other.*

ROBERT I thought we'd never get out of that alive!

BERNARD But we did get out of it quite well!

    BERTHA *enters from the kitchen with her coat, a suitcase and a tartan bag.*

BERNARD You again?

BERTHA Yes, I have something to tell you.

BERNARD What?

ROBERT What kind of bag is that?

BERTHA It's mine. A leftover from monsieur's past.

ROBERT Oh, what airline's that...?

BERNARD Yes. Let's move on. So, what do you want?

BERTHA I want to settle up.

BERNARD At this time of night? Why?

BERTHA Because I'm giving in my notice.

BERNARD What do you mean?

BERTHA Ask your friend, he'll tell you, I'm losing my mind here.

ROBERT Oh no, don't start with all your doom and gloom, woman.

BERNARD You heard him, go away.

BERTHA That's just what I'm doing.

ROBERT Go on, go back to your room and go back to sleep.

BERTHA No, I will not. I only have the one life and I want to hang on to it. My nerves can't take it here.

BERNARD You can't leave, Bertha. I'll do anything. I'll give you a raise.

BERTHA How much?

BERNARD We'll talk about it later.

BERTHA Twenty per cent at least.

BERNARD Yes, all right... Anything you like...but you cannot leave me. I need you, Bertha.

ROBERT We all need you, Bertha. What a very charming hat you've got on.

BERTHA Well, it still won't be easy – not even with a thirty per cent raise, it's still no life for a maid here!

ROBERT But that's all over and done with now, isn't it, Bernard? Life is changing.

BERTHA Three women in one household is too many, monsieur.

BERNARD But that's all done with now. He's taking one off my hands.

BERTHA Well, two's still too many.

BERNARD Bertha, I've reformed.

> **GLORIA** *enters through door 5.*

GLORIA Darling, aren't you ever coming to bed?

BERNARD Just coming, darling.

BERTHA Reformed? Well, prove it. Come on. People are waiting, monsieur... *(With a vague gesture towards door 5)* Here. And elsewhere.

BERNARD All right. All right. I'll sort it out.

GLORIA I'm waiting for you... Let your friend go to bed... Cute little hat, Bertie.

BERTHA Thank you, mademoiselle, that reminds me. There's a letter come for you this morning – from America. *(She gives* **GLORIA** *a letter)*

GLORIA For me? Thank you, Bertie.

BERNARD So, why don't you read it in bed?

GLORIA I'll read it here.

BERNARD Do read it in bed.

ROBERT Oh yes. Fabulous to read in bed.

GLORIA *(reading it)* Oh my gosh!

BERNARD What is it?

GLORIA I can't tell you.

BERNARD Why not? I'm your fiancé.

BERTHA Here we go again! I'm off.

BERNARD ⎱ *(together)* Wait!
ROBERT   ⎰

GLORIA This is marvellous!

BERNARD What is?

GLORIA Bernard! I'm in love!

BERNARD I know.

GLORIA No...not with you any more. I love you...lots...but we can't go on and on like this... I'm leaving!

BERTHA You're leaving?

GLORIA Yes.

BERTHA For good?

GLORIA Yes. It's this guy I met on the Mexico run. He wanted to make his first million before he married me. He's done it and he's waiting for me at the Acapulco Hilton.

BERTHA That's nice.

ROBERT Yes. Congratulations, Gloria! A Mexican!

BERNARD Look here, do you mean to tell me you had two men in your life at the same time?

GLORIA No, honey, no.

BERNARD Thank goodness for that.

GLORIA Three.

BERNARD Three?

GLORIA Yes, I was engaged to another guy in Los Angeles – I suppose I'll have to drop him now.

BERTHA Yes. Good idea, don't you think, monsieur?

GLORIA I'm with the guy who marries me first.

BERNARD But you can't just go off like this. It's not as simple as that.

GLORIA Yes, it's quite simple. There's a Super-Boeing leaving at midnight. I'll ask if I can take a friend's place and when I get home I'll resign my job. A married life is what I want. I'm sorry, honey.

GLORIA goes off through door 5.

BERNARD Blimey.

ROBERT That's it then.

BERTHA Right. Now let's get this straight. *(To BERNARD)* You've just got the one fiancée now – Mademoiselle Gabriella. Right?

BERNARD Right.

BERTHA And you'll take the German off his hands? Right?

ROBERT Right.

BERTHA Right, then I'll stay. With that forty per cent raise, who knows...a maid's life might get a bit easier round here. *(Indicating the tartan bag)* Air Caledonia, monsieur.

BERTHA goes out through door 3.

ROBERT laughs.

BERNARD Do you think this is funny?

ROBERT This morning when you arrived you were going on and on about the perfect three-woman life, and here you are, forced to make do with only one.

BERNARD Yes, I suppose so. Do you know, to be honest, it's quite a relief.

GABRIELLA is at door 7.

GABRIELLA Bernard, I'm waiting for you to come and say good-night.

BERNARD I'm just coming.

GABRIELLA It's so late, darling.

GABRIELLA *shuts the door.*

ROBERT She really is a marvellous girl.

BERNARD Yes, she is, isn't she? I loved the other two, very much of course, but Gabriella I adore.

GLORIA *enters, door 5, in uniform carrying her bag.*

GLORIA All set. *(She kisses* BERNARD*)* I'll think of you from time to time. Goodbye, Robert.

ROBERT Goodbye, Gloria.

GLORIA Say it again.

ROBERT Goodbye, Gloria.

GLORIA No, not that, the other thing.

ROBERT It's not impossible.

GLORIA Oh! It's just too kooky. *(She kisses* ROBERT *on the mouth)*

BERNARD Hang on, why are you kissing him?

GLORIA We've kissed each other lots...all evening.

BERNARD That really is the limit. The moment my back's turned!

GLORIA It was purely technical!

ROBERT Yes we were just exercising!

GLORIA Right! Goodbye then, my little pair of Frenchmen!

GLORIA *exits, door 4.*

ROBERT It must affect you quite a bit to see all your women taking off like that one after another.

The telephone rings. BERNARD *looks at* ROBERT *and shrugs.* ROBERT *shakes his head as* BERNARD *answers the telephone.*

BERNARD Excuse me... (*Answering the phone*) Hello...yes, it's me...oh it's you? (*To* **ROBERT**) It's my friend from Orly.

ROBERT Then hang up! Hang up!

BERNARD (*on the telephone*) No...no... Thanks... It's kind of you to think of me...but I'm not interested anymore. I'm getting married... Yes, yes! ...What? She does Paris-Guadalupe-Rio? ...No, thank you... No, I assure you... Even if she is a former Rio de Janeiro Samba queen... No really, it makes no difference...even if her legs are as long... No. I want nothing to do with it... I don't care...

ROBERT Get her details!

BERNARD What?

ROBERT Get her details... I'm telling you...

BERNARD (*speaking on the telephone*) Hello...hang on... (*To* **ROBERT**) Are you crazy? You don't want to start doing all this?

ROBERT A former Rio de Janeiro Samba queen? We can't let an opportunity like that go by! Go on, take the details.

BERNARD Just think about it!

ROBERT Right. I have! Go on!

BERNARD This is insane! (*On the phone*) Hello...are you there? Good...this is for a friend...is that possible? ...OK, I'll put him on... (*He hands the phone to* **ROBERT**) There! (*He picks up the book of time zone tables and passes it to him*) The "timetables".

BERNARD *exits, door 3, to the kitchen.*

ROBERT Thanks... (*On the phone*) Hello, hello there, monsieur, I'm the friend! So...where can I meet this Brazilian girl? ...Really? ...You have a Japanese girl as well? ...And one from Sweden? ...Good...good... Hang on, I'll take down the addresses...

GRETCHEN *enters, door 1, in night clothes.*

Just hang on!

GRETCHEN Robert, you know I'm waiting for you.

ROBERT Oh, right!

GRETCHEN Yes! Because I want to tell you that now that I've
met you I shall never again be able to fall asleep without
you wishing me good-night.

ROBERT Oh, right!

GRETCHEN Yes. Just as I shall never again wake up happy unless
your hazel eyes are there to say good-morning!

ROBERT Oh, right!

GRETCHEN So from tonight, I'm waiting for you before I fall
asleep!

GRETCHEN *goes out through door 1.*

ROBERT *(looking at the door)* Oh, right? Oh, right? *(He realizes
he's still holding the phone)* Hello, are you still there?
...Yes, the addresses... Oh, no, no... I've changed my mind...
I've got somebody else... A girl from all the countries of
the world rolled into one. Yes, isn't that fantastic? ...Thank
you... Tell me... Could you do me a favour?... Can you get
me two seats tomorrow to Aix? ...No, Aix-la-Chapelle?
...You can? Wonderful... On a Boeing? What's that? ...Oh
right, it's an aeroplane, yes... Ten o'clock! Perfect... We'll
be there. *(He hangs up)*

BERNARD *comes back in with a bottle of champagne
in each hand.*

BERNARD Well, all fixed up?

ROBERT All fixed up. Ha! All fixed up. Are you kidding? It's
amazing!

BERNARD No, I tell you what's really amazing – just one woman.
Now that's perfection!

ROBERT Each to his own!

BERNARD Whatever you say. Here, Robert, champagne? *(He gives him the bottle)* I'm going to toast my betrothal to Gabriella! Cheers!

ROBERT Cheers, Bernard!

They each head for a door and knock.

GRETCHEN *and* **GABRIELLA** *each open their doors.*

The men make to go into their rooms.

GRETCHEN Wait! *(She presses a pillow into* **ROBERT***'s arms)* We take marriage very seriously in Germany.

GABRIELLA *(pressing a pillow into* **BERNARD***'s arms)* Uh-uh, love is not to be treated flippantly.

GRETCHEN Wake me with your hazel eyes in the morning, my darling.

GABRIELLA We should think about these things, now that we're going to be married.

GRETCHEN ⎫
GABRIELLA ⎭ *(together)* Good-night.

  GRETCHEN *and* **GABRIELLA** *exit to their rooms.*

BERNARD You too?

ROBERT Me too.

BERNARD Champagne?

ROBERT Why not? Bernard, do you think they'll still love us in the morning when they know the whole truth?

BERNARD It's not impossible.

ROBERT Say that again?

BERNARD Say what?

ROBERT It's not impossible.

BERNARD It's not impossible.

ROBERT Say it again.

BERNARD It's not impossible.

ROBERT No. It doesn't look like a tiny flower to me.

Curtain.

FURNITURE AND PROPERTY LIST

ACT I

On stage: Mirror
Glasses
Bottle of cognac
Telephone
Desk
Chair

Offstage: Plate of pancakes and molasses (**Bertha**)
Coffee (**Bertha**)
TWA shoulder bag containing nail file (**Gloria**)
Letter (in pocket) (**Bertha**)

Personal: **Bernard:** book of timetables

ACT II

Offstage: Suitcases (**Robert**)
Towel, aftershave (**Robert**)
Cigarettes (**Bertha**)
Alitalia shoulder bag (**Gabriella**)

ACT III

Offstage: Tray. *On it:* cup of coffee (**Bertha**)
TWA bag (**Gloria**)
Lufthansa bag (**Gretchen**)
Suitcase, tartan bag (**Bertha**)
Bottle of champagne (**Bernard**)
Pillow (**Gretchen**)
Pillow (**Gabriella**)

LIGHTING PLOT

ACT I

To open: General interior lighting

No cues

ACT II

To open: General interior lighting

No cues

ACT III

To open: General interior lighting

No cues

EFFECTS PLOT

ACT I

Cue 1 **Bernard:** "Good."   (Page 8)
         Doorbell rings

Cue 2 **Robert:** "They're both engaged!"   (Page 24)
         Telephone rings

ACT II

Cue 3 To open   (Page 29)
         Telephone rings

Cue 4 **Bertha** hangs up   (Page 29)
         Doorbell rings

Cue 5 **Robert:** "We certainly have."   (Page 61)
         Telephone rings

ACT III

Cue 6 **Gloria** kisses **Robert**   (Page 79)
         Doorbell rings

Cue 7 **Gloria** kisses **Robert** again   (Page 79)
         Doorbell rings again

Cue 8 **Robert:** "...one after another."   (Page 107)
         Telephone rings

VISIT THE
SAMUEL FRENCH
BOOKSHOP
AT THE
ROYAL COURT THEATRE

Browse plays and theatre books,
get expert advice and enjoy a coffee

Samuel French Bookshop
Royal Court Theatre
Sloane Square
London
SW1W 8AS
020 7565 5024

Shop from thousands of titles
on our website

 samuelfrench.co.uk

 samuelfrenchltd

 samuel french uk

Milton Keynes UK
Ingram Content Group UK Ltd.
UKHW020615190124
436312UK00015B/242

9 780573 110245